WATERBIRDS

Most waterbirds seldom stray far from wetlands.
Those that do, like the gulls seen scavenging at
landfills, are easily recognized as waterbirds.

Aerialists Gulls and similar birds fly on long,
slender wings, s...
below in search o...

Swimmers Duc...
wide bodies and
the water is very
gull, and their fli...
like the slow, sea...

Wading birds b...
marshes and we...
with a sudden thr...

Shorebirds Sa...
others typically pr...
flats, or rock jett...
bills for deep prot...

Upland waterbir...
fish from a perch...
dipper probes alo...

14 AERIALISTS	Brown Pelican, Frigatebird	
15	Gulls, Skimmer, Terns	
25 SWIMMERS	Anhinga, Cormorants, Geese, Loons, Swans, White Pelican	
31	Coot, Ducks, Grebes, Moorhen, Purple Gallinule	
42 WADING BIRDS	Cranes, Herons, Ibises, Limpkin, Stork, Spoonbill	
48	Least Bittern, Rails	
50 SHOREBIRDS	Avocet, Oystercatcher, Sandpipers (large), Stilt	
	Sandpipers & Plovers (medi...	
	Sandpipers & Plovers (small... Wilson's Phalarope	
UPLAND WATERBIRDS	Dipper, Kingfishers	

The **American Bird Conservancy (ABC)** is a US-based, not-for-profit organization formed to unify bird conservation efforts across the Americas, and dedicated to the conservation of birds throughout the Western Hemisphere. ABC practices conservation through partnership: bringing together the partners whose expertise and resources are best suited to each task. ABC derives strength from being the US member of the BirdLife International, the world bird conservation partnership. It supports the work of BirdLife partner organizations throughout the hemisphere and the world. More than 500 research and education programs in Latin American and the Caribbean have been financially supported by ABC and its predecessor organization.

The **Policy Council** of the American Bird Conservancy has a membership of 60 organizations sharing a common interest in the conservation of birds. Composed of ornithologists, policy specialists, educators, and general bird enthusiasts, the Council is a forum for providing scientific and policy advice to conservationists; exchanging information and discussing critical and emerging bird conservation issues; stimulating a network of support for bird conservation policies through national, state, and local groups and their grassroots constituencies; and directly accomplishing conservation through ABC.

ABC is also a working member of **Partners in Flight (PIF),** an Americas-wide coalition of more than 150 organizations and government agencies dedicated to bird conservation. Initially begun to find ways to reverse the decline in neotropical migratory bird species, PIF has broadened its scope to include all nongame birds in the Americas. PIF links birders, hunters, government, industry, and citizens in a unified effort to conserve bird populations and habitats. PIF's bird conservation strategy, called *Flight Plan,* can be obtained from ABC, the National Fish and Wildlife Foundation, or the US Fish and Wildlife Service. PIF's national coordinator is on ABC's staff and ABC implements the *Flight Plan* through its Important Bird Areas initiative. ABC members receive *Bird Conservation,* the magazine about PIF and American bird conservation, and *World Birdwatch,* the magazine about world bird conservation.

AMERICAN BIRD CONSERVANCY'S FIELD GUIDE

ALL THE

BIRDS

OF NORTH AMERICA

CONCEPT AND DESIGN BY JACK L. GRIGGS

PRODUCED BY ROUNDTABLE PRESS, INC.

HarperPerennial

A Division Of HarperCollins*Publishers*

Want to Help Conserve Birds?

It's as Easy as ABC!

By becoming a member of American Bird
Conservancy, you can help ensure work is
being done to protect many of the species in
this field guide. You can receive Bird Conservation
magazine quarterly and learn about bird conservation throughout the
Americas and World Birdwatch magazine for information on international
bird conservation.

**Make a difference to birds. Copy this card and mail to the
address listed below.**

☐ *Yes,* I want to become a member and receive Bird Conservation magazine. A check in the amount of $15 is enclosed.

☐ *Yes,* I want to become an International member of ABC and receive
both Bird Conservation and World Birdwatch magazines. A check in
the amount of $40 is enclosed.

Name: _____

Address: _____

_____

Return to: American Bird Conservancy, 1250 24th Street, NW Suite 220,
Washington, D.C. 20037 or call 1-888-BIRD-MAG or e-mail: abcbirds.org.
Memberships are tax-deductible to the extent allowable by law.

ALL THE BIRDS OF NORTH AMERICA. Copyright © *1997* by Jack L. Griggs. All
rights reserved. Printed in Hong Kong. No part of this book may be used or reproduced in any manner whatsoever without written permission except in the case of
brief quotations embodied in critical articles and reviews. For information address
HarperCollins*Publishers*, Inc., 10 East 53rd Street, New York, New York 10022.

HarperCollins books may be purchased for educational, business, or sales
promotional use. For information, please write to:
Special Markets Department, HarperCollins Publishers, Inc.,
10 East 53rd Street, New York, New York 10022.
FIRST EDITION

Library of Congress Cataloging-in-Publication Data
Griggs, Jack.
    American Bird Conservancy's field guide to all the birds of North
America : a revolutionary system based on feeding behaviors and
field-recognizable features / by Jack Griggs.
         p. cm.
    ISBN 0-06-273028-2
    1. Birds—North America—Identification.   I. American Bird
Conservancy. II. Title.
QL681.G77 1997
598' .097—dc21   96-49679
97 98 99 00 01 10 9 8 7 6 5 4 3 2 1   CIP

Dedicated to the recreational bird-watcher

Illustrators
Jonathan Alderfer
F. P. Bennett
John Dawson
Dale Dyer
Larry McQueen
Alan Messer
John O'Neill
Hans Peeters
Doug Pratt
Bart Rulon
Andrew Vallely
Barry Van Dusen

Ornithological Consultants
Eirik Blom
Louis Bevier
Pete Dunne
Kimball Garrett
Kenn Kaufman
Paul Lehman
Larry McQueen
Nancy L. Newfield
Brian Patteson
Hans Peeters
Thede Tobish

Digital Illustrator Jack E. Griggs

Produced by Roundtable Press, Inc. Susan E. Meyer • Marsha Melnick • Amy T. Jonak • Abigail Anderson • Carol Healy • Sue Heinemann • Steven Rosen • Laura Smyth • Carol Spier • Rita Campon • Giga Communications, Inc.

Additional Production Elizabeth Raber • Digital Illustrations produced @ S&S Color Inc., NYC • **Additional Design** Barry Van Dusen

Special Thanks To Keith Bildstein • Glen Chilton • John Farrand, Jr. • Catherine Gibbons • Paul B. Hamel • Dan Lane • Ron Naveen • Pat Paul • Kate Rowe • Edward R. Tufte • George Barrowclough and The American Museum of Natural History • Jon Barlow and The Royal Ontario Museum • Kimball Garrett and The Los Angeles County Museum of Natural History • The Burke Museum Spread Wing Collection at the University of Washington • J. Philip Angle and the Smithsonian Institution • Jack McKeown, Linda Cunningham, and Patricia Leasure at HarperCollins Publishers

Credits for photos used in digital illustrations Catherine Gibbons • Jack E. Griggs • Bill Curtsinger • Derek Fell • Ed Reschke/Peter Arnold, Inc. • Anne Heimann • Stinger Guala • Gene Boaz

Extinct birds

DIGITAL ILLUSTRATOR **JACK E. GRIGGS**

After nesting, the numbers of any species are at their highest. During the following year individuals die from predation, disease, and a variety of hazards until the next year's nesting provides the opportunity to rebuild the population. When nesting consistently fails to replace the numbers lost over the course of a year, extinction becomes inevitable. It is not necessary that a population be small to be in trouble; only that it be unable to replenish itself.

Direct interference with nesting was a primary or significant cause in the extinction of most of the species and subspecies lost to North America in the last 200 years. Either the bird was slaughtered when attempting to nest (as was the great auk), had its nesting habitat destroyed (Bachman's warbler), or both (the passenger pigeon). Loss of nesting habitat continues to be the primary threat for many species.

Excessive losses between nesting seasons can result from many factors. Historically, birds were shot or captured in such large numbers that some disappeared from areas where good nesting habitat remained. Diminishing food supplies (on the winter range, in migration, or in nesting habitat) and toxic contamination are important causes of declines in some present species.

As a population declines, it becomes increasingly susceptible to extinction from disease or accident. Some suspect a hurricane delivered the mortal blow to Bachman's warblers, although habitat loss certainly set the stage. If the cause of an excessive loss is corrected, bird populations can usually replenish, but not without nesting habitat. Many of the species shot to scarcity in the 1800s recovered where nesting habitat remained. The Nature Conservancy is especially active today in working with government and developers to preserve habitat for birds and all wildlife.

Human needs are always cited to justify habitat destruction, but what we need most is a sustaining environment. Nature protects itself through diversity, and the productivity and efficiency of a habitat diminish as species become extinct. The loss of a species means that those remaining, ourselves included, are at greater risk. "Declining numbers of birds," warns ecologist Paul Ehrlich, "should be viewed with the sort of alarm that miners once felt when their canaries started to look ill." Yet private efforts to protect and increase our natural heritage remain minimal. In a recent year, almost $125 billion was donated to American charities. Religious causes received the most – nearly half. Environmental causes received just 2.5 percent of the total.

Great Auk *Pinguinus impennis* 30"
During the 16th and part of 17th century, great auks were numerous off New England and Newfoundland. Their range extended to waters off Greenland, Iceland, and Europe. They could not fly and lived at sea except to lay their eggs and hatch their young. The only known nesting colonies off North America were at Funk Island, a small rocky outcropping east of Newfoundland, and Bird Rocks in the Gulf of St. Lawrence, but it is probable they nested on suitable islands throughout the North Atlantic.

The Funk Island colony was last recorded in 1785. At that time it had already become well known among fishermen and sailors, who would come ashore, capture the helpless birds, and use them for food or bait. The great auk could be penned alive aboard ship and conveniently butchered as needed. The next recorded account on Funk Island is from 1841, when a naturalist recorded only heaps of bones and mummified remains. On June 3, 1844, at Eldey Rock off Iceland, the last known pair in the world were seen and shot.

Great auks were in summer plumage when they nested and were captured. There is a single specimen, collected in 1815 off Greenland and preserved in Copenhagen, of the bird in winter plumage. It has no oval white spot before the eye. There is a broad band of white above the eye and a gray eyeline extending back to a point just below the ear. The chin and throat are white.

Passenger Pigeon *Ectopistes migratorius* 16"
Accounts of the passenger pigeon by John J. Audubon, Alexander Wilson, and other early ornithologists seem beyond imagination. Audubon describes flocks that he calculates at more than a billion birds passing en masse for three days: "The light of the noon day was obscured as if by eclipse....The dung fell...not unlike melting flakes of snow." Passenger pigeons were, in fact, so abundant that they comprised more than a quarter of the US bird population.

The flocks lived on the nuts and fruits of the original eastern forest. They wandered irregularly, and where food was plentiful, they would nest in dense colonies up to 40 miles long and several miles wide. Their numbers made commercial harvesting by gunners, netters, and dynamiters profitable. "Wagon loads of them are poured into market...and Pigeons become the order of the day at dinner, breakfast and supper, until the very name becomes sickening," Wilson reported in 1814.

Passenger pigeons and the eastern forest were destroyed simultaneously. By the end of the 19th century little was left of either. The last major pigeon nestings occurred near the eastern shore of Lake Michigan in 1881 and in Wisconsin in 1882. Small flocks and pairs continued to nest into the 1900s, free from commercial persecution, but the passenger pigeon could not sustain itself in small or moderate numbers. The last one, "Martha," died at the Cincinnati Zoo in 1914.

Ivory-billed Woodpecker *Campephilus principalis* 20"
Audubon's "king of the woodpeckers" lived in the wet bottomlands of the virgin forest, habitat much like that of the Carolina parakeet. The beetles and grubs that infested dead and dying trees were the ivory-bill's principal foods, and it pursued them with exuberance. It would vigorously rip bark from a tree in large hunks and could shred a dead tree into a splintered trunk barely taller than the mound of chips and bark left around its base. The ringing echoes of the powerful blows from its beak were mixed with its loud, excited calls – *yamp, yamp, yamp,* like the sound produced by a clarinet mouthpiece.

The bill and crest of the ivory-billed woodpecker were valued as decoration by Native Americans and early hunters, and many birds were shot. However, they survived until the last of the old forests, with their dead and dying trees, were cleared. In 1939 an estimated 22 birds still existed, all in remote areas of Florida and Louisiana. Cutting continued until the only known remaining birds were in a 120-square-mile section along the Tensas River in Louisiana. Known as the "Singer Tract," it was cleared for agriculture in 1948. There was not sufficient national will to save the forest or the birds. Reported sightings continued for a number of years, but without large tracts of mature forest the ivory-billed woodpecker was doomed. A Cuban population suffered a similar fate.

IVORY-BILLED WOODPECKER

Labrador Duck *Camptorhynchus labradorius* 20"

The Labrador or sand shoal duck, as it was also known, frequented sandy bays and coastal estuaries in winter. Most of the museum specimens (only 54 exist, the least among the 7 birds in this section) were collected in winter from the shores of Long Island, New York, in the mid-1800s. Not much more is known about the Labrador duck. Some people speculate the ducks nested in Labrador, but because their nesting range was never found, others suppose it was fairly restricted, a few islands perhaps, and that their extinction may have resulted from habitat disruptions by man or introduced predators such as cats and dogs.

It is reliably reported that the Labrador duck was scarce, even in Audubon's day, and that it was hunted for market from at least 1840 to 1860. Perhaps hunting contributed to its extinction. It is also possible that the burgeoning human population along the eastern seaboard in the 1800s interfered with its food supply. This theory is based on its highly specialized bill, with a swollen cere and many lamellae (small, tooth-like projections), which bill implies a very specialized diet or foraging style. A specialist is in serious trouble if its food source is disturbed. It is not known what the diet or foraging style was, but because the Labrador duck was a sea duck, it probably dove for shellfish of some kind.

The last specimen, taken in 1875, is at the Smithsonian Institution in Washington, DC.

imm.

Carolina Parakeet *Conuropsis carolinensis* 16"
Cypress swamps and other wet, wooded bottomlands were home to the Carolina parakeet. It roosted inside large, hollow trees and fed on the seeds of the different forest trees and shrubs. Thistle seeds found at openings in the forest were a favorite food.

Numerous before the arrival of Europeans, the Carolina parakeet quickly disappeared wherever these settlers encroached. By 1832 it was gone from Ohio, although suitable habitat remained for perhaps another 50 years. By 1878 the only birds east of the Mississippi River were in remote parts of Florida. Reported sightings occurred into the 1900s, but a careful survey undertaken in 1938 found no birds. The last known individual died in 1914 in the Cincinnati Zoo.

People hunted Carolina parakeets for their plumage and captured them to sell as cage birds. They were said to become tame in 2 days. Many parakeets were shot as pests because they seriously damaged orchards. They would mischievously strip an entire tree of its fruit without bothering to feed on the seeds. Like other parrots, they lived in family flocks, and their strong social bonds made their eradication fast and sure. John J. Audubon describes the slaughter of a flock: "The living birds, as if conscious of the death of their companions, sweep over their bodies, screaming as loud as ever, but still return...to be shot."

"Heath Hen" *Tympanuchus cupido cupido* 19"
Now considered a race of the greater prairie-chicken, the "heath hen" lived on dry coastal plains partially overgrown with brush and dotted with occasional trees. It foraged widely on berries, seeds, nuts, and insects. As with other grouse, the males gathered at traditional sites to display for females (see Key 86). After mating, the female raised the chicks alone (not in the company of a male, as shown above for the sake of completeness).

Weighing about 3 pounds each, "heath hens" were hunted for food and considered a delicacy by early colonists. As early as 1791, the danger of overhunting was recognized. Laws enacted in New York that year proclaimed a limited hunting season on Long Island, where much of the market hunting for New York City was done. However, the law was not respected by the citizens, and by 1830 the "heath hen" was gone from Long Island and mainland New England.

As the native eastern birds disappeared, hunting organizations imported western birds and released them for shooting. It is not certain whether the population that survived on Martha's Vineyard, MA, into the 20th century was native or introduced from the mainland or the West. Laws passed in 1824 to protect it were successful for some time, but the perils of a small population – predation, disease, inbreeding, catastrophe – culminated in the extinction of the "heath hen'" in 1932.

Bachman's Warbler *Vermivora bachmanii* 4¾"

It is not certain that Bachman's warbler is extinct, but it is probable. Hope for this bird continues partly because it escaped notice for 50 years after being discovered by Dr. Bachman in Charleston, SC, in 1833. It is now thought to have been fairly numerous but seldom seen because it inhabited remote swamps, where it foraged in the canopy and nested in dense tangles of cane, briars, and palmettos. Avid birders still risk ticks, mosquitoes, and cottonmouths to explore suitable habitat in hopes of discovering a remnant population.

In the late 1880s there were regular accounts of Bachman's warbler being encountered in migration in Florida and Louisiana in sizable numbers. On Sombrero Key, FL, 21 Bachman's warblers struck the lighthouse on the single night of March 3, 1889. Continuing into the 1900s nests were discovered with regularity by collectors. But the clearing of the bottomland forest and canebreaks reduced the bird's habitat, and the population seriously diminished by the 1930s, never to recover. Similar changes occurred in Cuba, where the bird wintered.

The last specimen was taken in 1949 in Mississippi. Sightings of varying reliability extend into the 1980s, with photographs of a male taken near Charleston, SC, in 1958. An extensive search of suitable nesting habitat in the late 1970s did not reveal any birds.

Pelagic birds

CONSULTANT **BRIAN PATTESON**
ILLUSTRATORS (AERIALISTS) **BART RULON**
(SWIMMERS) **ALAN MESSER**

Most pelagic aerialists have external nostril tubes.

Pelagic birds live in a separate, larger world than we do – a world of open ocean. It wasn't until 1958 that scientists discovered how pelagic birds could survive without fresh water. Near the base of the bill all have salt glands that enable them to filter excess salt from their blood. The salty waste is expelled through external nostril tubes in many pelagic birds (tubenoses); it drips from the bills of others. Geese and other birds that regularly consume excess salt also have been found to have well-developed salt glands.

Some pelagic birds are swimmers, but most are aerialists that scan the ocean's surface from the wing for food. Albatrosses, shearwaters, gadfly petrels, storm-petrels, and the few gulls and terns that are pelagic mostly feed directly from the surface, often while in flight. Boobies, gannets, and tropicbirds specialize in plunge-diving. They often fly 20 feet or more above the surface and hover briefly before plunging headfirst, like a kingfisher, to the prey below. Other aerialists usually glide closer to the waves. None of the tubenoses are true plunge-divers, although some make shallow dives.

The remaining foraging strategy for a pelagic aerialist, in addition to fishing and scavenging from the open ocean, is to harass other seabirds into giving up their catch. That, in part, is how the strong-flying jaegers and skuas survive at sea. While nesting in the Arctic, jaegers also prey heavily on rodents and other land life. Most pelagic species continue to forage at sea when nesting.

Flight permits a bird to search a wide ocean expanse. Pelagic swimmers, almost all members of the auk family and called alcids, use a different strategy. Most of them gather at traditional fishing sites and begin their hunt for prey once they submerge. Unlike most divers, which use webbed feet for propulsion, auks use their wings to "fly" underwater. Feet are used as a rudder. The extinct great auk, like the penguins of the Antarctic, was so large and its wings so modified that it could "fly" only underwater. All our remaining alcids fly rapidly – in the air – on rather short, whirring wings.

Two phalaropes, members of the sandpiper family, are also found swimming far out in the ocean. They often spin on the water, apparently to stir up minute organisms, which they pick from the water with their finely pointed bills. Sexual roles are reversed in phalaropes. Females are larger, more brightly marked, and aggressive; males incubate the eggs and rear the young.

Although pelagic birding trips have become popular in recent years, and more specialists study pelagic birds, there is still much to learn about their ocean ranges and biology. When not nesting, some seem to wander according to shifting food sources and weather patterns. Others congregate at fixed areas or migrate in a continuous pattern. Some that nest in the Southern Hemisphere "winter" off our shores during our summer.

In addition to the occasional pelagic bird blown inland by hurricanes, there are several species, including the sooty shearwater, that are frequently seen from mainland North America. Black-vented shearwaters are regularly seen off the West Coast and gannets off the East Coast. On rare occasions pelagic birds can also be seen inland on the Great Lakes and at the Salton Sea, a lake near the Gulf of California. Pelagic trips are scheduled at several coastal points, including Westport, WA; Monterey Bay, CA; and Hatteras, NC. Still, few people will ever see a sooty shearwater, although flocks can include hundreds of thousands of birds.

The plumage marks of a distant bird can be difficult to see from a pitching boat under viewing conditions often encountered on the open ocean. Flight style and behavior, described on each Key, are important factors in identification.

Because their remote island and sea-cliff nesting sites were historically free of predators, nesting seabirds have developed no defenses against humans – or cats, rats, or other introduced predators. The names "booby" and "gooney bird" (for the Laysan albatross) were inspired by the odd inability of these birds to learn to defend themselves against threats on land. Even the open ocean is no longer a sanctuary for seabirds. Large numbers of birds are lost annually to gill nets and longlines. Alcids are the principal victims of gill nets. Bait set by longline fishermen often catches albatrosses, and many die. Ships at sea have altered some seabirds' behavior. A few – identified in the Keys – commonly follow ships in search of refuse. Trawlers and fish-processing ships also attract some species and have had an effect on their ranges and numbers.

Nesting islands off the coast of Maine that were historically plundered by man are now being restored through efforts of the National Audubon Society and the American and Canadian governments. Over 150 pairs of Atlantic puffins and a growing colony of terns now nest on isolated rocks like Eastern Egg Rock and Seal Island National Wildlife Refuge, and attempts to reintroduce gannets and murres are under way. In Bermuda, the Bermuda petrel, thought to be extinct for over 300 years, is slowly recovering with management of its nest sites.

imm.

**Laysan
Albatross**

The Laysan is the whiter albatross, although an old black-footed can become much lighter on the head and body than illustrated. Masters of the wind, albatrosses sail over the waves gracefully on very long, narrow wings. They alight to feed on fish, squid, and refuse. Without wind, they labor to fly and often rest on the water.

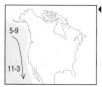

◄**Laysan Albatross** *Diomedea immutabilis* L 32" W 82"
Scarce in winter well off West Coast; more common in summer off Aleutians. Nests in Hawaii; known as "gooney bird." Has recently begun nesting on islands off Baja California. Sometimes follows ships. ● White with dark mantle, tail, eye smudge. Can show creamy tinge on head and neck. Complex underwing pattern. Imm. has gray bill with dark tip.

Short-tailed Albatross

adults

1st yr.

great
black-backed
gull Key 15

Black-browed
Albatross

Yellow-nosed Albatross

Black-footed Albatross

5-8

4-10

◀**Black-footed Albatross** *Diomedea nigripes* L 32" W 82"
Fairly numerous in spring and summer; rare at other times.
Has declined. Once nested widely in N. Pacific; most now
nest on Hawaiian Is. Follows ships. ● Mostly dark gray.
Whitish area around bill spreads onto face and crown with
age; rump and underparts also become paler.

Yellow-nosed Albatross *Diomedea chlororhynchos* L 31" W 80" S. Hemisphere;
a few records in N. Atlantic and Caribbean. ● White underwings with narrow
dark borders. Yellow ridge on black bill hard to see; absent on imm.

Black-browed Albatross *Diomedea melanophris* L 35" W 88" A few recent records
in N. Atlantic. ● Broad black underwing borders. Yellow bill; gray on imm.

Short-tailed Albatross *Diomedea albatrus* L 35" W 88" Very rare in N. Pacific.
Once abundant; nearly extirpated by Japanese plume hunters. A few hundred
now nest on Torishima I., Japan; increasing under protection. ● Pink bill, feet.
1st yr. dark brown; amount of white below gradually increases until adult.

juv.

Gannet

1st winter

Masked Booby

imm.

Gannets and boobies are large, heavy birds that taper to a point at both ends. Flying strongly on stiff wings, they climb high to plunge-dive for fish. Adults have distinctive plumages and brightly colored bills and feet, but identification of young birds requires care where species ranges overlap. Young birds take three or four years to acquire adult plumage. While gannets roost on the water, boobies also roost on remote islands, buoys, oil rigs, and trees.

◀**Gannet** (Northern) *Morus bassanus* L 36" W 72"
Abundant near nesting colonies in summer. Seen regularly from shore during migration and winter; often in flocks.
● White with black wing tips, yellowish wash on head. Gray bill. Juv. all dark at a distance. Head, underparts turn white first; tail, secondaries last. In contrast, boobies' head remains dark for most of 1st yr. or longer.

Red-footed Booby

white form

brown form

1st yr.

Blue-footed Booby

1st yr.

imm.

Brown Booby

imm.

western form

◀**Masked Booby** *Sula dactylatra* L 32" W 62"
Scarce in Gulf of Mexico, rare but regular in Gulf Stream to
NC.; usually alone. ● Black tail (white in gannet). Black
mask, wing tips, secondaries. Imm. has white patch on upper
back, rump; more white on breast, neck than brown booby.

◀**Brown Booby** *Sula leucogaster* L 29" W 57"
Rare off FL and in Gulf of Mexico; records north to MA.
● Brown upperparts, head, and breast meet white belly at
leading edge of wing. Western form (recorded in late sum-
mer at Salton Sea and coastal CA) has whitish head, neck.
Imm. brown overall with white wing linings.

Red-footed Booby *Sula sula* L 28" W 59" Tropical. Rare but regular at Dry
Tortugas, FL; several records off CA. ● Adults of both color forms have red feet;
1st-yr. birds, yellow-gray feet. Imm. brown, paler below with dark wing linings.

Blue-footed Booby *Sula nebouxii* L 31" W 62" Tropical. Rare, irregular at Salton
Sea, CA, in late summer, fall; often imms. ● Adult has streaked head, blue feet.
White nape, rump patches in all plumages. Imm. more streaked below, dull feet.

Red-tailed Tropicbird

Red-billed Tropicbird

imm.

imm.

White-tailed
Tropicbird

Tropicbirds fly with pigeon-like wing beats and plunge-dive for
fish from heights of over 100 feet. The upperparts are diagnostic
but hard to see from below. At all ages the black patch in the
primaries is larger in the red-billed tropicbird than in the white-
tailed, extending onto the primary coverts. The terns have forked
tails; adults resemble each other, but the bridled tern is paler
above than the sooty tern and has more white in its face and tail.

◀**Red-billed Tropicbird** *Phaethon aethereus* L 18-38" W 42"
Very rare. ● White with long tail streamers, black primaries
and primary coverts, red bill. Fine barring on mantle may
appear gray at a distance. Imm. lacks streamers; finely
barred above, with black collar on nape; yellow bill.

◀**White-tailed Tropicbird** *Phaethon lepturus* L 16-30" W 36"
Rare, well offshore and at Dry Tortugas, FL; singly or in
pairs. ● Slender, white with long tail streamers, black
carpal bar and outer primaries, white primary coverts. Bill
yellow to orange. Imm. lacks streamers; boldly barred.

Black Noddy　**Brown Noddy**

sooty tern

bridled tern

Bridled Tern

Sooty Tern

juv.

juv.

◀**Sooty Tern** *Sterna fuscata* L 15" W 34"
Nests abundantly at Dry Tortugas, FL; has nested in TX, LA, NC. Scarce away from nesting colonies; alone or in small groups. Often blown ashore by hurricanes. Feeds from surface in flight. ● Blackish above, white below, with white forehead patch, deeply forked tail. Juv. mostly dark brown with white wing linings; fine spots above in fresh plumage.

4-10

◀**Bridled Tern** *Sterna anaethetus* L 14" W 32"
Nests in Bahamas, W. Indies. Scarce in Gulf and Atlantic; singly or in small groups. Feeds like sooty tern. Often perches on flotsam, which sooty tern rarely does. ● Like sooty tern but slimmer, gray-brown above with indistinct white collar, narrow white line over eye. Juv. paler brown above than adult, whiter head.

6-9
4-10

Red-tailed Tropicbird *Phaethon rubricauda* L 18-38" W 42" Very rare far off CA.

Brown Noddy *Anous stolidus* L 15" W 32" Tropical. Nesting colony at Bush Key, Dry Tortugas, FL. ● Whitish cap, reduced in imm. Long, wedge-shaped tail.

Black Noddy *Anous minutus* L 13" W 28" Rare among brown noddies on Dry Tortugas, FL. ● Long, thin bill in all ages. Adult blacker than brown noddy, with bolder white cap. Imm. similar in color to brown noddy.

TROPICBIRDS / TERNS

3

summer   **Black-legged**   winter
          Kittiwake

imm.

Great Skua

Two gulls are pelagic for most of the year: Sabine's gull and the black-legged kittiwake. The adult wing patterns are obvious and diagnostic, but the pattern of a young kittiwake, seen from a distance, can suggest that of Sabine's gull. Skuas are strong-flying robbers, like the jaegers on the following Key. The white patches in their primaries are bolder and more extensive than in the jaegers'. The two skuas can be difficult to distinguish. The best clue is the overall color, which is a warmer brown in the great skua.

9-5

10-4   11-4

◀**Black-legged Kittiwake** *Rissa tridactyla* L 17" W 38"
Numerous in winter, esp. off NE Maritimes and in Gulf of
Alaska; scarcer to south. Seen occasionally from both coasts.
Most stay near nesting cliffs during summer. Feeds from
surface either in flight or while resting on water. Distinctive
buoyant flight with quick wing beats. Follows ships, attends
trawlers. ● Black wing tips and legs. Short yellow bill, round
forehead. Winter adult has head and nape smudged with
gray. Imm. has black bill, black hind collar and tail band, black

M on upperparts; compare with imm. Bonaparte's gull (Key 21). Like adult by 2nd winter. ♪ *Kittiwake*, high, nasal call.

◀**Great Skua** *Catharacta skua* L 23" W 55"
Rare far offshore; usually alone. ● Stout, hunch-backed appearance. Broad wings, with white base of primaries in upper- and underwing. Gold and reddish streaking on upperparts visible at close range. Dark cap. Imm. duller, but still warmer brown than South Polar skua.

9-4
12-4

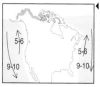

◀**South Polar Skua** *Catharacta maccormicki* L 21" W 50"
Antarctic. Scarce off West Coast, rare well offshore in Atlantic; typically alone. ● Colors vary from nearly solid cold brown to birds with pale heads and underparts. Most have distinctive gold wash on nape.

5-10
6-8
5-6

Sabine's Gull *Xema sabini* L 13" W 34"
Fairly numerous in migration in Pacific, often in small flocks; much rarer in Atlantic. Rare in interior during fall (mostly juvs.). Picks food from surface. Tern-like flight. Follows ships. ● Triangular wing pattern. Notched tail diagnostic but seldom conspicuous. Juv. lacks hood and yellow tip on bill; has brownish upperparts, dark tail band; molts after migration. Hood incomplete in 1st summer.

5-6
5-6
9-10
9-10

GULLS / SKUAS

4

Pomarine Jaeger

dark form

pale form

juv.

Long-tailed Jaeger

pale juv.

dark juv.

Jaegers are muscular, predatory cousins of gulls. The central tail feathers, when present, are diagnostic on juveniles as well as adults. When they are broken or missing, identification requires care. Plumages vary considerably within each species, and there are similarities among all species. Veteran observers study shapes, flight styles, and plumage details and still leave some birds unidentified. Most jaegers take four years to acquire adult plumage and the varied subadult plumages are still not well understood.

5-6

5-6

8-11

8-11

11-3

◀**Pomarine Jaeger** *Stercorarius pomarinus* L 18-22" W 48"
Fairly numerous in migration. Scarce in winter off CA and in Gulf of Mexico. Flight strong, like that of large gull.
● Largest, bulkiest jaeger. Long, twisted, blunt-tipped central tail feathers in adult. Pale form much more common than dark. Breast band (lacking in some pale adults) more mottled than in parasitic jaeger. Juv. can be much darker than shown, but usually rump is paler than nape and extensions of the central tail feathers are very short, blunt.

Parasitic Jaeger

parasitic jaeger
chasing tern

dark form

pale form

dark juv.

pale juv.

◀**Long-tailed Jaeger** *Stercorarius longicaudus* L 15-22" W 39"
Scarce in migration, usually well offshore. Flight buoyant,
tern-like. ● Smallest, slimmest jaeger. Narrower wings than
in parasitic jaeger, with long-tailed look even without streamers. Clean white throat and breast. Gray mantle contrasts
with blacker primaries, secondaries. Small, neat black cap.
Dark-form adults virtually unknown. Juvs. vary from pale to
dark, with pale birds grayer, colder brown than parasitic
jaeger. Barring on rump and undertail straighter, bolder than
in parasitic; less white in primaries; short, blunt tail streamers.

◀**Parasitic Jaeger** *Stercorarius parasiticus* L 16-19" W 42"
Scarce in migration, usually closer to shore than other
jaegers. Scarce off s. CA and rare off southeastern US
in winter. Often chases terns. Flight falcon-like with quicker
wing beats than in pomarine jaeger, deeper than in long-
tailed jaeger. ● The midsize jaeger. Adults have flat,
pointed central tail feathers. Pale form usually has smooth
breast band, unlike mottled band of pomarine jaeger. Juv.
variable, usually warm brown with nape paler than rump;
very short, pointed tail streamers; vague wavy barring on
rump and undertail. Juv. shows more white in wing than
does juv. long-tailed jaeger.

Sooty Shearwater

Greater Shearwater

Shearwaters fly on bowed wings, arcing up over the ocean swells and disappearing into the troughs. Their stiff-winged glides are interrupted by shallow, rapid wing beats. In high winds they make towering arcs and do little flapping. The sooty shearwater is the only common large, dark tubenose on the Atlantic. Cory's can be confused with the greater shearwater, but the greater is darker above with a sharply defined dark cap and a dark, not yellow, bill. The smaller shearwaters, Audubon's and Manx, closely resemble one another, but are seldom found together.

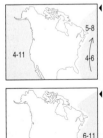

◀**Sooty Shearwater** *Puffinus griseus* L 17" W 40"
Numerous in Atlantic, abundant in Pacific and regularly seen from shore. Flocks can number in the hundreds of thousands and include other species. Attends trawlers, but seldom follows other ships. ● Grayish brown overall with contrasting whitish area on underwing coverts. Bill all dark, legs dark.

◀**Greater Shearwater** *Puffinus gravis* L 19" W 43"
Fairly numerous; can be in large flocks, sometimes mixed. Flight stiffer-winged than Cory's with shallower, more rapid stroke. Follows ships, attends trawlers. ● Distinct dark brown cap, dark bill. White collar often inconspicuous or

Cory's Shearwater

Audubon's Shearwater

Manx Shearwater

lacking. Very dark upperparts, usually with white tail coverts. Dark smudge on lower belly diagnostic but hard to see.

5-10

◀**Cory's Shearwater** *Calonectris diomedea* L 20" W 46"
Fairly numerous, sometimes in mixed flocks with greater and Audubon's shearwaters. Usually feed in warm waters, often over tuna. Wing stroke looser, deeper, slower than in other large shearwaters. ● Yellowish bill with gray tip. Smooth brown above, blending to white below. Usually shows whitish uppertail coverts.

◀**Manx Shearwater** *Puffinus puffinus* L 13" W 33"
Scarce but increasing; mostly off NE Maritimes. A cold-water species, most often in waters colder than 60° F. Rare in winter off Southeast; very rare but annual off West Coast. Flies with stiff wing beats in short bursts, followed by long glides, much like greater shearwater. ● Black above, white below. Longer wings, shorter tail than in Audubon's. Undertail coverts white, never dark.

3-10

5-10
4-10   1-12

◀**Audubon's Shearwater** *Puffinus lherminieri* L 12" W 27"
Fairly numerous over warm southern waters, rare to NY and in winter in Gulf Stream off southeastern US. Prefers waters over 70° F. Often in flocks. Nests in Caribbean. Fluttery wing beats, short glides, quick turns. ● Dark brown or black above, white below, but undertail coverts usually dark. Whiter face than in Manx shearwater; longer tail and more extensive black margins on underwings.

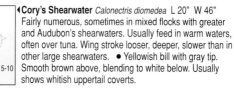

On the Pacific, two regularly seen shearwaters closely resemble the dark and abundant sooty. The flesh-footed is often found in mixed shearwater flocks and is distinguished from the sooty by its bulkier shape, slower wing beat, and pale bill and legs. The short-tailed usually is not seen south of Alaska until late fall, when most sootys have left. Other Pacific shearwaters are white below and easy to identify. The dark M across the upperparts of Buller's can suggest a gadfly petrel (Key 8), but Buller's is larger and has a longer bill.

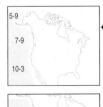

Sooty Shearwater See Key 6.

◀**Short-tailed Shearwater** *Puffinus tenuirostris* L 16" W 37"
Abundant off AK, numerous from B.C. to CA in winter.
Follows ships. ● Like sooty shearwater but slightly smaller with shorter, slimmer bill; steeper, rounded forehead. Wing linings variable but usually grayer, more evenly colored than sooty's. Birds with pale wing linings often have small white throat patch, can show pale mottling on breast and belly.

◀**Flesh-footed Shearwater** *Puffinus carneipes* L 19" W 43"
Scarce. Usually found individually at trawlers in mixed flocks of shearwaters. Wing beats slower than in sooty

Streaked Shearwater

Wedge-tailed
Shearwater

Buller's
Shearwater

Pink-footed
Shearwater

Black-vented
Shearwater

4-10

8-11

10-4

shearwater, with longer glides. ● Blackish brown with pale legs, pale bill with dark tip, dark wing linings.

◀**Pink-footed Shearwater** *Puffinus creatopus* L 19" W 43"
Fairly numerous offshore; rare in winter. Often in flocks, sometimes among sooty shearwaters. Follows ships.
● Grayish brown above, whitish below with mottled sides and wing linings. Pink feet and pink, dark-tipped bill.

◀**Buller's Shearwater** *Puffinus bulleri* L 17" W 40"
Scarce; often in flocks, seldom mixed with other shearwaters. Fairly deep, slow wing beats; buoyant, wheeling flight.
● Bright white below with white underwings. Upperparts gray with dark M pattern, dark cap, dark wedge-shaped tail.

Black-vented Shearwater *Puffinus opisthomelas* L 14" W 33"
◀Fairly numerous, often close to shore. Fluttery wing beats, little gliding. ● Dark brown above blending to white below. Dusky sides sometimes form breast band. Undertail coverts dusky brown. Compare with Manx shearwater (Key 6).

Streaked Shearwater *Calonectris leucomelas* L 19" W 48" W. Pacific. Recorded off CA. Slow, lumbering flight. ● Pale head with darker streaks. Pale bill.

Wedge-tailed Shearwater *Puffinus pacificus* L 17" W 40" Tropical. Recorded off CA. Most like Buller's shearwater in shape, flight style. ● Dark bill. Slender with long, wedge-shaped tail. Dark form (not shown) sooty brown, paler on underwing.

Fulmars are bulky with bulging foreheads and thick, pale bills. They vary from an overall dark gray to pale birds with a gull-like gray mantle. Like shearwaters, fulmars and gadfly petrels pick food from the ocean's surface, but gadfly petrels often sail higher and more acrobatically, with wings bent more at the wrist. Note the gadfly petrel's short, stout bill. The black-capped petrel resembles the greater shearwater (Key 6), but the petrel's white rump is more prominent and the underwing pattern is different.

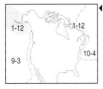

◀**Fulmar** (Northern) *Fulmarus glacialis* L 18" W 42"
Abundant in Far North; scarcer to south, sporadic to dashed line on map. Sometimes scavenges from trawlers, ships. Flies on flat wings with stiff, shallow strokes and arcing glides. ● Stocky with bull neck, prominent forehead, stout yellow bill; nostril tubes conspicuous. Pale form predominates in Atlantic, dark form in Pacific, with many gray intergrades.

◀**Black-capped Petrel** *Pterodroma hasitata* L 16" W 37"
Fairly numerous in warm waters of Gulf Stream. Nests in Hispaniola mountains; has seriously declined. ● Dark gray above, with white collar and rump patch, but collar can be hard to see and rump patch reduced. Black cap, white forehead, diagonal black bar on white underwing.

Stejneger's Petrel

Cape Verde Petrel

Herald Petrel

dark form

pale form

Murphy's Petrel

Cook's Petrel

◀**Mottled Petrel** *Pterodroma inexpectata* L 14" W 32"
Fairly numerous well offshore in Gulf of Alaska; rare to
south. Flies rapidly, sails in great arcs. ● Gray belly. White
underwings with black bar, dark M across upperparts.
Blackish eye patch and gray cap evident at close range.

▶**Murphy's Petrel** *Pterodroma ultima* L 16" W 38"
Abundance uncertain, probably variable; scarce to numerous far offshore. Typical gadfly flight. ● Gray-brown above
with dark M contrasting less than in other petrels. Pale flash
in underwing extends toward body. Pale throat.

Cook's Petrel *Pterodroma cookii* L 12" W 30"
Possibly fairly numerous, but uncertain. Typically far offshore.
● Small with long, narrow wings. Gray above with black M
◀across upperparts, black eye patch, white outer tail feather.
White below except for narrow black markings on underwing.

Stejneger's Petrel *Pterodroma longirostris* L 12" W 30" Several records far off CA.
● Similar to Cook's but contrasting dark cap, dark tail lacks white edges.

Cape Verde Petrel *Pterodroma feae* L 14" W 35" Several records, most off NC.
● Underwings mostly dark, pale gray tail. Often shows dark M on upperparts.

Herald Petrel *Pterodroma arminjoniana* L 15" W 37" Several records off NC.
● Variable, but all forms have jaeger-like white flash in underprimaries.

Bermuda Petrel *Pterodroma cahow* L 15" W 35" (Not shown) About 50 pairs nest
on Bermuda. Pelagic range uncertain. ● Like small black-capped petrel but
with smaller bill; smaller, grayer rump patch; hooded, not capped appearance.

Leach's Storm-Petrel

Baja California form

typical

Wilson's Storm-Petrel

Band-rumped Storm-Petrel

Wilson's is the common Atlantic storm-petrel. It flies directly and has a larger white rump patch than the band-rumped or Leach's storm-petrels. The band-rumped inhabits warm waters. Leach's prefers cold water and has a distinctive erratic bounding flight. Over much of the Pacific, Leach's shares range with the fork-tailed storm-petrel, our only gray species. Off California, three more storm-petrels complicate identification. The sparrow-size least storm-petrel is distinctive with its wedge-shaped tail, but the ashy and black storm-petrels resemble each other as well as Leach's, which, off southern California, can lack the white rump.

◀**Leach's Storm-Petrel** *Oceanodroma leucorhoa* L 8" W 18" Abundant in Maritimes and at scattered island nesting colonies along West Coast. Migrates off continental shelf. Nighthawk-like bounding flight; raises wings well above horizontal, takes deep wing strokes. ● Long wings bent at wrist. Forked tail can be hard to see. Off-white rump patch (usually clearly divided) may be faint or lacking in birds off s. CA.

◀**Wilson's Storm-Petrel** *Oceanites oceanicus* L 7" W 16" Abundant in Atlantic, often in flocks and often seen from shore; scarce in Gulf; very rare in Pacific. Skims over waves like swallow with some glides on flat wings. Usually feeds by pattering feet on water. Follows ships. ● Short wings held straight at wrist. Square tail. Broad, U-shaped white rump patch extends onto undertail coverts. Feet extend beyond tail; yellow webs on toes visible at very close range.

Wedge-rumped Storm-Petrel

White-faced Storm-Petrel

Least Storm-Petrel

Ashy Storm-Petrel

Black Storm-Petrel

Fork-tailed Storm-Petrel

◀**Band-rumped Storm-Petrel** *Oceanodroma castro* L 8" W 18" Scarce over warm, deep water. May form small flocks. Shearwater-like glides on bowed, sickle-shaped wings interrupted by strong, rapid wing beats, shallower than in Leach's storm-petrel. ● Smaller white rump than in Wilson's storm-petrel, with less white extending below.

◀**Black Storm-Petrel** *Oceanodroma melania* L 9" W 20" Numerous, sometimes in flocks. Small colony nests off s. CA. Graceful flight; deliberate strokes with wings raised well above horizontal, sometimes mixed with glides, shallower strokes. ● Dark brown with long, pointed wings; forked tail.

◀**Fork-tailed Storm-Petrel** *Oceanodroma furcata* L 8½" W 18" Abundant off AK, increasingly scarce south to n. CA; often in flocks. Flight similar to ashy storm-petrel's. ● Gray above, paler below, with dark wing linings, ear patch; forked tail.

Ashy Storm-Petrel *Oceanodroma homochroa* L 7½" W 17" Scarce except around nesting islands in summer and stag-◀ing areas in fall; in flocks. Direct flight, with shallower wing beats than in black storm-petrel; wings raised barely above horizontal. ● Paler wing linings than in black storm-petrel, rounder wings. Very long, forked tail.

◀**Least Storm-Petrel** *Oceanodroma microsoma* L 6" W 13" Numerous visitor in some autumns, rare in others; alone or in flocks. Swift, direct flight; deep, rapid wing beats. ● Small and dark with short wings, short wedge-shaped tail.

Wedge-rumped Storm-Petrel *Oceanodroma tethys* L 6½" Tropical. Recorded off CA.

White-faced Storm-Petrel *Pelagodroma marina* L 8" W 17" W. Atlantic. Rare off East Coast. ● Unmistakable; bounces kangaroo-like across water on long legs.

STORM-PETRELS

9

Common Murre

summer

"bridled" form

winter

Thick-billed Murre

summer

winter

The dark brown upperparts that help distinguish the common murre from the thick-billed murre can be hard to discern at a distance. In winter the common murre has more white on the sides of its face and a dark line behind the eye. Differences in bill shape can be seen at close range. Young razorbills have smaller bills than the adults; their thicker bodies and longer tails help distinguish them from murres. The dovekie is the only tiny Atlantic alcid.

◀**Common Murre** *Uria aalge* 18"
Numerous off West Coast, less numerous in Atlantic; alone or in small flocks. Nests in colonies on rocky coasts, cliffs.
● Bill longer, more slender and pointed than in thick-billed murre; flanks streaked. Head, neck brown in summer. Atlantic "bridled" form has white eye-ring and eye stripe. In winter has dark eyeline on white face. Juv. and 1st summer like winter.

Thick-billed Murre *Uria lomvia* 18"
More numerous and widespread than common murre off East Coast. Same habits as common murre. ● Shorter,

Dovekie

summer

winter

Razorbill

summer

imm.

winter

◄thicker bill than in common. White stripe on edge of upper mandible visible at close range. Black above, white below. In summer usually has sharper white point at throat than in common; in winter, more extensive black on face and cheek than in common. Juv. and 1st summer like winter.

Razorbill *Alca torda* 17"
About 25,000 pairs. Numerous off New England in winter, ◄scarcer to south; usually in small groups. Numbers increasing off ME; and range may be expanding south: fairly numerous some years south to Cape Hatteras, NC. Nests on cliffs with murres, also in boulder fields, crevices. ● Bulky, with large head, thick neck. Blade-like bill has vertical white stripe. Horizontal white stripe in front of eye in summer. In winter shows white foreneck and side of face. Long, pointed tail often held cocked when swimming. Juv. and imm. like winter but with smaller bill, more extensive black on face.

Dovekie *Alle alle* 8"
Abundant, but irregular, in flocks in winter; scarcer to south. Nests in Greenland. A few resident in northern Bering Sea and Baffin I. Flocks in fall sometimes blown ashore by storms. ● Tiny, plump, with tiny bill. White breast, throat, and side of face in winter. Dark underwings.

ALCIDS

10

Atlantic Puffin

summer

horned puffin
Key 164

imm.

winter

Tufted Puffin

imm.

summer

winter

Outsize, brilliantly colored bills characterize the puffins. In fall the outer layers are shed but the bills are still massive. The head plumes of the tufted puffin in summer add to its bizarre look. Guillemots have slender bills and slender necks; they seldom show the hunched profile while swimming that is common in other alcids. In all plumages, adults have black wings, each with an oval white patch. The pigeon guillemot has a black bar across the white wing patch and dusky wing linings. Guillemots are usually seen near shore, in bays or on rocks in the intertidal zone.

1-12

12-4

◀**Atlantic Puffin** *Fratercula arctica* 12"
Numerous near nesting colonies in summer. Small numbers nest in high Arctic. Colonies being restored on islands off ME. Nests colonially in burrows or on rocky island slopes, headlands. Scarce in winter, usually seen singly or in small flocks well offshore. ● Smaller overall and more compact than razorbill, murres (Key 10). Unmistakable in summer with large colorful bill. Winter birds and imm. have dusky faces, much smaller and duller bills. Adult bill develops over 5 yrs.

white-winged scoter
Key 38

summer

Black Guillemot

winter

winter

winter

summer

winter

summer

Pigeon Guillemot

◀**Tufted Puffin** *Fratercula cirrhata* 15"
Abundant in nesting colonies in Arctic, scarcer to south; range contracting northward. Nests in diverse habitats: burrows, sea cliffs, rocky slopes. Usually seen singly or in pairs in winter, far from shore. Swims low, back often underwater.
● Huge, blade-like red-and-yellow bill in summer with white face, yellow head plumes. Plumage dark gray in winter; bill smaller, duller. Imm. like winter adult but can be pale, nearly white, on belly and has smaller, yellowish bill.

1-12
10-5

◀**Pigeon Guillemot** *Cepphus columba* 13"
Numerous in coastal waters, esp. in summer. Pairs nest alone or in small groups on rocky shores, often near high-tide line. ● Black in summer with white wing patch crossed by black bar. Bright red legs, dusky wing linings. Winter adult retains black wings, white patches; underparts white, upperparts white with dark barring. 1st-winter birds darker and with dark mottling on white wing patch. 1st-summer birds patchy black and white.

1-12
3-9

◀**Black Guillemot** *Cepphus grylle* 13"
Fairly numerous in coastal waters in summer. Pairs nest alone or in colonies along rocky coasts. Winters farther offshore, singly or in small groups. ● Much like pigeon guillemot but lacks dark bar on white wing patch, has white wing linings. Wing patch mottled in 1st summer.

1-12   1-12

ALCIDS

11

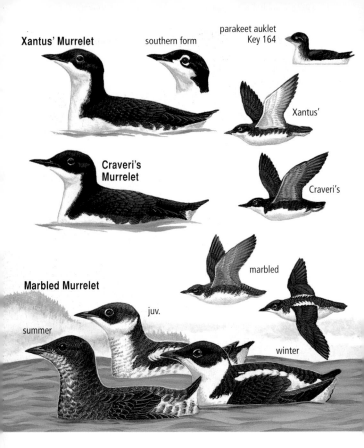

Xantus' and Craveri's murrelets are very difficult to separate; both have crisp black and white markings and long, slender bills. The marbled murrelet is mottled brown in summer; in winter it shows a distinctive white stripe at the base of the wing. The ancient murrelet has a gray back, contrasting with its black crown, and a short, pale bill; summer birds have wispy white head plumes. Cassin's auklet often seems uniformly dark but has a pale belly, stubby bill, and more rounded wings than murrelets. The larger rhinoceros auklet is also dark but has a yellow bill, with a pale "horn" and white head plumes in summer. The auklets and the ancient and marbled murrelets come ashore at night to visit their nests and return to the ocean before sunrise to avoid predators.

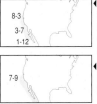

◀**Xantus' Murrelet** *Synthliboramphus hypoleucus* 10"
Scarce, often in pairs. Rides low with head high, alert. Flies straight, close to water. Nests north to San Miguel I. off s. CA.
● White throat and breast; long, thin bill; white wing linings. Southern form, rare off CA in fall, has white above eye.

◀**Craveri's Murrelet** *Synthliboramphus craveri* 10"
Rare but regular off s. CA. ● Like Xantus' but has partial black breast band, most noticeable in flight; slightly

winter

summer

Rhinoceros Auklet

rhinoceros

Cassin's Auklet

Cassin's

juv.

winter

summer

Ancient Murrelet

1-12

1-12

11-4

1-12

11-4

1-12

10-4

longer and thinner bill; black on face extending under bill. Dusky wing linings distinctive but can be hard to see as bird often flies directly away from boat.

◀**Marbled Murrelet** *Brachyramphus marmoratus* 10"
Numerous in north, scarcer to south. Usually alone or in family groups, but shy, seldom seen. Nests separately, high in mature trees of old-growth forest; seriously declining with loss of habitat. Also nests on ground in Far North.
● Mottled brown in summer, darker above. In winter, dark gray above with white scapulars, white below. Juv. like winter but shows some mottling below.

◀**Ancient Murrelet** *Synthliboramphus antiquus* 10"
Fairly numerous in small flocks, usually just offshore. Nests colonially in burrows. ● Small, pale bill; black head, throat; gray back. Less black on throat in winter, little or none on juv.

◀**Cassin's Auklet** *Ptychoramphus aleuticus* 9"
Numerous. Nests in burrows, rock slides. Often well offshore in winter. ● Plump, neckless look. Mostly gray with white belly, pale eyes, pale spot on lower mandible. Juv. paler overall with whitish throat.

◀**Rhinoceros Auklet** *Cerorhinca monocerata* 15"
Fairly numerous in winter in flocks, near shore and offshore; increasing off CA. Nests in burrows or caves. Actually a misnamed puffin. ● Large, brownish gray with pale yellow bill. In summer, horn on bill, white plumes on head.

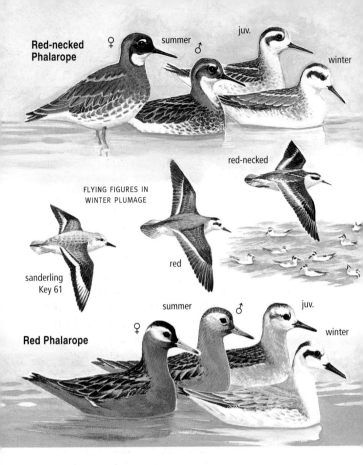

The dark "phalarope patch" behind each eye in winter phalaropes distinguishes them from their shorebird relatives. The red-necked's bill is thinner than the red's; its winter plumage darker with a streaked back. Summer birds have distinctive colors, and females are brighter than males. Phalaropes sit high and cork-like, often spinning in tight circles, feeding on tiny marine life.

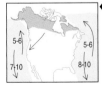

◀ **Red-necked Phalarope** *Phalaropus lobatus* 7½"
Numerous in flocks during migration on Pacific; some migrate over land. Less common migrant on Atlantic but still fairly numerous. ● Thin, needle-like bill. In winter, white below, dark gray above with streaked back, dark ear patch. Summer female has chestnut collar, gray head, white throat; male duller. Juv. similar to winter adult but with bright buff stripes on back.

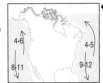

◀ **Red Phalarope** *Phalaropus fulicaria* 8½"
Scarce; in flocks at sea during migration. Rare off CA and southeastern coast in winter. ● Stockier than red-necked, with stouter bill. In winter, unstreaked pale gray above, white below with dark ear patch. Summer female chestnut below with white face; male duller. Juv. buffier than winter adult with mostly gray back.

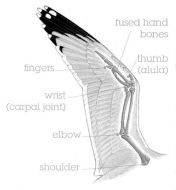

fused hand bones

thumb (alula)

fingers

wrist (carpal joint)

elbow

shoulder

Bones corresponding to our index and little fingers are missing in a bird's "hand."

Aerialists

CONSULTANT **EIRIK BLOM**
ARTIST **BARRY VAN DUSEN**

The birds that forage from the air along our coasts (mostly gulls and terns) have distinctively long, narrow wings, which are perfectly adapted for effortless gliding on light shore breezes. Gulls scavenge, feeding on anything edible that floats to the top of the water or washes ashore. The larger gulls also take whatever they can kill, or steal from other birds. Live fish, squid, or other morsels that swim too close to the water's surface are popular meals, and flying insects are taken by some gulls. Bugs are a major source of food for terns, but their most common meal is fish caught by plunge-diving (diving while airborne, rather than from the water's surface). In all cases the strategy depends on gliding efficiently over large areas to collect food – at least it did until gulls discovered garbage dumps. Our refuse has become a major source of food for some gulls, especially in winter.

Gulls and terns are the only shoreline aerialists found along lakeshores, rivers, and inland marshes. But along the seacoasts there are also magnificent frigatebirds, black skimmers, and brown pelicans. Each has developed strikingly distinctive adaptations for foraging, as described in the first two Keys of this section.

The vast number of gull plumages and the similarity of many of them present one of birding's most complex challenges. Adults are gray or black above, with many showing only subtle differences between species. Juveniles are mostly brown above, very

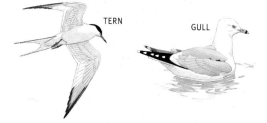

TERN

GULL

Terns are sleeker, more streamlined than gulls, with forked tails and pointed bills. They often fly with their bills pointed down as they scan the water for food; they seldom sit on the water as gulls do.

different from adults but very much like each other. Between the brown juvenal plumage and the gray adult plumage most species undergo more than half a dozen distinct plumage changes. Furthermore, some large gulls hybridize extensively, producing confusing combinations of features.

Identifying gulls may be challenging, but you will seldom run out of gulls to identify, even when shores are otherwise deserted. Rarities are easier to discover in a large flock of gulls than among warblers, for instance, simply because gulls are easier to find and examine in large numbers. A flock of gulls can be readily scanned for the small differences in size, shape, and shade that can be a hint of a rare hybrid or an out-of-range wanderer.

First learn to recognize and separate adult gulls. The smaller species have dark-hooded heads in summer, while the larger ones are white-headed. It is the large, white-headed adult gulls that present the most difficulty. In some cases ornithologists still have trouble deciding these birds' identities. Thayer's gull (Key 17) has, in recent times, been considered a race of the herring gull, a dark form of the Iceland gull, and a cross between herring and Iceland gulls.

On some white-headed gulls virtually every observable distinction is worthy of note, even the color of the eye and the fleshy orbital ring that surrounds it. The bill is always an important mark, and so is overall size, the shade of the upperwing, and the pattern on the wing tip. Two marks important in gull identification have imposing names but are quite easy to see. Just below midback on a standing bird is the scapular crescent. At the rump is the tertial crescent. Scapular and tertial crescents can be narrow, wide, or absent; they are always white on adult gulls.

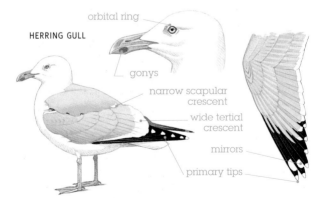

HERRING GULL

orbital ring

gonys

narrow scapular crescent

wide tertial crescent

mirrors

primary tips

Gull identification includes several unique marks. Wing-tip markings often include a dark patch of variable size, contrasting white mirrors within the dark patch, and a small white tip to each primary.

Young gulls acquire adult plumage gradually in a series of molts extending over two years for the smallest gulls and up to four years for the largest ones. Leg, bill, and eye color change along with the plumage. The first-winter plumage is the darkest brown and the most important plumage to learn after the adult. All the other plumages are intermediate. A gull that reaches adult plumage by its fourth year undergoes the biggest change between the second and third years. Second-year birds are brown but not as extensively so as first-year birds. Third-year birds show more gray than brown. Because of mortality, there are usually as many first-year birds in a flock as there are second- and third-year ones combined. Immature plumages are illustrated on Keys 20 and 21.

Tern identification can also be difficult. Head markings and bill color are usually sufficient, but separating some species can be as vexing as the toughest gull identification, and every mark becomes important. Like gulls, terns often stand on beaches in flocks facing into the wind, permitting leisurely inspection with binoculars and telescopes. Young birds are browner and have shorter tails but otherwise are generally similar to winter adults.

Sabine's gull, sooty and bridled terns, kittiwakes, and noddies are in the pelagic section of the Keys. Except when nesting on remote shores, they are seldom seen from land.

All the shoreline aerialists breed in colonies, often on beaches or islands where humans have had a considerable impact. Not all the impact is negative. On the West Coast, Caspian terns have become more common because they've begun nesting on islands and banks of fresh dredge-waste. Least terns have taken to nesting on flat, gravel rooftops. But these species and many others have suffered from human competition for their precious beaches. Least terns are the hardest hit, but all terns are nervous birds and will abandon their colonies if disturbed too often.

Pesticides have also interfered with breeding among these birds. In the 1960s DDT nearly eliminated the brown pelican over much of its range by causing thinning of its eggshells. It has since recovered in many areas. Chemical contamination is still a problem, with PCBs causing birth defects in gulls and terns.

The most dramatic impact on gulls has been produced by garbage dumps and commercial fish waste. During much of this century, such species as the herring gull, glaucous-winged gull, and great black-backed gull have been on the increase, exploiting the vast food resources the dumps provide. Because these large gulls are also predators fond of the eggs and young of smaller species, they have become a serious and increasing threat to smaller birds – tern colonies in particular.

white pelican
Key 26

Brown Pelican

winter

summer

1st yr.

Brown pelican diving in mangroves of Florida Keys

Pelicans and frigatebirds have varying plumages, but their shapes are so distinctive that they can be recognized even when seen as specks in the distance. The brown pelican makes dramatic plunge-dives amid schools of fish, using its huge bill and throat pouch to scoop them up. It also frequents fishing piers and marinas in hopes of a handout or to feed on the entrails of cleaned fish. Too often brown pelicans get tangled in fishing lines and hooks. The graceful magnificent frigatebird uses its very long bill to snatch fish near the water's surface. It is also a pirate, chasing gulls and other aerialists and stealing their catch. Hurricanes regularly blow frigatebirds far inland.

osprey
Key 70

bald
eagle
Key 70

**Magnificent
Frigatebird**

♂

♀

♂

imm.

◀**Brown Pelican** *Pelecanus occidentalis* 48"
Decimated in 1960s by pesticides; now numerous on East
Coast and CA; still scarce on Gulf. Often flies in long lines,
flapping and gliding low over water. ● Stocky; huge bill.
Gray-brown with golden head, white neck in winter. Head
fades to white in summer, hind neck becomes chocolate
brown. Imm. has dark head. 1st-yr. bird brown with white
belly; 2nd-yr. grayer with darker belly. Adult by 3rd yr.

◀**Magnificent Frigatebird** *Fregata magnificens* 40"
Numerous off s. FL, scarcer elsewhere. Nests in FL Keys.
Glides and soars singly or in small groups, sometimes far
offshore. Never alights on water. ● Slender, with long,
narrow wings; long, forked tail; long, hooked bill. Male
glossy black with red throat pouch, inflated during courtship
display. Female has white breast. Imm. has variably white
head and breast. Attains adult plumage in 4-6 yrs.

Black Skimmer

The black skimmer is our only bird whose upper beak is shorter than the lower one. This oddity is seldom overlooked since the bill is an attention-grabbing bright red at the base. The size and black back of the great black-backed gull are its best marks. The back color of the lesser black-backed gull is usually nearer that of the laughing gull (Key 19), although they have little else in common.

◀**Black Skimmer** *Rynchops niger* 18"
Fairly numerous but declining on quiet coastal lagoons, estuaries, salt marshes, sandy islands. Fishes by flying close to water with lower mandible slicing surface; bill snaps shut on prey. Often forages at night. ● Black above, white below. Red bill with black tip, long lower mandible. Winter adults have white collar. Imm. has mottled brown upperparts, bill initially darker. ♪ Soft, yapping notes.

lesser

great

Great Black-backed
Gull

winter

summer

Lesser Black-backed Gull

◀**Great Black-backed Gull** *Larus marinus* 30"
Numerous in N. Atlantic. Increasing and extending range
south. Occurs farther offshore in winter than most coastal
gulls. Scavenges; also predatory, taking birds, small mammals, live fish. ● Large. Black mantle, pink legs, heavy
yellow bill with red spot near tip. In winter, head and neck
can show some fine dark streaking. In flight, black subterminal bar on underwings separates this species and next
from other large eastern gulls. Imm. on Key 20. ♪ *Kyow*,
harsh, throaty call.

◀**Lesser Black-backed Gull** *Larus fuscus* 21"
European, incl. Iceland. Rare, but increasing in winter, esp.
on East Coast. Individuals recorded throughout N. America.
Usually seen singly in flocks of gulls. ● Smaller than great
black-backed gull; usually with dark gray mantle, but birds
with black mantles have been noted. Yellow bill, red spot
near tip; yellow legs. Summer birds, rare in N. America,
lack brown streaking on head, neck. Imm. on Key 20.

The yellow legs on these gulls often show grayish or greenish tones in winter. The gray mantles and black-and-white wing-tip patterns are similar to those of the larger, pink-legged herring and Iceland gulls (Key 17). The bill shape and markings are usually diagnostic, but care is required. Both mew and California gulls often show a narrow, dusky ring on the bill in winter, and the dark spot on the California's bill can be reduced or absent in summer.

◄ Mew Gull *Larus canus* 16"

Numerous in Far North and in winter along coast. ● Bill short, slender, yellow; greenish in winter, often with faint ring. Mantle slightly darker than in ring-billed. More white, less black in primaries than in ring-billed or California gulls. (A few from Europe seen on East Coast each winter have wing tips like ring-billed's.) Extensive white scapular and tertial crescents on perched bird. Brown eyes. Streaking in winter birds more diffuse than in ring-billed or California. Imm. on Key 21.

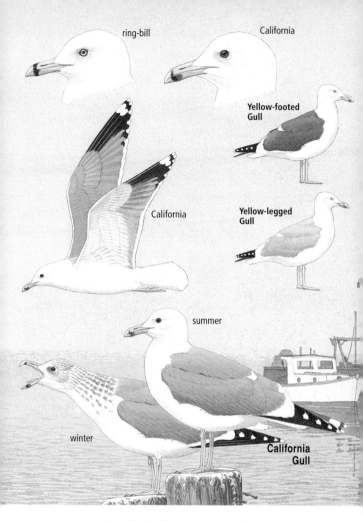

ring-bill

California

Yellow-footed Gull

California

Yellow-legged Gull

summer

winter

California Gull

◀**Ring-billed Gull** *Larus delawarensis* 18"
Abundant, widespread, increasing on fresh and salt water;
also parks, urban areas. ● Bill yellow with distinct black
ring. Mantle pale gray with small tertial crescent, no scapular crescent. Extensive black in primaries with small white
tips, one or two white mirrors. Yellow eyes. Imm. on Key 21.

California Gull *Larus californicus* 21"
◀Numerous on fresh water in summer; most winter on coast.
● Legs yellow to greenish yellow. Bill yellow, usually with red
and black spots near tip of lower mandible (also in herring
gulls approaching adulthood). Prominent white tertial and
scapular crescents as in mew gull, but mantle darker except
on some inland-wintering birds. Wing tips similar to ring-billed
gull's. Dark eyes. In flight, faint gray subterminal bar on
underwing contrasts with white trailing edge. Imm. on Key 20.

Yellow-footed Gull *Larus livens* 27" Mexican. Summer visitor to Salton Sea, CA;
most common large gull there. ● Like western gull (Key 18), but yellow legs.

Yellow-legged Gull *Larus cachinnans* 26" Old World. Several records in East.
● Like herring gull (Key 17) but slightly larger, darker; yellow legs.

YELLOW-LEGGED GULLS

16

glaucous

Iceland

glaucous

Iceland

summer

Glaucous Gull

winter

Loafing at the landfill

The differences in these gulls are subtle. The glaucous is large and very pale with white wing tips. Iceland gulls are smaller and typically show some gray in the wing tips, but some individuals are as white-tipped as the glaucous. At the other extreme, a few Iceland gulls are as dark-tipped as a Thayer's gull. In the herring gull it is the amount of black in the wing tip that best separates it from Thayer's, not the shade. Standing birds can be distinguished by eye color. All winter birds have streaks on the head, neck, and breast.

◀**Glaucous Gull** *Larus hyperboreus* 27"
Numerous in North, scarce to US in winter on rocky coasts, large lakes, at garbage dumps. ● Larger than Iceland or herring gulls. Bill stout, yellow (never greenish) with reddish spot on lower mandible. Bill extends more than half of head length. Sloping forehead, pale yellow eye. Paler gray mantle than in Iceland, with translucent, white-tipped primaries. Folded primaries do not extend far beyond tail, usually less than length of bill. Imm. on Key 20.

Thayer's

herring

Thayer's

herring

summer

Iceland Gull

winter

summer

Herring & Thayer's Gulls

winter

◄**Iceland Gull** *Larus glaucoides* 22"
Fairly numerous; coastal. ● Smaller than glaucous gull, with shorter, more slender bill (often greenish yellow); rounder forehead. Yellow eye, dark orbital ring. Pale gray mantle. Form seen in N. America ("Kumlein's gull") has small amount of gray in primaries but can be pale, missing. Wing tips extend farther beyond tail than in glaucous. Imm. on Key 20.

◄**Thayer's Gull** *Larus thayeri* 23"
Fairly numerous, but less common, more coastal than herring gull. ● Typically smaller than herring with slightly shorter, more slender bill; rounder forehead. Brown eye. Extent of dark in primaries less than in herring, esp. as seen in underwing; shade can be gray to black. Scapular crescent typically more prominent than in herring. Imm. on Key 20.

Herring Gull *Larus argentatus* 25"
◄Abundant, widespread, increasing; most common large gull over most of N. America. ● Pale gray mantle. Extensive black in primaries with small white tips (can be worn off), two white mirrors. Sloped forehead, yellow eyes, yellow or orange orbital ring. Large yellow bill with reddish spot on lower mandible. Scapular crescent on perched bird small or can be lacking. Imm. on Key 20.

GULLS

17

Glaucous-winged Gull

glaucous-winged

glaucous-winged
or western

example of
glaucous-winged
and western intergrade

winter

summer

Western and glaucous-winged gulls are pink-legged like those on
Key 17. They commonly interbreed, so individuals range from
being as pale-backed as a herring gull and without any dark contrast in their wing tips to having very dark backs and black wing
tips. Mantles and wing tips of some intergrades are like those in
herring or Thayer's gulls (Key 17). A good mark for hybrids or
either parent is the large bill, slightly swollen at the tip. Heermann's
is one of the few gulls not likely to be confused with others.

◀**Glaucous-winged Gull** *Larus glaucescens* 26"
Numerous in North. Fairly numeous to s. CA in winter;
scarce inland. ● Stocky, with stout yellow bill, heaviest at
tip; reddish spot near tip; in winter often with fine, dark line
zigzagging across tip. Forehead nearly as rounded as
Iceland gull's (Key 17); eyes usually dark, never yellow.
Primaries same color as mantle except for white tips and
1-2 white mirrors (much less white than in glaucous gull,
Key 17). In winter, streaks on head, neck. Imm. on Key 20.

western
(dark form)

Heermann's

imm.

**Heermann's
Gull**

summer

winter

summer

summer
(pale form)

Western Gull

◄Western Gull *Larus occidentalis* 25"
Numerous along coast; scarce inland. ● Size, overall
shape, bill, and forehead as in glaucous-winged. Mantle
much darker than in glaucous-winged and with contrasting
blackish area in primaries. Birds breeding in southern half of
range have darker mantles, usually paler eyes, and little or
no streaking on their heads in winter. Northern-breeding
birds have paler mantles, usually dark eyes, head streaking
in winter like glaucous-winged. Northern birds can be found
south to Mexico in winter. Imm. on Key 20.

◄Heermann's Gull *Larus heermanni* 19"
Mexican. Fairly numerous summer and fall visitor to West
Coast. ● Gray body, black tail, red bill. Usually seen in win-
ter plumage (streaked head) or imm. (dark head and body).

HYBRIDS   Glaucous-winged and western gulls hybridize from
OR to B.C. In this range hybrids are more numerous than parental types. In winter
they spread south as far as Mexico. The most troublesome intergrades have mantle colors and wing tips suggesting herring or Thayer's gulls. Most can be identified
by carefully noting other marks, esp. overall size/shape and bill/head structure.
Glaucous-winged also hybridizes with herring and glaucous gulls. Any combination of parental features is possible, but these hybrids are rare south of AK.

GULLS

18

The dark hoods displayed by these birds in summer are reduced to patches or spots by winter. Franklin's retains about half of its hood – much more than the similar laughing gull does. In summer Franklin's has less black in the wing tip than the laughing gull and a white band bordering the black tip. Bonaparte's best mark is the white wedge on the leading edge of the wing. The rarer black-headed gull (whose hood is actually brown) has a similar white wedge, but the rest of its underwing primaries are distinctively dark. The underwings of the aptly named little gull are almost entirely dark. All hooded gulls can be pinkish below in summer.

◄**Franklin's Gull** *Larus pipixcan* 15"
Numerous in summer on prairie marshes, lakes. Migrates in large flocks. Feeds heavily on insects, often following farm machines. ● Thinner bill, rounder head than in laughing gull; less black in wing tips, extent of white varies considerably. Legs, bill red in summer. Bold white eye crescents seem to join at rear of eye and are obvious even in winter because of contrast with dark half-hood. Tail gray in center, unlike any other gull's. Imm. on Key 21. ♪ *Wee-a, wee-a*, shrill call.

Bonaparte's
summer
winter

black-headed
summer
winter

black-headed

little

little
summer
winter

Little Gull

Bonaparte's
Gull

Black-headed
Gull

◀Laughing Gull *Larus atricilla* 17"
Abundant on or near coasts. Declining north of VA. Noisy, aggressive. ● Black wing tips without white mirrors. Large, drooping bill; sloping forehead. Legs, bill usually dull red in summer but can be bright. White eye crescents not obvious in winter when hood reduced to dark wash on nape. Imm. on Key 21. ♪ *Ha-ha-ha-ha-ha-ha,* loud, high-pitched call.

◀Bonaparte's Gull *Larus philadelphia* 13"
Numerous in summer on lakes, marsh in boreal forest; nests in trees. Fairly numerous in migration, winter on lakes, rivers, coasts. ● Translucent white wedge in primaries with black border on trailing edge; pale underwings. Small black bill, red legs. Eye crescents not visible in winter when hood reduced to dark ear spot. Imm. on Key 21. ♪ *Kreeer,* nasal call.

Black-headed Gull *Larus ridibundus* 16"
◀Scarce winter visitor from Old World; rare nester in eastern Canada. ● Larger edition of Bonaparte's, with dark brown hood, red bill, dark underwing primaries. Imm. on Key 21.

Little Gull *Larus minutus* 11"
◀Rare in summer in marshes, often among marsh terns. Winters along coasts, often among Bonaparte's. Old World; first New World nesting 1962. ● Small size. Plain wings are pale above, dark below with white border. Imm. on Key 21.

HOODED GULLS

19

1st winter
typical

dark

1st summer

2nd winter

Herring Gull

1st winter

2nd summer

3rd winter

Thayer's Gull

1st winter

2nd summer

3rd winter

California Gull

1st winter

2nd summer

Glaucous-winged Gull

2nd summer

1st winter

3rd winter

Western Gull

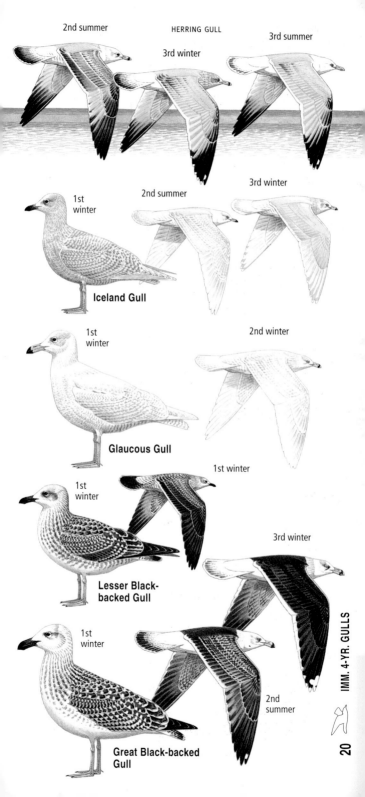

2nd summer

HERRING GULL

3rd winter

3rd summer

1st winter

2nd summer

3rd winter

Iceland Gull

1st winter

2nd winter

Glaucous Gull

1st winter

1st winter

Lesser Black-backed Gull

3rd winter

1st winter

2nd summer

Great Black-backed Gull

IMM. 4-YR. GULLS

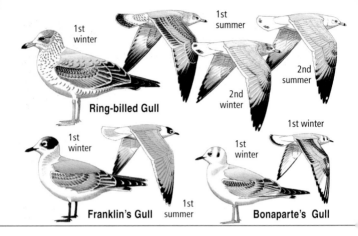

1st winter

1st summer

2nd summer

2nd winter

Ring-billed Gull

1st winter

1st winter

1st winter

Franklin's Gull

1st summer

Bonaparte's Gull

The size and structure of a gull, especially of its bill and head, are the first clues to its identity in any plumage. A young gull's shape is like an adult's, as described on the previous Keys, except that the bill continues to grow a little over the first year.

IMM. 4-YR. GULLS (KEY 20) All molt through a series of changes as in herring gull. Brown juveniles molt to 1st-winter plumage before leaving nesting colonies. Plumage continues to lighten over 1st yr. Individuals develop at different rates; adult gray (or black) in mantle usually visible in standing bird by 2nd summer. By 3rd winter, mantle is like adult's but with dark marks remaining on wing tips, secondaries, tail. These disappear over 3rd yr. Most birds adult by 4th winter.

Herring Gull Juv. has black bill. By 1st winter, black blends distinctively to pale base on all but darkest birds. Overall color varies from dark brown to much paler with scaly pattern on mantle and whitish head, breast. Tail almost all dark, paler at tip and rump. When standing, primaries are blackish brown with little or no contrasting Vs on wing tips. In flight, blackish brown appears only on outer primaries; inner primaries paler even on darkest birds; dark secondary bar. Eye becomes pale in many by 2nd winter; yellow in 3rd year.

Thayer's Gull Bill can have pale base but usually darker than herring gull's for 1st yr. Standing birds show medium brown (not blackish) tail and primaries, with pale Vs at tip of each primary. Wing-tip pattern in flight same as in adult but less contrast. Dark secondary bar broken with paler webs.

Iceland Gull Pale birds separated from glaucous gull by structure and, during 1st yr., darker bill. Wing tip in 1st yr. varies from white to buff with little contrast with rest of wing; entire primaries can appear translucent from below.

California Gull Plumage similar to herring gull's in 1st yr., but well-defined black tip to pale bill, no pale windows in inner primaries. Shows gray back (darker gray than in herring) in 2nd yr. In 3rd yr. bill pattern like adult's.

Glaucous Gull Fairly even pale brown, fading to whitish with some dark barring by 1st summer. Pale bill has well-defined dark tip for 1st yr., much as in smaller, darker California gull. Broad, white, translucent tips to primaries at all ages.

Glaucous-winged Gull Dark bill (some have small pale area at base) distinguishes 1st-yr. bird from glaucous and paler herring gulls; present on many birds throughout 2nd yr. At all ages, wing tips and tail are same shade as mantle. Pale tip on each primary shows as chevron on folded wing tip as in Thayer's gull.

Lesser Black-backed Gull Similar to herring gull. Bill all-black in 1st yr., rump pale with few dark bars. Wings lack herring gull's pale inner primaries. Dark bar on secondaries and row of equally dark coverts above it, unlike any other gull.

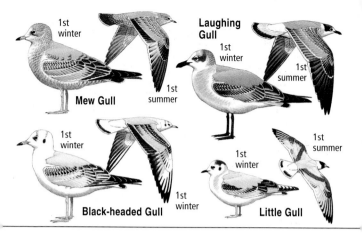

Mew Gull
1st winter
1st summer

Laughing Gull
1st winter
1st summer

1st winter
Black-headed Gull
1st winter

1st winter
Little Gull
1st summer

Western Gull 1st-winter birds average darker brown than herring gull, but difference often fades away by 1st summer. Best mark is structure, esp. head and bill. Bill color as in glaucous-winged gull; often remains darker than in herring gull until 2nd summer, when mantle color can be seen.

Great Black-backed Gull Bill black in 1st yr. except for frequently present whitish tip. Mantle similar to herring gull's, but more black-and-white contrast, producing checkered effect. Shows pale patch in inner primaries, suggesting herring gull; outer primaries more blackish.

IMM. 3-YR. GULLS Even on 1st-winter birds, some adult back color can be seen. By 1st summer it is obvious in perched birds, and some begin to show adult bill and leg colors. Bonaparte's and black-headed gulls mature in just 2 yrs. and show nearly complete hoods in their 1st summer.

Ring-billed Gull Blackish secondary bar, carpal bar, outer primaries contrast with rest of upperwing in flying 1st-yr. birds. When perched, note heavy spotting on head, neck, chest. Bill dark-tipped, with ring forming by 2nd winter. 1st-yr. can be confused with small-looking 2nd-yr. herring gull, but ring-billed has whiter tail.

Mew Gull Plumage as in young ring-billed gull but brown rump, paler carpal bar both standing and in flight. Can show diffuse ring on bill, but bill always thinner. Brown wash, not spots or streaks, on head and breast.

Laughing Gull All-black bill; gray breast, flanks. Head pattern like winter adult's but more extensively gray.

Franklin's Gull All-black bill; nearly white below. Head pattern like winter adult's.

Bonaparte's Gull All-black bill. Shows much white in outer primaries like adult and has dark ear spot like winter adult. Blackish carpal bar.

Black-headed Gull Like large Bonaparte's gull but with pale black-tipped bill, black underwing primaries.

Little Gull Small with distinct W on mantle in 1st yr. Compare with imm. black-legged kittiwake (Key 4). Pale underwing darkens as in adult by 2nd summer.

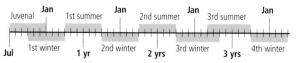

Juvenal | Jan | 1st summer | Jan | 2nd summer | Jan | 3rd summer | Jan
Jul | 1st winter | 1 yr | 2nd winter | 2 yrs | 3rd winter | 3 yrs | 4th winter

Dates of immature plumages. Plumage is freshest in winter after the full fall molt. Only body feathers are replaced in spring, and flight feathers become increasingly worn. Late summer birds can be very disheveled.

Its bulky body and heavy red bill distinguish the Caspian tern in all seasons. Even seen flying at a distance, it can be separated from the royal tern by the large dark patch on the underside of the primaries. The royal tern, which has a more slender and more orange bill, also has a white forehead most of the year. The elegant tern is smaller and has a shaggier crest than the royal, but its best mark is the bill, which is very slender and usually yellowish orange.

◄**Caspian Tern** *Sterna caspia* 21"
Fairly numerous but local on fresh and salt water, esp. gravelly lakeshores, coastal beaches. Sometimes pirates from others. Seen singly or in small groups. ● Heavy-bodied, with thick neck, large head. Bill very thick, red or red-orange with black tip. Shallowly forked tail. Broad wings with black in underside of outer primaries. Black cap, streaked with white in winter. Imm. like winter adult but dusky patches in wings, dusky tail tip, often red legs. ♪ *Kraa*, harsh, deep call.

elegant

peak breeding

nonbreeding

royal

elegant

summer

juv.

Elegant Tern

summer

juv.

Royal Tern

◀**Royal Tern** *Sterna maxima* 20"
Numerous but local, esp. on isolated sandbars. Exclusively
marine. Often in large flocks. Dives for fish, other marine
life. • Large orange to orange-yellow bill. Full black cap
held briefly during breeding in spring or early summer. At
other times dome is white and well-defined black crest suggests fringe on a balding man; it does not usually encom-
pass eye. Narrow dark edges on underwing primaries. Tail
deeply forked. Legs usually black but can be orange. Juv.
like winter adult but duskier above and with dusky tail tip.
♪ *Kee-er,* high-pitched, bleating call.

◀**Elegant Tern** *Sterna elegans* 17"
Fairly numerous in summer and fall after dispersal from
nesting colonies in Mexico and, since 1959, San Diego Bay.
Usually in flocks. • Like royal tern but smaller; bill more
slender, slightly downcurved with no apparent gonys, usually yellower. Crest shaggier than in royal tern, extending
around eye and further onto dome during nonbreeding.
Juv. like winter adult but with dusky wings and tail; bill
often yellow. ♪ *Ker-rrick,* high-pitched, grating call.

arctic summer

common summer

winter

arctic

late summer

common

Arctic Tern

summer

juv.

Common Tern

summer

winter

juv.

Only common and Forster's terns are present in most areas. In summer plumage, Forster's has "frosted" wing tips that are paler than the mantle; the common's wing tips are dark. By fall, the common tern begins to show a shoulder bar. The common usually has a redder bill than Forster's, but colors overlap. Bills on all four species start turning black by fall. Arctic and common terns are difficult to separate. The best mark is the narrower, longer, sharply defined black trailing edge on the arctic's underwing. The roseate has plain underwings and a very pale mantle; most are long-tailed.

◀**Arctic Tern** *Sterna paradisaea* 15"
Abundant in Arctic; local south to MA. ● Translucent primaries with less black than in common tern; shorter neck, legs; rounder head; upperwing more evenly gray. Blood-red bill can have dusky tip. Gray wash on underparts contrasts with white cheeks. Molts after fall migration. Juv. white below and on forehead, black bill, short tail. ♪ Like common's.

Common Tern *Sterna hirundo* 14"
Numerous, widespread. ● Primaries darker than mantle in upperwing and with prominent black trailing edge in under-

summary (Forster's) summer

Forster's summer · roseate summer · winter

Forster's · roseate

Roseate Tern

Forster's Tern

summer · summer

juv. · winter

◀wing. Gray tinge below; throat, face white. Tail white with narrow dark edges; does not extend beyond folded wing as in other 3 terns. Very few winter in US: white forehead; dark shoulder bar; black nape, bill, legs. Juv. like winter adult but mottled above; short tail. ♪ *Kee-ar*, rasping, drawn-out call.

Forster's Tern *Sterna forsteri* 14"
Numerous on fresh and coastal marshes, lakes; on salt
◀water in migration, winter. ● Pale gray mantle with silvery white upperwing primaries, gray tail, white underparts. Bill thicker than in other 3 terns, black-tipped, usually orange in summer. Black cap reduced to mask over eyes by fall. Some show dark nape like winter common tern, but all lack common's dark shoulder bar. Juv. like winter adult but tail shorter, brown flecking on mantle. ♪ Like common's.

◀**Roseate Tern** *Sterna dougallii* 15"
Rare, local; exclusively marine. Often nests on rooftops in FL Keys. ● Pale mantle does not contrast with white rump or tail. White (or rosy) underparts. Bill briefly has more red at base. Molts after fall migration. Juv. has white forehead, scaly upperparts. ♪♪ *Chewee-che*, musical call.

IMMATURES 1- and 2-yr.-olds usually remain on wintering grounds, but some return and suggest worn winter adults. Imm. Forster's has primaries darker than mantle, as in adult common, but cap seldom extends over forehead.

PROBLEM TERNS

23

The sandwich and gull-billed terns are black-capped and of medium size, like those on Key 23, but note the distinctive bills. The slender black bill of the sandwich tern is tipped with a bit of "mayonnaise," while the heavy bill of the gull-billed lives up to its name. The black-tipped yellow bill of the least tern, our tiniest tern, is one of its best marks, along with the white forehead. Black terns become mottled in summer as they molt from black to white body plumage. The small, dark side-breast patch is diagnostic.

◀**Sandwich Tern** *Sterna sandvicensis* 15"
Scarce, declining. Often with royal terns. ● Shaggy black crest. Forehead becomes white with black streaks by mid-summer. Yellow-tipped black bill; deeply forked tail. Juv. mottled with brown above, shorter crest, shorter dusky-tipped tail; bill often lacks yellow tip. ♪ *Ki-rick*, grating call.

Gull-billed Tern *Sterna nilotica* 14"
◀Scarce; on salt marshes. Also summers at Salton Sea, CA. Feeds heavily on flying insects. ● Stocky with stout black bill, very pale upperparts, shallowly forked tail. Black cap in summer reduced to black ear patch and dusky nape patch

least summer

black summer

black winter

White-winged Tern

least

black summer

fall (molting)

juv.

juv.

summer

Black Tern

summer

Least Tern

by fall. Juv. like winter adult, with brownish mottling on head and mantle. ♪ *Za-za-za* or *kay-wick,* raspy call.

◄**Least Tern** *Sterna antillarum* 9"
Scarce, local; on beaches, sandbars along coasts, rivers. Easily disturbed; declining over most of range. Has adapted in some areas by nesting on rooftops or islands of dredge-waste. ● Bill yellow with black tip; cap black with white forehead. Gray mantle with contrasting dark outermost primaries. Fall molt can start before migration; bill turns brown, crown pattern becomes blurred. Juv. has black bill; whitish head with black through eye, on nape; dark shoulder bar. ♪ *Kip, kip, kip,* and *Kiddeek!* Loud, high-pitched calls.

◄**Black Tern** *Chlidonias niger* 10"
Seriously declining, esp. in East. Locally numerous on some freshwater marshes. Migrates mostly along coasts. Feeds heavily on insects. ● Black bill, head, and body contrast with gray wing and tail, white undertail coverts and shoulder. Winter adult white below with black crown, nape, ear coverts; dark patch in front of wing. Juv. similar to winter adult but heavily mottled with brown above. ♪ *Krik,* metallic call.

White-winged Tern *Chlidonias leucopterus* 10" Eurasian. Rare; usually among black terns. ● Like black tern but bill shorter, black on underparts extends to underwings in summer; lacks side patches in front of wing in fall.

TERNS

24

GOOSE

CORMORANT

Swimmers have webbed toes; all four are webbed in pelicans, cormorants, and the anhinga.

Goose-size
Swimmers

CONSULTANT **KIMBALL GARRETT**
ILLUSTRATOR **JONATHAN ALDERFER**

Most birds would soon drown if they fell into water – as sometimes happens in migration. Others, through remarkable adaptations, make their home on water, some coming ashore only to nest. The large swimmers include geese, swans, the white pelican, loons, cormorants, and the anhinga. All have wide bodies, flattened for stability while floating. Their feet are webbed, set back for efficient paddling, and driven by large leg muscles. The plumage is dense and can capture air for insulation and buoyancy, but surprisingly it is not waterproof in all swimmers. Cormorants and the anhinga are frequently seen with wet wings spread to dry in the sun.

Most swimmers can submerge in an emergency, but among the large swimmers only the loons and cormorants dive to feed, catching mostly small fish of little economic value. The white pelican also feeds on fish, scooping them up in its large bill while floating on the surface. Geese and swans are mostly vegetarians, grazing on plants in shallow water and on land.

As divers, loons and cormorants frequent the deep waters of large lakes or seacoasts. Some can be seen far offshore. Divers don't have the buoyancy of surface feeders; they wouldn't be able to dive if they did. They are heavy birds that usually swim low in the water. Their wings alone can't lift their heavy bodies into the air; they need the assistance of their powerful legs, running along the water's surface.

Loons and cormorants usually dive with a headfirst flip, but sometimes they sink slowly beneath the surface, grebe-like, by expelling air from internal air sacs and holding their feathers

COMMON LOON

DOUBLE-CRESTED CORMORANT

Divers usually submerge for less than a minute and stay within 50 feet of the surface, but dives of 200 feet and lasting up to 5 minutes have been reported.

close so that less air is captured. Underwater, they propel themselves with synchronous paddling of their webbed feet. Because they live almost entirely on the water, no birds are more threatened by oil spills than loons and cormorants.

The legs of loons are set so far back that they can barely stand. Cormorants, on the other hand, are frequently seen standing erect on pilings or rocks. Often they gather in groups, and they nest colonially. Loons are usually seen singly or in pairs; in summer they are more often heard. The haunting call of the common loon has become a symbolic sound of the wilderness.

The legs of swans and geese are positioned sufficiently forward to allow them to walk easily. They have always grazed on land to some extent, but the loss and pollution of wetlands, combined with the increased availability of croplands, have made many flocks frequent land grazers. Canada geese, in particular, have become pests in some communities. Because they live and migrate in flocks, swans and geese are rarely encountered singly. The integrity of flocks results in numerous distinct subspecies. There are more than ten different subspecies of Canada goose, for example, which range widely in size.

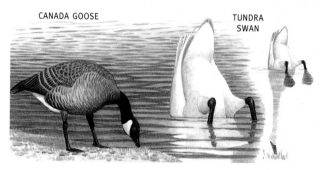

CANADA GOOSE

TUNDRA SWAN

Grazers feed on land or in shallows. Long necks help them reach bottom vegetation. Water is pressed out through tooth-like projections on the edges of their bills.

Swans, geese, and ducks are often termed waterfowl. The United States government classifies them as migratory game birds, and most can be hunted under regulations. Like the ground-walkers (grouse, turkey, quail, pigeons), they have always been prized as food. Geese have been domesticated since the Stone Age.

Swans were shot from existence over most of their range before hunting was regulated in the early 20th century. Other waterfowl populations, having survived in better shape, now benefit from their value to sportsmen. Much of the National Wildlife Refuge system was designed and is maintained to preserve waterfowl.

Trumpeter Swan

trumpeter

imm.

trumpeter

tundra

imm.

Tundra Swan

Voice is the best mark for tundra and trumpeter swans. The tundra is the more common and usually shows a yellow spot near the eye. The mute swan is the swan of European fairy tales. It was introduced in North America to decorate parks and estates, swimming with its neck gracefully curved and its wings partially flared. It now nests in the wild. Note its orange bill with a black knob at the base.

historical range

◀ **Trumpeter Swan** *Cygnus buccinator* 60"
Recovering but still scarce, local. Most birds nest in AK on marshes, lakes; winter in flocks on remote coastal estuaries, shallow lakes. A smaller number nest and winter in Rockies; those nesting in Canada migrate south as waters freeze. Flocks being reintroduced in historic range, esp. near western Great Lakes. Shy, requires wilderness. Habits like tundra swan's. ● White head and neck often stained from iron in water. Imm. gray-brown with pink on bill.
♪ *Oh-óh*, loud, trumpeting notes given in flight or on ground.

tundra

imm.

mute imm.

Bewick's form

Mute Swan

◀**Tundra Swan** *Cygnus columbianus* 52"
Numerous. Flocks in winter and migration on shallow fresh water, esp. coastal estuaries, nearby grainfields. Usually holds neck straight when swimming. Flies in lines and Vs.
● Smaller than trumpeter swan but can be inseparable except by voice. Yellow lore spot can be absent in tundra, present rarely in trumpeter. Black skin near eye forms wider angle in trumpeter, joining eye more strongly to bill. Tundra's bill slightly more concave on ridge, forehead slightly more rounded than in trumpeter. Both can have salmon "grin mark" on lower mandible. Imm. gray-brown (white by 1st spring), bill and legs marked with pink. Eurasian race, "Bewick's swan," recorded in West; shows more yellow on bill. ♪ *Oh,* up to 3 syllables; higher, less harsh than in trumpeter.

◀**Mute Swan** *Cygnus olor* 60"
Scarce, local, but spreading. May be found anywhere in shallow fresh or brackish water; saltwater bays and marshes in winter. Bold, can be aggressive. ● Bill orange with black knob at base. Imm. gray-brown (paler in 2nd yr.) with blue-gray bill, no knob. ♪ Usually silent; loud wing beats.

chick-feeding stage

courtship

brown pelican
Key 14

White Pelican

winter

White pelicans are an identification problem only when seen flying at a distance. Other large white birds with black wing tips include the geese on this Key and several waders (Keys 43-46). Snow and Ross' geese usually flock together and are very similar. Both often have rust stains on their heads and necks. Check the bills closely. The snow goose's is longer and has a black "grinning patch" or "lips." Ross' bill is stubbier, often with "warts" at the base. Snow geese also occur in a "blue" form (Key 27).

◀**White Pelican** (American) *Pelecanus erythrorhynchos* 62"
Fairly numerous in colonies on shallow freshwater marshes and lakes in summer. Most winter on protected coastal shallows; scarcer inland. Flies in lines or Vs, neck folded; sometimes soars. Often forages cooperatively, herding small fish to shallows for capture. Does not dive. ● White with black wing tips, huge orange bill. Pale yellow crest and breast patch in spring courtship, large plate on bill. Both sexes shed plate after eggs laid, head turns grayish. Imm. has pale bill.

domestic goose

Ross'

snow

Ross' Goose

Snow Goose
(white form)

imm.

◀**Snow Goose** *Chen caerulescens* 28"
Abundant locally in large flocks. Winters in shallow coastal bays, salt and freshwater marshes, nearby grass and grain-fields. "Blue" form (Key 27) most common in Gulf, less so in West, rare but annual in East. Called "wavies" for flying in undulating lines. ● White form is white with black wing tips. "Blue" form has dark body with white head and neck. Intergrades occur. Adults of both forms have pink legs, pink bills with black grinning patch. Imm. white form grayish above. Imm. "blue" form very dark; bill and legs dark.
♪ Shrill barking yelp, given continuously by flocks in flight.

◀**Ross' Goose** *Chen rossii* 23"
Regaining former numbers and fairly numerous with flocks of snow geese, although most do not intermingle. Most winter in CA. Very rare among eastern snow geese flocks; some of these may be hybrids. ● Like white form of snow goose but smaller; stubby pink bill with blue-gray at base. Mature birds, esp. males, have "warts" at base of bill. "Blue" form (like "blue" form of snow goose) has been recorded very rarely. Imm. whiter than imm. snow goose.
♪ Like snow goose's but higher-pitched, even less musical.

domestic goose

Barnacle Goose

juv.

White-fronted Goose

Canada Goose

endangered Aleutian race

large race

small race "cackling goose"

The white-fronted goose gets its name from the white at the base of its pink bill. Its orange legs are another easy mark. Canada geese, or "honkers," are as well known for their resonant calls as for their distinctive black necks and white chin straps. Smaller races – some are duck size – have high-pitched cackles instead of deep honks. "Blue geese" are a dark form of the snow goose (Key 26). The brant is barely larger than a mallard. Seen swimming, it is dark above except for paler sides, a stylish white design on the neck, and a white rear that flashes when it tips to feed.

◄**White-fronted Goose** (Greater) *Anser albifrons* 28"
Numerous in winter, grazing in flocks on grains, grasses; also in shallow fresh water, salt marshes, bays. Flies fast, agile in Vs or lines. ● Gray-brown with barred underparts, white forehead, orange legs, pink bill. Juv. has plain face, belly; leg and bill shade can vary. Larger, darker form, "tule goose," winters in marshes of Sacramento Valley, CA.
♪ High-pitched, 2-note "laughing" call given in flight.

western
"black brant"

Brant

eastern

"Blue Goose" form
of Snow Goose

intergrade

juv.

◀**Canada Goose** *Branta canadensis* 24"-48"
Most races abundant. Increasing dramatically in East, expanding range rapidly to southeast. Summers on coastal marshes, shallow fresh water. Winters in flocks on fresh and salt water, nearby fields, farmlands, parks. Can be bold. Flies in Vs. Endangered Aleutian race *(B.c. leucopareia)* rare in West in winter; now increasing. ● Black head and neck, white chin strap. Several subspecies show white neck ring. ♪ Large birds honk; smaller ones cackle or yelp.

"**Blue Goose**" See Snow Goose, Key 26.

◀**Brant** *Branta bernicla* 25"
Numbers fluctuate greatly. Nests farther north than other waterfowl, with unpredictable success. Winters in saltwater shallows in family groups. Feeds at low tide, often tipping up; prefers eelgrass. Flies rapidly in diagnostic shifting bunches. ● Small. Black head, neck, breast; white sides, rump. White neck mark can be inconspicuous. Neck mark absent in imms. Western birds, "black brant," have dark belly; white neck mark forms collar. ♪ Low, guttural croaks.

Barnacle Goose *Branta leucopsis* 26" Eurasian; also breeds in Greenland. Several records in Maritimes. Common in captivity.

The common loon is the most numerous and widespread, and the only one that nests south of the tundra. Its back and neck have a gloss and detail that look hand-painted. In winter loons are best separated by bill shape and the pattern on the side of the neck. Sizes overlap, and head shapes vary with the way feathers are held.

◀**Red-throated Loon** *Gavia stellata* 25"
Fairly numerous along coast in winter, alone or in loose flocks; rare inland. Often on more protected waters than Pacific loon. Nests on fresh water. ● Slender bill with upward-angled lower mandible, usually held tilted up. Reddish throat, gray head, plain back in summer. In winter, border of dark and white on neck more diffuse than in Pacific loon (esp. in juv.); white often surrounds eye; upper back has tiny white spots. ♪ Usually silent in winter.

◀**Pacific Loon** *Gavia pacifica* 26"
Fairly numerous along coast in winter; singly or in flocks. Often on turbulent waters, open ocean. Migrates in long flocks along coast. ● Straight, slender bill held horizontally. In summer, pale gray crown, nape; iridescence on throat can be purple, green, or appear black. In winter, white on

WINTER LOONS

red-throated

Pacific

yellow-billed

common

winter

juv.

summer

Common Loon

foreneck and cheek shows clean border with dark on sides of neck and crown; usually has faint chin strap; no white above eye. Juv. like winter adult. ♪ Usually silent in winter.

◀**Common Loon** *Gavia immer* 32"
Numerous, nesting on shores and islands of northern lakes and rivers shortly after spring thaw. Shy, requires wilderness. Winters along coasts and deep inland waters, usually singly or in pairs. Migrates in small groups. ● Heavy, dark bill with angled lower mandible. In summer, black head and neck with green gloss, striped partial collar; black back with white spots; white underparts. In winter, dark hind neck meets white foreneck in jagged line, like pieces of jigsaw puzzle; usually has pale border around much of eye. Juv. shows pale barring on back over most of winter. ♪♪ Variety of yodeling, wails, and maniacal "laughter" in summer. Usually silent in winter.

Yellow-billed Loon *Gavia adamsii* 34" Nests on Arctic tundra. Scarce in winter off s. AK coast, progressively rarer to south and inland; recorded south to CA. ● Larger than common loon and paler overall, with pale yellow bill in summer. Culmen straighter than in common loon; bill appears upturned. In winter, outer half of culmen pale (dark in common); distinct dark ear spot.

Arctic Loon *Gavia arctica* 29" Fairly numerous in summer on Seward Peninsula of w. AK; few records in winter south of AK. ● Like Pacific loon but larger with proportionally larger bill. Rear flanks white at waterline. Green neck gloss in summer.

LOONS

The anhinga's pointed yellow bill and snake-like head and neck are often all that is visible as the bird swims, body submerged. The double-crested cormorant is on all coasts and is the only cormorant commonly seen inland; note the yellow or orange throat pouch. Great cormorants have white throat straps and are larger. The neotropic cormorant suggests a small double-crested, but the neotropic's tail is comparatively much longer. Cormorants fly silently in lines or Vs. In spring and early summer they have modest crests and wispy white plumes or small white patches.

◀ **Anhinga** *Anhinga anhinga* 35"
Fairly numerous at freshwater swamps, ponds; less so in salt and brackish marsh. Dives and spears fish. Flies with neck kinked, more so than in double-crested cormorant. Often soar in groups, looking like tiny crosses high in sky.
● Cormorant-like, but longer tail, longer neck, pointed bill. Male dark with faint iridescence, silver plumes on wings, back. Female and imm. similar with tawny neck and breast.

neotropic

great

double-crested

Great Cormorant

early summer

imm.

◀**Neotropic Cormorant** *Phalacrocorax brasilianus* 26"
Fairly numerous on fresh and brackish waters, often with
anhinga or double-crested. A few also in s. AZ ● Small
with slender bill and neck; no head bulge visible in flight.
Dull yellowish throat pouch angled sharply at base of bill,
bordered in white and with short white neck plumes in early
summer. Lacks stripe of bare yellow on lores as in double-
crested. Long tail. Imm. browner, esp. on underparts.

◀**Double-crested Cormorant** *Phalacrocorax auritus* 32"
Numerous, widespread, and increasing on fresh and salt
water. Flies with kink in thick neck. ● Yellowish orange
throat pouch. Short tail. Western birds have white tufts on
head and some white plumes on neck early in summer;
tufts dark, inconspicuous on eastern birds. Imm. brown
above, whitish on breast.

◀**Great Cormorant** *Phalacrocorax carbo* 36"
Fairly numerous, increasing in summer in Maritimes. Scarcer
but expanding range along coast to south in winter; recorded
to FL. ● Large with heavy bill. Yellow throat pouch bordered
by white throat strap. White flank patches and head plumes
in summer. Imm. brown above, white below with dusky
breast (reverse of pattern of imm. double-crested).

CORMORANTS / ANHINGA

29

These cormorants and the double-crested (Key 29) are the only ones seen on the Pacific Coast. Brandt's, the most common, has a bright blue throat pouch in summer. The buffy patch bordering its throat pouch is a good mark all year. Pelagic cormorants are more slender; their red facial skin is seen only at close range.

◀**Pelagic Cormorant** *Phalacrocorax pelagicus* 26"
Fairly numerous. Seldom far from rocky shores with heavy surf, usually alone. Flies with neck straight; no head bulge. ● Small. Slender neck, thin bill, relatively long tail. In early summer has small crest, white flank patch. Imm. brown, darker below than other imms.

Brandt's Cormorant *Phalacrocorax penicillatus* 35"
Most common cormorant on Pacific Coast, often in flocks, well offshore. Flies with neck straight, distinct
◀head bulge. ● Large with short tail. Buff patch behind and below throat pouch. Blue throat pouch in summer (never shows yellow), fine white plumes on back and neck. Imm. dark brown above, paler on breast.

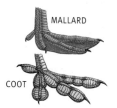

MALLARD

COOT

Grebes and coots have lobed toes instead of webbing.

Duck-size
Swimmers

ORNITHOLOGIST **KIMBALL GARRETT**
ILLUSTRATOR **JONATHAN ALDERFER**

Ducks swim with webbed feet, like their larger cousins, geese and swans. The only birds in this section other than ducks are grebes and the coot, which swim very proficiently with lobed toes, and the purple gallinule and moorhen, which often swim, although their extremely long toes are primarily adapted for walking on floating vegetation. Coots and moorhens are opportunists and can eke out a living from an oversized puddle. They are omnivorous, exploiting much of the edible life in and around their favored marshy ponds.

Ducks are often divided into dabblers and divers. "Dabbler" is the name given to ducks that feed on vegetation along the edges and at the bottoms of shallow marshes or other still waters. They are often seen tail up, stretching for bottom vegetation, or waddling along a shore. Some make short dives. Others, like wigeons, often graze on grasses some distance from water.

The diving ducks pursue fish or devour shellfish or vegetation from bottoms that can be 100 feet or more beneath the water's surface. Sea ducks, like scoters and eiders, specialize in shellfish, which they swallow whole, grinding the shells in their gizzards. Large numbers of sea ducks often congregate in "rafts" over particularly good shellfish beds (often around pier pilings) and may be rare elsewhere. The bay ducks, which include the redhead and canvasback, feed mostly on bottom vegetation and are among hunters' favorites. Mergansers feed heavily on fish and have serrated edges on their bills to hold the slippery prey.

For grebes diving is more than a way to forage, it is the preferred means of escape. Large grebes are the only ones that take many fish. Smaller grebes collect insects, larvae, and other small animal and plant edibles from still waters and their edges and bottoms. Many ducks also collect insects, larvae, and small crustaceans in summer when nesting on interior wetlands.

The legs of diving ducks and grebes are positioned for efficient swimming but are too far back on their bodies for easy walking. These birds tend to live almost entirely on water, some nesting in marsh reeds just above the water's surface. Most have heavy bodies and often ride low in the water, seemingly tailless. Few can jump into flight like a dabbler; most diving ducks and all grebes must run on the water, using legs and wings to power their bulk into flight.

MANDARIN DUCKS ♂

MUSCOVY

DOMESTIC AND
MALLARD HYBRIDS

The mallard is the ancestor of most domestic ducks, and mixes are common in park ponds. Domesticated varieties of Muscovy and escaped mandarin ducks are also common. Female mandarin ducks resemble female wood ducks (Key 31).

Flocks of migrating ducks are a familiar sight. Unlike geese, which are noisy in flight, ducks are usually silent, except for the whistling wings of the goldeneyes. Waterfowl flocks are at their largest in fall, when birds move south from their northern nesting grounds. Licensed hunting during fall migration reduces the flocks to calculated winter levels. Most of today's sportsmen contribute to the health of goose and duck populations by supporting duck stamp and other conservation programs.

Adult ducks molt all their flight feathers simultaneously and replace them before fall migration. Other birds molt and replace their flight feathers sequentially so that they can continue to fly, but nearly all ducks experience an eclipse, during which they lose all their flight feathers and are very shy and vulnerable. Males go through eclipse first, while the females stay on the nest. Males gather in a "safe" area to molt, and for a few weeks they wear a dull, female-like plumage. When alarmed they dive or paddle away.

Even during eclipse, dabblers have a brightly colored wing patch, the speculum, which is diagnostic. It is visible at close range on flying birds and usually on swimming ducks as well. However, at a distance, it is often the silhouette of the head that experienced birders use to make identifications.

Only a few ducks are commonly recognized by their voices. Many do little vocalizing except when courting. The well-known *quack-quack* is given only by the females of several species.

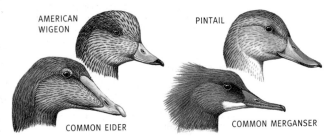

AMERICAN
WIGEON

PINTAIL

COMMON EIDER

COMMON MERGANSER

The shape of a duck's bill and head is often diagnostic. Note especially the angle at which the bill meets the forehead.

fulvous whistling-duck

Black-bellied Whistling-Duck

wood duck ♂

wood duck ♀

♂

Fulvous Whistling-Duck

Wood Duck

The long neck and legs of the fulvous whistling-duck give it a goose-like appearance. It has a rich tawny head and underparts. Also note the dark upperparts and the white rump and side stripe. Male wood ducks look like imaginatively painted decoys. Females are much duller but have a distinctive tear-shaped white eye mark. Wood ducks are often seen in trees, where they nest in cavities.

◄**Fulvous Whistling-Duck** *Dendrocygna bicolor* 20"
Scarce, declining. Few in West except at Salton Sea, CA. Usually in grainfields, esp. rice. Also dabbles and dives in freshwater marshes. Small flocks often wander far north of range. Active at night. ● White rump, dark wings. Legs often droop in flight. ♪ *Pi-wheeeoo*, whistled flight call.

◄**Wood Duck** *Aix sponsa* 18"
Fairly numerous in wooded wetlands. In pairs or small flocks in summer, often large flocks in winter. Wary, but uses nest boxes in parks, reserves. ● Short bill, steep forehead, crest. Long dark tail, white belly, blue speculum with white border. Male brilliant; red bill, eye. Female has gray head, white eye mark, black bill. ♪ Loud, rising whistle.

Black-bellied Whistling-Duck *Dendrocygna autumnalis* 21"
Tropical. Local in summer in s. AZ; resident in s. TX.

All dabblers (Keys 32-34) tip up to feed on bottom vegetation. Male mallards are familiar and distinctive, but females are like black or mottled ducks, two species in which the sexes look similar. Note the female mallard's orange bill with black markings. Others have yellow or greenish yellow bills. Also, the black duck is dark-bodied and lacks bold white borders to its purple, not blue, speculum. Mottled ducks are an intermediate shade of brown; many have white behind, but never in front of, their speculum.

◀**Mallard** *Anas platyrhynchos* 23"
Abundant, widespread on virtually any shallow wetland, esp. freshwater; least common on Northeast and Gulf coasts.
● Medium-size bill, rounded head. Speculum bright blue with white borders. Wing linings and tail white. Male has yellow bill, metallic green head, white collar, chestnut breast. Female has orange bill with black saddle mark on top, mottled brown plumage. Eclipse male and juv. male resemble female; bill slightly duller than in adult male. Mallards hybridize with black ducks and mottled ducks, complicating identification in some regions. "**Mexican Duck**" *(A. p. diazi)* is Mexican race of mallard. Mostly hybrids near US-Mexican border from se. AZ to

w. TX. Looks like mottled duck; bill greenish yellow.
♪ *Quack!* Given loudly by females. Males give softer notes.

◀**Black Duck** (American) *Anas rubripes* 23"
Still numerous and widespread in Northeast but declining, already scarce in interior from competition and hybridization with mallards. More common in salt water than mallards. Often in small, wary groups in flocks of mallards. ● Bill and head similar to female mallard's, but bill typically yellow on male, yellowish green with some black flecking on female. Purple speculum bordered in black. Feathers on flanks show pale edges but no interior markings as in mottled duck and mallard. No white in tail as in mallard. White underwing linings contrast with dark body in flight. ♪ Like mallard's.

◀**Mottled Duck** *Anas fulvigula* 22"
Numerous, more common than mallard on coastal marshes. Often considered race of mallard. ● Much like female mallard, but darker body shows more contrast with pale head and unstreaked cheek and throat. Bill yellow to olive-yellow, with some black flecking on female's. No white in tail as in mallard. Speculum usually more greenish than mallard's; white borders often not evident in field. ♪ Like mallard's.

Muscovy Duck *Cairina moschata* 28" Wild birds from Mexico scarce along lower Rio Grande. ● Black with large white wing patches.

Seen standing or swimming, the male gadwall is one of the least distinctive dabblers. The best mark is the contrast of the black rear end with the gray body; the brownish head and neck are less distinctive. In flight the gadwall displays a white speculum, the only dabbler to do so. The other males shown are distinctive, but females of all four species suggest a female mallard (Key 32) when not flying. Note the female gadwall's steeper forehead and gray bill with orange edges. Pintails are sleek-looking, with a long, slender neck, small head, and gray bill. Female wigeons have a steep forehead and a short, bluish bill with a black tip.

◀ **Gadwall** *Anas strepera* 20"
Numerous in West and in winter in South; fairly numerous and expanding range in East. Widespread in shallow fresh water, nearby grainfields. Usually in small flocks, often with pintails. ● Blocky head with fairly steep forehead, flattened crown. Narrow gray bill, with orange edges on female. White speculum. Male has gray body with black rump and undertail coverts, white belly, brownish head and neck, rusty shoulder. Female plumage mallard-like except for dark tail, white belly and speculum. ♪ High, reedy quack given by males.

White-cheeked Pintail

American wigeon

♂

♀

Eurasian wigeon

♂

♀

♀

Eurasian Wigeon

American Wigeon

♂

♀

♂

Pintail (Northern) *Anas acuta* ♂ 27" ♀ 21"
Abundant, esp. in West. Widespread on shallow freshwater wetlands, often in large flocks; also salt marshes, grainfields in winter. Wary; flight fast, agile. ● Slender neck, rounded head, blue-gray bill, gray legs. Male has long, pointed tail; brown head with white line on neck extending from breast; green speculum. Female mottled brown; bronze speculum with white rear border. Juv. and eclipse male like female.

American Wigeon *Anas americana* 20"
Abundant in West; fairly numerous in East. Widespread, incl. salt marsh, grainfields in winter. A grazer, but often with diving ducks, stealing vegetation they bring to surface. Flies swiftly in compact, noisy, agile flocks. ● Stubby blue bill with black tip, steep forehead. Male has white crown, green sheen behind eye, rufous sides. Female brown with grayish head, white belly. In flight both sexes show green speculum, large white patch on forewing (grayish in female).

Eurasian Wigeon *Anas penelope* 20"
Eurasian; very rare but regular in winter, almost always in flocks of American wigeon. ● Male has rufous head with buff crown, pale gray sides. Female has barred wing pits, darker upperwings than American wigeon; most have rustier head, no color contrast between head and flanks.

White-cheeked Pintail *Anas bahamensis* 17" W. Indian. Nearly annual straggler to s. FL. Other sightings probably escapes.

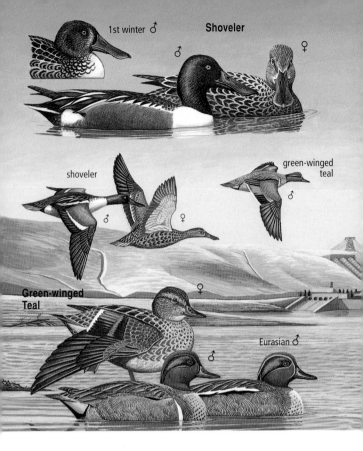

The male shoveler's green head suggests a mallard (Key 32), but the outsize bill on both sexes leaves no doubt about the true identity. Shovelers are closely related to teal and have blue wing patches as some teal do. Teal are the smallest dabblers; all fly rapidly in tight flocks. On males the bright colors and patterns are obvious, but female teal are much alike when swimming – small and mottled brown with dark bills. The green-winged teal has the smallest bill, and it lacks the bright blue forewing patch that both cinnamon and blue-winged teal show in flight. Female cinnamon and blue-winged teal are difficult to separate in the field.

◀**Shoveler** (Northern) *Anas clypeata* 19"
Numerous in West in shallow, often stagnant, water. Less common in East and on coastal bays in winter. Often in small flocks. Swims low in water; feeds by straining tiny crustaceans and seeds through highly specialized bill.
● Long, spatulate bill; sloping forehead. In summer, male has green head, white breast, rufous sides and belly; remains in drab, female-like eclipse until early winter. 1st-winter males often show whitish crescent on face as in blue-winged teal. Both sexes have dark green speculum and light blue upperwing coverts, duller in female.

Cinnamon Teal

blue-winged teal

cinnamon teal

Blue-winged Teal

◀ Green-winged Teal *Anas crecca* 14"

Abundant, widespread on shallow fresh water, mudflats, nearby fields. Often in flocks. ● Short bill, fairly steep forehead, squarer head than in other teal. Green speculum. Male has chestnut head with glossy green eye patch outlined in white, buffy yellow undertail coverts, vertical white side stripe. Female, eclipse male, imm. male mottled brown with whitish undertail coverts. Eurasian form rare but annual; males have horizontal white side stripe instead of vertical stripe.

◀ Blue-winged Teal *Anas discors* 16"

Numerous, esp. in shallow freshwater marshes on midwestern prairies in summer. Often in small flocks, sometimes large flocks in winter. ● Longer bill than in green-winged teal, but shorter, less spatulate than in cinnamon teal; rounded head. Light blue forewing patches (can appear whitish in poor light), green speculum. Male has prominent white facial crescent, white flank patch. Female grayer than female cinnamon teal, with distinct dark eyeline, pale lore spot. Eclipse male and imm. male like female.

◀ Cinnamon Teal *Anas cyanoptera* 16"

Fairly numerous, but rare east of Rockies. In fresh or brackish marshes and ponds. ● Bill fairly long, dark, and slightly spatulate as in shoveler; rounded head. Light blue forewing patches, green speculum. Male has chestnut-colored body; female, mottled brown. Eclipse male and imm. male closely resemble female.

SHOVELER / TEAL DABBLERS

34

The diving ducks here and on Keys 36 to 39 are usually found on deep water. The ruddy duck has a large head and bill and a long, stiff tail, which is often raised and fanned. Male ruddy ducks are bright in summer. The white cheeks that mark winter males are dusky in females. Ring-necked ducks might better be called ring-billed ducks; even so, the male's best mark is his black back. Scaups have pale gray backs. Separating greater from lesser scaups is best done by head shape and wing pattern. Note the peak of the lesser scaup's crown. Female scaups, ring-necks, and redheads (Key 36) must be distinguished with caution.

◄**Ruddy Duck** *Oxyura jamaicensis* 15"
Numerous, on freshwater marshes in summer. Winters in flocks (seldom mixed) on bays, larger lakes, marshes. Low, fast, jerky flight. ● Chunky, with sloping forehead, broad bill, thick neck, long tail. Male has blue bill in summer, white cheek, chestnut body. Winter males dull gray-brown with dark cap, contrasting white cheek. Female, imm. like winter male but cheek grayer with dusky stripe through center.

Ring-necked Duck *Aythya collaris* 17"
Fairly numerous on fresh water, esp. in woodlands. Also on

brackish coastal marshes, bays in winter. Usually in groups, sometimes large flocks in winter. Leaps into flight like dabbler, also sometimes tips up to feed. ● Peaked crown; blue-gray bill with white ring, black tip. Gray secondaries in flight. Male has black back with white spike on side before wing. Female brown with thin white eye-ring and line behind eye.

Greater Scaup *Aythya marila* 18"
Numerous in winter, often in rafts. Declining on East Coast. ● Round head; pale blue bill, black tip. Long white wing stripe in flight. Male dark with white sides, pale gray back; head has green gloss. Female gray-brown with white patch around bill; often shows pale cheek from wear by late spring (not present on female lesser scaup). Eclipse or imm. males like female.

Lesser Scaup *Aythya affinis* 17"
Numerous in summer on fresh water. Also on coasts in winter, usually in protected waters. ● Peaked head. Smaller, narrower bill than in greater scaup with smaller black tip. Wing stripe white on inner wing, gray at tip. Head gloss on male usually purplish, can be green. Female gray-brown with white around bill; eclipse male and imm. similar.

Masked Duck *Oxyura dominica* 13" Tropical. Rare on Gulf Coast from TX to FL. Secretive.

Tufted Duck *Aythya fuligula* 17" Eurasian. Annual on both coasts, often with ring-necks, scaups. ● Male has black back. Female lacks eye-ring and bill ring of female ring-neck.

Redhead ♂

♀

redhead   king eider

♂

♀

1st winter ♂

King Eider

♂   ♀

Maine coast in winter

The plumage of the male redhead is very similar to that of the male canvasback, but their heads and bills are strikingly different. Female redheads resemble the female scaups and tufted duck (Key 35) but lack the white in the wings of those species. Eiders dive for mollusks in frigid ocean waters. The bill on male eiders extends in a colorful shield well up the forehead. These shields, along with their showy black-and-white plumage, make mature males conspicuous. Females and young males are much less colorful but can be identified by their distinctive bill and forehead shapes.

◀**Redhead** *Aythya americana* 19"
Numerous, but much reduced by loss of marsh habitat used in summer and migration. Most winter off coasts, esp. on Gulf; often in large rafts. Also on freshwater lakes in winter.
● Round head with fairly steep forehead, blue bill with black tip bordered in white. Shows gray wing stripe in flight. Male has chestnut head, darker gray back and sides than in male canvasback or greater scaup (Key 35). Female tawnier brown than scaups or ring-neck (Key 35); pale area near bill tip. Eclipse and imm. males resemble female.

Canvasback

common eider ♀

♂

♀

Canvasback

♂ canvasback

western race

Common Eider

1st winter ♂

♂

♀

King Eider *Somateria spectabilis* 22"
Numerous in Arctic. Rare in winter south of AK in Pacific or NY in Atlantic; very rare on Great Lakes. • Male has magnificent head, bill, and shield. Female similar to female common eider, but forehead more rounded, bill shorter with feathering farther down top of bill, less down side. Crescent-shaped marks on flanks and back. Imm. male dull brown to black, usually with yellow-orange bill and white breast.

Common Eider *Somateria mollissima* 24"
Numerous in Far North. Fairly numerous in winter south to NY; often well offshore. • Sloping forehead, long bill, shield extends nearly to eyes. Shape and color of shield vary with range. Male black and white with green tinge on nape; western form has yellow-orange bill and shield, thin black V on throat. Females rusty brown with barred flanks, back. Imm. male usually has whiter back than imm. male king eider.

Canvasback *Aythya valisineria* 21"
Numerous but declining. In small flocks on lakes and marshes in summer and migration. Winters on large lakes, bays; often in large flocks. • Long, flat forehead and bill; tip of bill slightly dished. Male has chestnut head and neck, black breast and tail, nearly white back and sides. Female, imm., eclipse male have brownish head and foreparts, pale gray back and sides.

Oldsquaw ♂ spring ♀

♂ winter ♀

oldsquaw (winter) ♂ ♀

common goldeneye ♂ ♀

Common Goldeneye ♂ ♀

The male oldsquaw has a very long tail, but it is often submerged. In winter, when usually seen, both sexes have small, mostly white heads and short bills. Buffleheads and male goldeneyes each have a differently shaped white patch on the head. The heads of the male goldeneyes look flat black if the reflective sheens are not visible. Female goldeneyes are best distinguished by head and bill shape; note the steep forehead and stubby, triangular bill of Barrow's. In flight, goldeneyes' wings whistle distinctively.

◄ **Oldsquaw** *Clangula hyemalis* ♂22" ♀16"
Numerous in winter in loose rafts over deep-water shellfish beds. Dives to depths of over 100 ft. Flocks very active, noisy, esp. in spring. ● Small head, with fairly steep forehead, flattened crown, short bill. Dark wings, no speculum. Winter male has bold black-and-white pattern best seen in flight; short, black bill with pink stripe; long tail. Summer male has dark brown breast, neck, head, with white face patch. Females have dark backs and dark head patches. Eclipse and imm. males similar to female but with pink on bill. ♪ *Ow-owdle-oo,* loud yodel, given during courtship.

Bufflehead

Barrow's goldeneye ♂ ♀ ♂ ♀ bufflehead

Barrow's Goldeneye ♂ ♀

Common Goldeneye *Bucephala clangula* 18"

Numerous. On woodland lakes, ponds in summer; nests in tree cavities, nest boxes. Winters on sheltered coasts, large lakes; usually in small flocks. ● Triangular head shape created by sloping front and rear of head. Large white wing patches in flight. Male has round white spot at base of bill, glossy green head. Female brown-headed; small yellow patch on bill can be absent. Eclipse male, juv. like female.

Barrow's Goldeneye *Bucephala islandica* 18"

Scarce. Rare, local in East. Habitat, behavior as in common goldeneye, but most winter on coasts. ● Steep forehead, puffy nape giving skinny-necked look. Short, triangular bill. Less white in wings than in common goldeneye. Male has crescent-shaped white spot on face, purple head sheen. Female, juv., and eclipse male darker overall than female common goldeneye; bill of female usually has more yellow.

Bufflehead *Bucephala albeola* 14"

Numerous. Habitat, behavior as in common goldeneye, but flocks more active, not so wary. Can spring directly into flight, unlike most divers. ● Small overall with large, puffy head; steep forehead; short bill. Male has glossy black head and neck with white patch from eye to rear crown; bold black-and-white pattern best seen in flight. Female gray-brown with white oval cheek patch, belly, speculum.

In poor light the dapper male harlequin can look as dark overall as the female. In females the white spots below and before the eye can merge or be indistinct, but the white ear spot is always sharp. Scoters are also dark ducks. The white-wing's namesake speculum is not always visible on swimming birds. Note how far the feathering extends down the side of the white-wing's bill. A male black scoter has an orange bulb on his bill; a male surf scoter has a very colorful bill and white head spots. The distinctive pale patches on the faces and necks of females and young can show little contrast, especially in poor light. Scoters do not have an eclipse plumage.

◀**Harlequin Duck** *Histrionicus histrionicus* 16"
Fairly numerous in West, scarce in East. Winters in small flocks feeding in turbulent surf along broken, rocky, northern coasts; increasingly scarce to south; rare inland. Nests on rushing mountain streams and cold Arctic shores.
● Small, chunky with short bill, steep forehead, rounded head. White scapulars of male contrast with dark back and wings in flight. Female dark gray-brown with white face spots. Eclipse and imm. males resemble female.

Surf Scoter

White-winged Scoter

◀**Black Scoter** *Melanitta nigra* 19"
Fairly numerous but local in large coastal rafts in winter; scarcer to south. Least common scoter. ● Round head. Dark bill usually parallel with water, not pointed down as in other scoters. Silvery flight feathers contrast with black wing linings. Female brown with pale cheek, foreneck. Imm. like female but whitish belly; male develops yellow bulb on bill.

White-winged Scoter *Melanitta fusca* 21"
Numerous in winter on both coasts, often in rafts. Rare, but ◀most likely scoter to occur inland in winter. Small numbers of all scoters also winter on Gulf Coast and Great Lakes. ● Slightly rounded forehead, long bill feathered nearly to nostrils, white speculum. Male black; has white eye spot, orange bill with black bulb at base. Female brown with 2 obscure pale spots on side of face; spots most evident on imms., which also show whitish bellies.

Surf Scoter *Melanitta perspicillata* 19"
◀Numerous in winter on both coasts, often among breakers or just beyond. Most common western scoter. ● Long bill, swollen at base and partially feathered on top. Nearly flat forehead, slightly more rounded in female. Male black with bright bill, white forehead and nape spots. Female and imm. brown with face spots like female white-winged scoter's but lack white speculum.

Hooded Merganser

♂ ♀

common

hooded

Common Merganser

♀ ♂

Mergansers are rakish-looking ducks. Most sport swept-back crests, and all have long, slender bills. Only the hooded merganser has a dark bill (note the yellow-orange at the base of the female's lower mandible), and the male hooded certainly has the most arresting crest. The crest is scant in the male common merganser. The best mark for separating female common and red-breasted mergansers is the clean line beween the neck and breast in the common. Also, note the white collar on the male red-breasted. On the pied-billed grebe the bill changes color seasonally, but the chicken-like bill shape is constant. The pied-billed is more easily confused with the birds on Key 41 than with the grebes on Key 40.

◄**Hooded Merganser** *Lophodytes cucullatus* 18"
Fairly numerous on fresh water, esp. woodland streams, ponds; rarely on salt water. Often in small flocks in winter. Can jump into flight like dabbler. ● Bushy crest, steep forehead, thin bill with serrated edges. Male has white patch on crest. Female dull brown with rufous tinge to crest, yellow on bill. In flight, male shows some white in wing; female, less. In all mergansers, eclipse and imm. males resemble female. Imm. male molts to adult during 1st winter and spring.

Least Grebe

winter   summer

Pied-billed Grebe

summer   winter

downy young

red-breasted   ♂
             ♀

Red-breasted Merganser

♂ molting
imm.

♂

♀

◀**Common Merganser** *Mergus merganser* 25"
Numerous, widespread on fresh water, occasionally brackish inlets in winter; often in large flocks. • Long red bill, thicker than in other mergansers; sloping, elongated head. Male mostly white with dark, greenish head. Female has chestnut-brown head, ragged crest, well-defined border to white throat patch and breast. In flight, male shows single black bar crossing white on upperwing; female has white speculum crossed by bar.

◀**Red-breasted Merganser** *Mergus serrator* 22"
Numerous along coasts in winter. Can be tame, attend fishing piers with cormorants. In summer, most migrate to fresh water. • Forehead steeper than in common merganser; bill thinner at base, nostrils closer to base; eyes red in adults. Male has dark breast, shows two dark bars on upperwing in flight. Brown on female's head blends into white breast.

Pied-billed Grebe *Podilymbus podiceps* 14"
◀Numerous on fresh and brackish water; scarce on salt water in winter. Usually alone. Often submerges with only head remaining above water; other grebes seldom do this. • Stubby, chicken-like bill; round head; dark eye with white eye-ring. Brown with black throat, black band on bill in summer. In winter, pale throat, plain bill. Juv. has striped head.

Least Grebe *Tachybaptus dominicus* 10" Scarce, local resident in s. TX. Records to se. AZ and along TX coast. • Thinner bill than in pied-billed, yellow eyes.

Eared Grebe

summer

winter

Clark's Grebe

nest

reed dancing

typical

Western Grebe

pale

These grebes all have thin, pointed bills. Western and Clark's grebes are often together and are distinguished by bill color and slight differences in face pattern. The other grebes are all brightly marked in summer. Separating them in winter is more difficult; the head, neck, and bill shapes are important marks. Note the large, yellow bill of the red-necked grebe. The eared grebe has a steeper forehead and thinner bill than the similar horned grebe, and a darker, smudged face and neck. Grebes seldom fly except in migration.

◀**Eared Grebe** *Podiceps nigricollis* 13"
Numerous in summer on marshy portions of fresh water. Nests in colonies. Often in large flocks in winter, when many migrate to coasts; rare on Gulf Coast. ● Thin, black, slightly upturned bill; steep forehead and crest; red eyes. Spray of golden feathers behind eye in summer. Winter birds darker than horned grebe, with dusky foreneck and cheek (well below eye); rear end usually loosely fluffed.

Western Grebe *Aechmophorus occidentalis* 25"
Clark's Grebe *Aechmophorus clarkii* 25"
Numerous in summer on freshwater marshes, lakes. Nests

winter

Horned Grebe

summer

rushing display

summer   winter

Red-necked Grebe

juv.

◀in colonies, often mixed, with western grebe predominating
in interior. Winters mostly along coasts or in bays, usually in
flocks, with western grebe predominating in north. ● Long,
graceful, black-and-white neck. Bill thin, long, pointed;
orange-yellow in Clark's, duller greenish yellow in western.
Clark's paler on flanks; black cap does not extend over eye;
but intermediate plumages exist, esp. in winter. ♪ *Krrik*,
loud, given by Clark's; doubled, *krrik, krrik,* by western.

◀**Red-necked Grebe** *Podiceps grisegena* 20"
Fairly numerous in summer on marshy, freshwater ponds,
lakes. Most winter on bays, coasts; often seen alone just
beyond breakers; scarce on East Coast. ● Long, stout,
yellow bill; sloped forehead with flat crown, dark eye. In
summer, chestnut neck, white cheek and throat, black cap.
In winter, dusky foreneck and cheek, white throat strap (can
be obscure on 1st-winter birds). Juv. has striped cheek.

◀**Horned Grebe** *Podiceps auritus* 14"
Fairly numerous in summer on freshwater marshes, ponds.
Winters mostly on coasts, bays; some on nearby deep fresh
water; usually alone or in small, loose flocks. ● Dark bill
with white tip, red eye, fairly flat crown. In summer has
rufous foreneck and sides, black head with contrasting
golden "horns." In winter has sleeker shape, crisper pattern
on head and neck than in eared grebe.

GREBES DIVERS

40

These birds have chicken-like bills and colorful forehead shields. They not only swim, but dive, dabble, wade, *and* graze on land. All pump their necks while swimming. Purple gallinules are distinctive. The white side stripe is a good mark for the moorhen. Coots are dark except for the contrasting white of the bill and under the tail.

COOT AND ALLIES

Purple Gallinule *Porphyrula martinica* 13"
Scarce. Habits and habitat like moorhen's. ● Red bill with yellow tip, blue shield. Colorful body sheen. Juv. tawnier brown than juv. moorhen; greenish tinge above.

Moorhen (Common) *Gallinula chloropus* 14"
Numerous on fresh water with marsh vegetation; scarce on brackish water. Uses large feet for swimming, walking on marshy shores. Warier than coot. ● Red shield and bill in summer with yellow tip. Brown back, white flank stripe. Juv. grayer, with whitish belly; lacks bright shield and base of bill.

Coot (American) *Fulica americana* 16"
Abundant on freshwater marshes in summer; also on coasts in winter, often in large rafts. Fairly tame; grazes on lawns. ● Ivory bill with dark band near tip; white shield, dull reddish at top; dark red eyes. Slate black with white on outer undertail coverts. Juv. paler.

Wading birds

CONSULTANT **PAUL LEHMAN**
ILLUSTRATOR **HANS PEETERS**

A bird's leg appears to bend in the opposite direction from man's because its "knee" is actually its ankle. The lower leg is composed of fused foot bones, and what we often call its feet are really only toes.

Most wading birds are large and have long legs that help them wade in shallows to catch fish and other aquatic prey. Their size makes them relatively easy to see. However, the bitterns and rails are smaller and conceal themselves in marsh vegetation. Most of them are also very thin, the better to squeeze through dense vegetation. John J. Audubon discovered that a least bittern he kept as a pet could squeeze its two-and-one-quarter-inch-wide body through bookends placed only one inch apart.

The large wading birds have long, flexible necks to allow them to reach prey underwater or on the ground. A heron typically coils its neck when hunting and then slings its long, pointed bill at prey with blurring speed. A heron with its neck fully extended looks quite different when its neck is folded so that its head sits squarely on its shoulders. Herons, which include the egrets and bitterns, usually stalk slowly or "still-hunt" – freeze until prey appears. But they can also be seen in mad chase.

Other wading birds have their own feeding specialties. Cranes are omnivorous. They and the herd-following cattle egrets range beyond wetlands onto dry prairie and pasture. Wood storks and the roseate spoonbill feed in shallow water by sense of touch, clasping whatever food their bills encounter. Ibises also often depend on touch. Their long, curved bills are a special threat to aquatic animals, such as crayfish, that live in burrows.

Some rails and herons tend to be nocturnal, and tides influence the foraging periods of birds living in coastal marshes. They usually feed at low tide, when prey is exposed or concentrated in shallow pools. When flood tides fill the marshes, rails are forced into the open, and it is their turn to be exposed to predators. Marshes don't provide much food for waders when the weather turns cold. Most wading birds are migratory and, come winter, leave North America, except for its warm southern wetlands.

All the wading birds can swim and briefly dive, but the birds that do so regularly are grouped with the swimmers. The herons and ibises roost and nest in trees or bushes, usually in fairly dense colonies. The birds are so obviously built for wading that

LITTLE BLUE HERON

GLOSSY IBIS

Herons (including egrets and bitterns) typically fly with their necks folded; the other waders extend their necks. Ibises and spoonbills fly in diagonal lines or Vs.

they seem incongruous in a tree, but that is where they are safest.

Most wading birds have distinctive shapes and markings, but the sexes are usually similar. In the nesting season herons have showy plumes, usually on their heads, necks, or backs. The facial skin, bill, or legs can become brightly colored in some species for a few days at the peak of breeding. In southern swamps and marshes breeding and nesting may not occur in summer; they can take place in midwinter. After nesting, individuals of many species wander far north of their nesting range, both inland and along the coasts, before returning to their wintering grounds.

Many of the wading birds, especially the larger ones, were shot nearly to extinction at the end of the 19th century. Plume hunters destroyed entire rookeries, disrupting even the nesting of species they were not hunting. The breeding plumes of the great egret became more valuable than gold before opposition to the wanton killing coalesced into the Audubon movement and brought the era of millinery slaughter to an end. Cranes, hunted for food, have had much of their habitat overtaken by man and will never reoccupy it. Some rails, "marsh hens" to sportsmen, continue to be hunted for the table, but because they reproduce rapidly, they are less threatened. Habitat destruction and pollution are now the biggest threats to rails and most other wading birds.

Marshes, swamps, and other low-lying wetlands were once thought of as forbidding, bug-infested, unhealthy places that could become useful only if filled in. Some wetlands can be very inhospitable, but they are now widely understood to be a rich environment for wildlife. Still, North America continues to lose wetlands to development and coastal erosion, with the result that most wading birds are diminishing. Marshes are also at risk of being buried in silt or poisoned by pesticides, fertilizers, and chemicals. Silt and industrial and agricultural contaminants all eventually concentrate in low wetlands, deposited there by flowing water. Rails in some marshes have ingested so much mercury that hunters are advised not to eat them. While their toxicity may save a few rails from the hunter's table, ultimately the entire marsh ecosystem is at peril.

Whooping Crane

imm.

Drained wetlands – lost habitat

At over four feet, the whooper is North America's tallest bird.
It once ranged widely, but by 1937 its numbers had been reduced
to 15 wild birds wintering in coastal Texas. Under protection, this
last wild flock now numbers over 100. Still, one serious disease
or oil spill could be disastrous, so conservationists are attempting
to establish a second flock, so far unsuccessfully.

historical
range
nesting
winter

◀ **Whooping Crane** *Grus americana* 52"
Rare and local in winter in coastal marshes at Aransas
National Wildlife Refuge, TX. Nests in wetlands at Wood
Buffalo National Park, Canada. Attempts to create a second
flock from eggs placed in nests of sandhill cranes at Grays
Lake NWR, ID, failed when hatchlings reached maturity
but did not reproduce. Efforts to establish second flock
currently under way in central FL. ● Tall with long neck,
legs. White with black primaries, red on crown and
cheek. Imm. white with rusty brown head, neck; washed
with brown elsewhere; starts molting to adult by 1st fall.
♪ Loud, rolling, trumpeting call.

Jabiru

Greater Flamingo

Sandhill Crane

imm.

Sandhill cranes forage in noisy flocks on dry prairies and stubble fields as well as in wetlands. They are similar in size to great blue herons (Key 45) and sometimes confused with them. Spoonbills and wood storks feed blindly, closing their bills on food by touch. Spoonbills swing their slightly open bills from side to side through shallow water. Wood storks drag their bills along shallow bottoms.

◀**Sandhill Crane** *Grus canadensis* 42"
Fairly numerous on wetlands, prairies. Many congregate along Platte River, NE in spring. Mississippi race, about 100 birds, endangered. Most birds in Southeast are resident; average 12" shorter than migrants. Flocks soar on thermals.
● Gray, often mottled with rust stains; crown naked, red. Imm. reddish brown with feathered crown. ♪ Long, hollow, bugling call given on ground and in flight; heard for miles.

imm.

Wood Stork

imm.

Roseate Spoonbill

◄**Roseate Spoonbill** *Ajaia ajaja* 32"
Local; in small flocks in mangroves, salt marshes, coastal lagoons. Once hunted nearly to extinction; only partially recovered. Also suffers from habitat destruction. ● Long, flat, spatulate bill. Pink wings with red shoulders, red-orange tail. Imm. white, gradually becoming pink.

◄**Wood Stork** *Mycteria americana* 40"
Scarce, local in small flocks in shallow salt- and freshwater wetlands; seriously declining due to habitat destruction. Often soars high on afternoon thermals. ● White with black flight feathers. Dark, naked head and neck; stout, dark, decurved bill. Imm. has pale yellow bill and feathered, gray-brown head and neck. ♪ Voiceless except for low grunts, hisses; much bill clacking.

Jabiru *Jabiru mycteria* 52" Tropical. Several records in TX. ● Huge.

Greater Flamingo *Phoenicopterus ruber* 46" Tropical. Once locally numerous in FL. Now recorded regularly only in s. FL; most are escapes.

breeding

high breeding

"great white heron," form of great blue heron Key 45

nonbreeding

Cattle Egret

Great Egret

Merritt Island National Wildlife Refuge

Usually, white herons can be told by their size and by the color of their bare parts (legs, bills, and the skin before the eye). However, young birds often show different colors from adults, and bare parts in adults can become vividly colored at the peak of breeding. Sure marks for the cattle egret are its small size and comparatively short bill. Great egrets are clearly larger than all but the yellow-legged "great white heron" of Florida. Snowy egrets are midsize, like young little blue herons but with bright yellow toes.

◀**Cattle Egret** *Bubulcus ibis* 20"
Numerous African immigrant; in flocks, esp. in pastures feeding on insects disturbed by grazing livestock; also in wetlands. Arrived in US in 1940s, now most common heron in many southern areas; scarcer, local nester to north.
● Small, stocky. Bill yellow or yellow-orange most of year, legs dark green (appearing black) with yellowish feet. In nest-

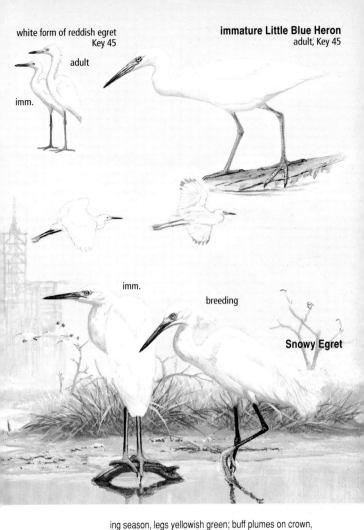

white form of reddish egret
Key 45

adult

imm.

immature Little Blue Heron
adult, Key 45

imm.

breeding

Snowy Egret

ing season, legs yellowish green; buff plumes on crown, neck, back. Bill and legs bright red just before egg-laying.

◀**Great Egret** *Ardea albus* 39"
Numerous, widespread in wetlands. Rare nester in western interior. Recovered from decimation by plume hunters. Feeds alone or in groups, mainly on fish caught by still-hunting.
● Large. Bill yellow, legs black. Long, lacy plumes on back and breast in breeding. Green lores at high breeding.

◀**Snowy Egret** *Egretta thula* 24"
Numerous in salt water, fairly numerous inland. Hunted closer to extinction than great egret; now recovered. Often feeds in flocks, frequently sprinting through shallows in pursuit of fish. ● Slim, with slender neck and bill. Bill and legs black, lores yellow, toes golden yellow (orange-red at high breeding). Breeding adults have prominent long plumes on crown, back, breast. Imm. has dull yellow toes, dull yellow stripe up back of black legs.

Little Egret *Egretta garzetta* 23" (Not shown) European. Several eastern records.
● Like snowy but 2 long head plumes in summer; bill slightly larger, lores duller.

WHITE HERONS

44

imm.

breeding

"Würdemann's
heron"

**Great Blue
Heron**

little blue heron

"calico"
phase

breeding

**Little Blue
Heron**

These dark herons are slender with straight, dagger-like bills, in contrast to the curve-billed waders and stocky herons that follow. The great blue is the size of a sandhill crane (Key 43), much larger than other herons. Little blue herons pass through a "calico" phase as white young birds become slate-blue adults with maroon-tinged heads and necks. The tricolored heron is the only dark heron with a white belly. The pink-and-black bill of the reddish egret is often dark in nonbreeding plumage, but its legs remain cobalt blue.

◀**Great Blue Heron** *Ardea herodias* 46"
Numerous in wetlands, also fields. Usually stalks slowly or still-hunts, alone. ● Large, gray-blue. White crown, black stripe over eye, black head plumes, some yellow on bill, dark legs. Plumes on back, neck in breeding. Imm. duller. "Great white heron" of FL is white form; has yellow bill, legs. Intermediate form, "Würdemann's heron," has white head.

Little Blue Heron *Egretta caerulea* 24"
Numerous, widespread in wetlands. Adults tend to stalk

Western Reef-Heron

dark form breeding

Reddish Egret

imm.

reddish egret

breeding

imm.

Tricolored Heron

singly; imms. often in active groups. ● Appears all-dark at distance. Dull maroon head; neck turns richer and shaggier in breeding. Bill bluish with black tip; legs dull blue. Imm. (Key 44) white with greenish legs, gray-green lores, dusky wing tips; patchy when molting to adult during 2nd yr.

Tricolored Heron *Egretta tricolor* 26"
Fairly numerous along coast, less so in nearby freshwater marshes. Often stalks in deep water; alone or in groups. ● Long, slender neck and bill. Blue-gray with white belly, foreneck; pale rump. Long plumes on head and back in breeding. Imm. has rusty neck, wing coverts.

Reddish Egret *Egretta rufescens* 30"
Scarce, local on shallow salt flats, coastal lagoons. Partially recovered from plume trade; about 2,000 pairs breed in US. Forages alone or in small flocks, often sprinting after fish or stalking with wings spread, providing shade for better visibility. ● Pale eye. Dark form gray with rusty brown head and neck, long blue legs. White form rare outside of FL. Shaggy neck plumes, pink bill with black tip in breeding. Nonbreeding adults and imms. have dark bills.

Western Reef-Heron *Egretta gularis* 22" African. Recorded in MA.

DARK HERONS

45

Limpkin

White Ibis

molting imm.

imm.

The only two curve-billed waders likely to be confused are the nearly identical glossy and white-faced ibises – dark birds whose ranges overlap only slightly. The limpkin is a slightly larger, brown bird with streaked foreparts and less curve to its bill. It tends to be nocturnal and is best known for its wailing call. The white ibis, with its red bill, face, and legs, could hardly be more obviously marked.

◄**Limpkin** *Aramus guarauna* 26"
Hunted to near-extinction by 1920s, now fairly numerous but local. Wades alone in freshwater marshes, feeding heavily on apple snails; sometimes swims. Seldom flies but has crane-like upward flip of wings in flight. Largely nocturnal.
● Long, heavy bill, slightly curved. Dull brown, streaked and spotted with white. ♪ *Kar-r-ee-ow, kra-ow,* loud wailing call, often given at night, earning it the name "crying bird."

White Ibis *Eudocimus albus* 25"
Fairly numerous but declining in both salt- and freshwater

Scarlet Ibis

winter · breeding

GLOSSY

winter · breeding

WHITE-FACED

winter

White-faced & Glossy Ibises

imm.

◀wetlands. Probes for wide variety of aquatic animals, usually feeding in groups. ● White with red bill and legs, black wing tips. Imm. has brown body and wings, white belly. Molting imm. boldly mottled brown and white.

White-faced Ibis *Plegadis chihi* 23"
◀Fairly numerous but local in freshwater marsh in West, salt or brackish marsh along Gulf. Often feeds in groups, preying on aquatic animals, esp. crayfish. ● Glossy overall but often looks black. Breeding birds have bright chestnut body, white feathers bordering pinkish red facial skin. Winter birds heavily streaked on head and neck. Adults have red eyes. Imm. has brown eyes; plumage lacks gloss until 2nd yr.

Glossy Ibis *Plegadis falcinellus* 23"
◀Fairly numerous in wetlands, esp. salt marsh. Habits like those of white-faced ibis. ● Similar to white-faced ibis but with brown eyes. Adults lack white feather border on face but have narrow pale blue border of facial skin, which can look similar. Imm. like imm. white-faced.

Scarlet Ibis *Eudocimus ruber* 25" Tropical. Records in FL, TX.

CURVE-BILLED

46

American Bittern

black-crowned imm.

2nd yr.

Black-crowned
Night-Heron

imm.

These birds are bulky and often sit hunched up. The American bittern is secretive and well camouflaged, but its peculiar call is easily recognized. Night-herons, on the other hand, are tame and often conspicuous. Adults have distinctive plumages, but young birds resemble each other and are best separated by the longer legs and stouter all-dark bill of the yellow-crowned night-heron. Green herons usually permit a close approach before flushing with a sharp call. They're a dark bluish green, with short, bright legs.

◀**American Bittern** *Botaurus lentiginosus* 28"
Locally numerous in fresh and brackish marshes; seriously declining with loss of habitat. Shy, solitary. Hides by freezing, bill pointed skyward; sways like wind-blown reed, even in the absence of reeds. Usually forages at dusk, night.
● Heavy brown streaking, contrasting black neck stripe. Dark flight feathers obvious in flight (usually low over marsh). Imm. lacks neck stripe. ♫ *Pump-per-lunk*, loud, distinctive call.

Black-crowned Night-Heron *Nycticorax nycticorax* 25"
Fairly numerous, widespread in wetlands. Habits similar to yellow-crowned night-heron's but more gregarious; takes

Green Heron

imm.

yellow-crowned
imm.

**Yellow-crowned
Night-Heron**

imm.

JULIAN

fish by still-hunting. • Black back and crown, gray wings,
white underparts. Narrow white plumes on nape (longest
in breeding). Feet barely extend beyond tail in flight. Imm.
heavily spotted; some yellow at base of lower mandible.
♪ *Quok!* Loud call, deeper than yellow-crowned's.

Yellow-crowned Night-Heron *Nyctanassa violacea* 24"
Fairly numerous in salt- and freshwater wetlands, even
near suburbs. Active day and night, roosting in trees,
shrubs when not feeding. Forages alone or in small groups,
preying mostly on crabs, crayfish. • Gray body with black-
and-white head; yellowish forehead. White head plumes
in breeding. Stouter bill, longer legs than in black-crowned
night-heron; feet extend well beyond tail in flight. Imm.
grayer brown above with finer spotting than in black-
crowned night-heron. ♪ *Quok!* Loud call.

Green Heron *Butorides virescens* 18"
Fairly numerous, widespread on wetlands, esp. ponds,
streams. Forages alone, frequently still-hunting or stalking
slowly. Usually stretches neck when first disturbed, gives
loud call and defecates on take-off, flies short distance.
• Small, dark, compact; neck can be greatly extended.
Back and wings blue-green, head and neck chestnut with
dark crest sometimes erect, legs orange to yellow. Imm.
steaked below. ♪ *Kowp!* Loud call given when flushed.

STOCKY HERONS

47

Least Bittern

least bittern

♂

♀

King Rail

The least bittern is a small, secretive heron. It is most often glimpsed in brief flight and identified by its contrasting buff wing patches. Large rails are laterally compressed – thin ("as a rail") when viewed from the front. The largest are the similar king and clapper rails. In the East the clapper occupies salt marshes, whereas the king prefers fresh water. Both can occur in brackish water, and the species have interbred. Some western and Gulf Coast clapper rails are as richly colored as king rails.

◀**Least Bittern** *Ixobrychus exilis* 13"
Scarce, local in fresh and sometimes brackish marshes; local in West. Declining with habitat loss in East. Feeds on variety of aquatic animals, usually by still-hunting. Shy, secretive, usually seen singly; freezes with bill pointed skyward to avoid detection. Expert climber, often seen in reeds several feet above water. ● Small. Large buff wing patches obvious in flight. Rich chestnut on portion of wing, sides of neck. Crown and back black in male, brown in female. Imm.

pale form

dark form

Clapper Rail

like female but more heavily streaked. In rare dark form, "Cory's least bittern," buff wing patches replaced by chestnut. ♪ *Wack-wack-wack*, raspy 3-noted call; also *coo-coo-coo*, soft, dove-like call given during breeding season.

◀ King Rail *Rallus elegans* 15"
Scarce in freshwater and some brackish marshes. Has declined seriously because of habitat loss and pollution. Shy, solitary, and secretive, preferring to run rather than fly. Feeds on aquatic animals and some plants. • Heavy body, long bill. Rich cinnamon-rust on breast and shoulders, flanks barred with black and white. Back feathers have darker centers, more colorful fringes than in clapper rail. ♪ *Kek-kek-kek-kek-kek-kek*, dry, chattering call.

◀ Clapper Rail *Rallus longirostris* 15"
Fairly numerous in salt and brackish marshes in East; rare and endangered in West, where it can also be found in freshwater marshes. All populations threatened by habitat loss, pollution. Habits like king rail's. • Eastern birds similar to king rail but duller with gray-brown breast, olive-brown shoulders, grayer back. Some Gulf Coast and western birds have rusty breasts but lack rusty shoulders of king rail, usually show more gray on face. ♪ Like king rail's.

These small rails are usually secretive, but when found they may seem oblivious to humans, as if they were still hidden. They forage alone, often at night, and are usually identified by their calls. Both the yellow and the black rail are so tiny that they can pass through dense vegetation even though they are not laterally compressed, as larger rails are. The adult sora has a short yellow bill and a black face. Young soras can be mistaken for yellow rails, especially by flashlight, when both can seem a pale buff. The Virginia rail has a long, slightly curved bill and suggests a half-size king rail (Key 48) with gray cheeks. Black rails are often confused with the chicks of larger rails, which are also black.

◀**Yellow Rail** *Coturnicops noveboracensis* 7"
Fairly numerous but secretive and seldom seen. In grassy marshes and wet meadows. ● Tiny. Warm buff below and on face; dark above with buff, white, and blackish bars and streaks. Broad white tips on secondaries visible in flight, but seldom flushes. ♪♪ *Tic-tic-tic, tic-tic, tic-tic-tic*, in groups of 2 or 3; like 2 pebbles being tapped together.

Jacana

Black Rail

juv.

Virginia
Rail

chick

◀**Sora** *Porzana carolina* 9"
Numerous, in same habitat and with same habits as
Virginia rail. ● Short yellow bill, black face and throat,
gray neck and breast, barred flanks. In winter black face
and throat obscured by feather edgings. Juv. lacks black
face and throat, has buff-brown breast. ♪♪ *Ker-wee?* or
keek, loud calls.

Virginia Rail *Rallus limicola* 9½"
Numerous, local in fresh and brackish marshes; also salt
◀marshes during migration, winter. Sometimes shy but often
forages in full view. ● Long bill, rusty breast, gray cheeks,
barred flanks. Juv. has blackish underparts. ♪♪ *Ti-dick, ti-
dick, ti-dick,* loud call; also *wack,* repeated in series.

Black Rail *Laterallus jamaicensis* 6"
Scarce, local, in eastern salt marshes; rare in West and
inland wetlands. Shy, seldom seen. ● Tiny. Dark gray with
barred flanks, white flecks on upperparts, chestnut nape,
◀bright red eye. ♪♪ *Kee-kee-der,* male call note; *who-whoo,*
deeper female note.

Jacana (Northern) *Jacana spinosa* 9½" Tropical. Rare visitor
to s. TX; has nested in TX. Extremely long toes allow walking on floating vegetation. ● Bright yellow flight feathers.

RAILS

49

The little surf-chasing sanderlings are abundant on most beaches.

Shorebirds

CONSULTANT **KIMBALL GARRETT**
ILLUSTRATOR **JONATHAN ALDERFER**

Shores, mudflats, and estuaries offer a bounty of mollusks, tiny crustaceans, aquatic insects, and worms that a large number of shorebirds exploit. Nearly all are plovers or sandpipers, although they have a variety of names. The exceptions are the oystercatchers, the avocet, and the stilt, which are all easily recognized by their distinctive bills. It is hard to miss the long, flattened, red bill of an oystercatcher. The stilt has a needle-thin bill, and the avocet's bill is shaped like a scythe.

Plovers also have distinctive bills – pigeon-like, short, and slightly swollen at the tip – which help distinguish them from sand-pipers. Plovers are small to medium-size birds. Smaller species have neck bands; most medium-size ones do not. When feeding, plovers have the habit of sprinting a short distance, abruptly paus-ing to look about or pick for food, then dashing off again.

Sandpipers vary in size from little six-inch peeps to curlews and godwits with bills nearly that size. When living on beaches, they often roost on spits or sandbars in mixed flocks at high tide. As the tide recedes, each species moves to its favorite foraging area. Some prefer mudflats; others choose wet sand. The larger ones have long legs and are often observed wading at the edges of tidal pools and coastal lagoons. Sanderlings and some other sand-pipers scamper along the edge of the surf, collecting whatever they can find in the wet sand.

Sandy ocean beaches, mudflats, and estuaries are not the only sandpiper habitats. Some sandpipers specialize in probing among stones and kelp on rocky shores. They are sometimes called rock pipers. A few sandpipers live exclusively on freshwater shores, and

OYSTERCATCHERS   STILT

AVOCET

Oystercatchers search for mollusks at low tide. Avocets sweep their bills through bottom mud or muddy water.

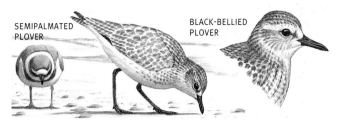

SEMIPALMATED
PLOVER

BLACK-BELLIED
PLOVER

Plovers use their bills to pick from the surface instead of probing beneath it, as many sandpipers do. This allows them to exploit drier upper beaches and upland fields.

freshwater wetlands are critical for nearly all species during nesting and migration. The snipe and woodcock (both sandpipers) have abandoned shores altogether. They use their long bills to probe for earthworms and insects in the soft earth of wet meadows and wooded bogs. The general appearance and ground-walking habits of all shorebirds set them apart wherever they are encountered.

Virtually all our shorebirds are migratory. Many winter on our southern coasts, but some winter south of our borders, nest in the Arctic, and are seen in populated North America only during migration. Spring migration is fairly concentrated, with birds massing at major staging wetlands on the coast and in the interior. In fall, the migration is usually along a broader front and is often staggered, with adults leaving first and young birds following weeks later. In many species, some individuals, especially those in their first summer, may not nest. Those not nesting often remain on their wintering grounds throughout the summer.

Although the larger shorebirds typically can be identified by their structure, especially bill and leg shape, some of the medium-size and smaller birds are very similar in structure and can require a careful study of their plumage. In spring, each species wears its most distinctive plumage, with few of the smaller birds

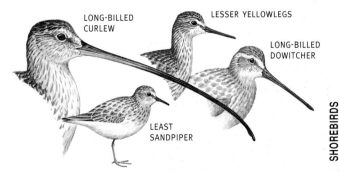

LONG-BILLED
CURLEW

LESSER YELLOWLEGS

LONG-BILLED
DOWITCHER

LEAST
SANDPIPER

Sandpipers' bills are slender and specialized for probing at different depths. Every level from the surface to eight inches deep is exploited.

SHOREBIRDS

fresh spring
adult

worn, molting,
fall adult

fresh winter
adult

fresh juvenal
(typical fall
migration)

Wing coverts and scapulars are usually the first feathers to be molted by summer adults. Young birds may retain juvenal wing coverts and scapulars well into winter.

showing any sex or age variation. But by fall migration most adults have dull, worn plumage and have begun their molt into winter dress. Compounding the identification problem in fall are the numerous young birds. They are in fresh plumage with bright, crisp feather edges, especially noticeable on the mantle. Most juveniles molt to winter plumage on the wintering grounds and become inseparable from adults.

Calls are often useful in identifying confusing fall individuals. Most species have distinctive and diagnostic calls, and the odd bird in a flock will often first call attention to itself by its different call. The complex songs are usually heard only on the nesting grounds.

Most shorebirds once existed in far greater numbers than they do today. Early naturalists told of clouds of shorebirds taking flight before them as they walked the beaches. Now it is people that crowd the beaches. Species such as the snowy and piping plovers, which nest directly on sandy beaches, have experienced disastrous declines. Their future now depends on our active intervention to secure patches of beach where they can nest without disturbance. Some species have taken to nesting on dredge-spoil islands, man-made mounds of dredge waste avoided by people.

The large sandpipers, and even many of the littlest ones, were shot for food in the 19th century. They were protected under federal laws beginning in 1918, and most have gradually recovered. Some have not, and the future of the Eskimo curlew is uncertain at best. Once abundant, this bird is now virtually unreported.

The most serious present threat to shorebirds is the destruction or mismanagement of critical stopover areas for migrating birds. The Western Hemisphere Shorebird Reserve Network works to identify and protect these critical staging areas, some of which support literally millions of birds. Many refuges currently maintained for the benefit of waterfowl could also be managed for the benefit of migrating shorebirds.

Black Oystercatcher

American Oystercatcher

juv.

Oystercatchers are large, chunky shorebirds with long, red bills that are flattened laterally and used for prying open mollusks. They also probe for crabs and marine worms. Ranges of the black and American oystercatchers normally do not overlap north of Mexico.

◀Black Oystercatcher *Haematopus bachmani* 17"
Fairly numerous. Feeds noisily in intertidal zone on rocky coasts at low tide; singly or in small flocks, sometimes with sandpipers shown on Key 56. Roosts and nests on nearby beaches or rocks above tide line. ● Blackish body, red bill, pink legs. Juv. browner; bill has dusky tip during 1st yr.
♪ *Wheep!* Loud, sharp flight call given singly or in series.

American Oystercatcher *Haematopus palliatus* 18"
Fairly numerous in pairs or small, noisy flocks on coasts, ◀salt marshes; roosts on sandbars, secluded beaches at high tide. Sometimes in large flocks during migration, winter. Often nests on dredge-spoil islands. Very rare in CA.
● Black-and-white plumage, white wing stripe, red bill. Juv. has back scaled with buff-edged feathers. Bill dusky orange with dark tip for 1st yr. ♪ Like black oystercatcher's.

OYSTERCATCHERS

50

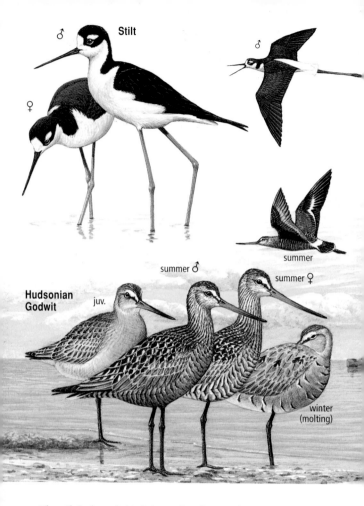

The stilt is the only bird shown that does not have an upturned bill. It and the avocet can be told, even at a distance, by their bold patterns and exceptionally long legs. The godwits show the typical subtle streaking and barring of sandpipers (which they are). The Hudsonian is distinguished from the larger and more common marbled godwit by its white wing stripe and black-and-white tail pattern. Female godwits are larger and longer-billed than males.

◀**Stilt** (Black-necked) *Himantopus mexicanus* 14"
Numerous in West, Gulf Coast, FL; now rare, local on East Coast with loss of wetlands. Feeds in still waters, singly or in groups, picking insects from surface, probing in bottom mud. Prefers salt or brackish water in East, fresh or alkaline in West. ● Long reddish legs, bold black-and-white pattern, needle-like bill. Female brownish above. Juv. like female but with buff feather edges. ♪ *Yip-yip-yip*, sharp.

Hudsonian Godwit *Limosa haemastica* 15"
Scarce; in flocks on wetlands in spring migration. Rare on

Avocet

summer

♂

winter

♀

winter

♂

summer

winter

summer ♂

summer

♂

♀

Marbled
Godwit

◀Atlantic Coast in fall. Never recovered from market hunting.
● Long, upcurved bill with pink base. Black-and-white tail,
black wing linings. In spring, male has chestnut underparts;
paler in female. In winter, adults gray above, whitish below;
usually in molt during fall migration.

Marbled Godwit *Limosa fedoa* 18"

Numerous in loose nesting colonies near prairie potholes in
summer. Winters in flocks on coastal bays, marshes, mudflats; numerous on Pacific Coast, less so on Gulf, scarce in
◀East. ● Long, upturned bill with pink base. Brownish overall with black mottling above, fine barring below. Cinnamon
wing linings. Winter birds and juv. paler, less barring below.
♪ *Ka-rah,* flight call given with laughing quality.

Avocet (American) *Recurvirostra americana* 18"

Numerous; locally abundant in West. On still waters in
summer, esp. alkaline lakes, prairie potholes; sometimes
in large colonies. Winters on coastal mudflats, marshes.
◀Sweeps bill from side to side when feeding. Swims readily
in deep water. ● Slender, upturned bill; black-and-white
wing pattern. Head and neck rusty in summer, gray in winter. Female's bill shorter, more sharply bent. Juv. has rust
on hind neck only. ♪ *Kleep,* sharp flight call.

Eskimo Curlew

Little Curlew

Eskimo

Long-billed Curlew

juv. ♂

The long-billed curlew is the largest of the shorebirds with down-curved bills. Its unstriped crown further distinguishes it from the smaller whimbrel. The nearly extinct Eskimo curlew has crown stripes and resembles a whimbrel, but it is smaller and has a straighter bill, only one and a half times its head length.

historical range

Eskimo Curlew *Numenius borealis* 14"
Once abundant, but not wary; shot to scarcity by 1890, now virtually unreported. Most likely to be seen on TX coast during spring migration. Known to associate with American golden-plovers (Key 57) in spring. ● Like small or young whimbrel with shorter, straighter, thinner bill; slightly darker upperparts, cinnamon tint to wing linings. Only absolute difference is unbarred primaries, nearly impossible to see in field. ♪ *Tee-dee*, 2 or 3 soft syllables, often repeated.
Little Curlew *(N. minutus)* of Eurasia similar but lacks cinnamon tint to wing linings; several recent records in CA. Also compare with straight-billed upland sandpiper (Key 55).

Eurasian Curlew

Whimbrel
European race

long-billed

whimbrel

Whimbrel

◀**Long-billed Curlew** *Numenius americanus* 23"
Fairly numerous but declining. On grasslands in summer;
feeds on insects, berries, seeds. Winters on marshes, mudflats, beaches, nearby fields, grasslands; usually in small
groups. Migrates in large, noisy flocks. Once regular eastern migrant before overhunting. ● Long curved bill, plain
crown, cinnamon wing linings. Female's bill longer than
male's; juv. male's shortest. ♪ *Cur-lee,* loud, ascending,
usually repeated; also *kli-li-li-li,* loud, rapid.

◀**Whimbrel** *Numenius phaeopus* 18"
Now numerous after overhunting in 19th century. Winters
on all types of coasts, nearby grasslands. Feeds singly
or in small, loose groups; migrates and roosts in flocks.
● Decurved bill, striped crown, gray-brown wing linings.
Rump, tail, primaries barred with black. European race
(*N. p. phaeopus*) has white rump; several records from
East Coast. ♪ *Pip, pip, pip,* clear, loud whistle.

Eurasian Curlew *Numenius arquata* 22" Eurasian. A few recent records from
Northeast. ● Larger than whimbrel. White rump, no crown stripes.

Lesser Yellowlegs

summer

Greater Yellowlegs

summer

winter

Low tide in coastal salt marsh

Size differences of the lesser and greater yellowlegs can be hard to judge; calls and bill lengths are surer marks. The greater's bill is half again its head length and slightly upturned; the lesser's bill is thinner, straighter, and about as long as its head. Both species move constantly, bobbing their heads and tails. Yellowish legs are also seen on the stilt sandpiper (Key 60) and the wandering tattler (Key 56). The willet seems nondescript until it takes flight and surprises us with its bold black-and-white wing pattern.

◀**Lesser Yellowlegs** *Tringa flavipes* 11"
Numerous in East during migration, less so in West; often in flocks of several dozen. Widespread, esp. in marshes, small pools, tidal mudflats. Approachable. Most winter south of US. ● Long yellow legs; relatively short, straight, all-black bill. Streaked neck, breast; white belly. Neck and breast streaking finer and grayer in winter. White rump

patch obvious in flight. Juv. slightly browner above, breast more finely streaked. ♪♪ *Tew*, often doubled, given softly.

◀ **Greater Yellowlegs** *Tringa melanoleuca* 14"
Numerous in winter and migration, alone or in small groups. Widespread, versatile feeder at ponds, marshes, mudflats, sandy shores. Often wades, sweeping bill through water. Wary; quickly takes alarm. ● Like lesser yellowlegs but bill longer, slightly upturned, pale at base. In summer, barring and streaking often extend onto belly. Fine breast streaking in winter. Juv. slightly darker and browner above than winter adult. ♪♪ *Tew-tew-tew*, ringing alarm call.

◀ **Willet** *Catoptrophorus semipalmatus* 15"
Fairly numerous; recovered from overhunting. Western birds nest on prairie potholes; eastern ones in coastal marshes, nearby grasslands. In winter on coasts; alone or in loose groups. Migrates, roosts in flocks. ● Black-and-white wing pattern, white rump. Relatively heavy bill. Streaked and barred in summer (western birds less heavily marked than shown), plain gray in winter. Juv. browner above than winter adult. ♪ *Pill-will-willet*, loud, shrill.

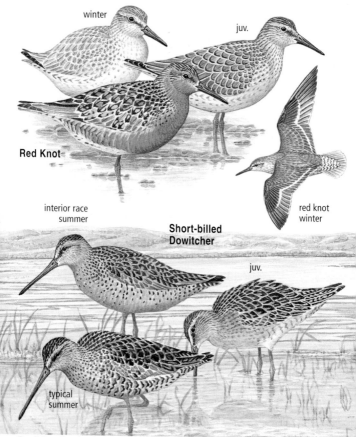

winter

juv.

Red Knot

interior race
summer

**Short-billed
Dowitcher**

juv.

red knot
winter

typical
summer

Dowitchers in migration on midwestern river bottomlands

The red knot and the dowitchers are chunky birds of similar size, but the dowitchers have very long bills. All have reddish breasts in summer and are drab in winter. The only winter shorebirds as large and with such pale backs as the red knot are the dowitchers and the black-bellied plover (Key 57), all of which have distinctive bill shapes. Like dowitchers, the woodcock and snipe (Key 55) have long bills, but they lack the long white rump seen in flight, and they don't feed in flocks in muddy water as dowitchers often do. Voice, rather than bill length, is the sure way to separate dowitchers.

◀**Red Knot** *Calidris canutus* 10"
Scarce, seriously declining; in winter most numerous in s. FL, s. CA. Local, in flocks during migration on coasts, esp. mud-flats, beaches at low tide. Often with sanderlings (Key 61) or dowitchers. ● Robin-like below in summer. In winter, gray above, white below with some breast streaks. Medium-size black bill. Gray barring on white rump in all plumages. Juv. like winter but more scalloped above. ♪ *Knut,* low, soft call.

Short-billed Dowitcher *Limnodromus griseus* 11"
Fairly numerous in flocks in winter on tidal mudflats. Fall

winter ♂ **Ruff** summer ♂

♀
juv.

♀ juv. ruff

**Buff-breasted
Sandpiper**

Snipe

◄**Woodcock** (American) *Scolopax minor* 11"
Fairly numerous but declining. Probes for earthworms in
moist forest, day or night. Early migrant. Male's wings whistle during high, circling spring courtship flight. ● Chunky,
cryptically patterned. Long bill. Large, bulging eyes set far
back and high. ♪ *Bzeep,* nasal courtship call by male.

Snipe (Common) *Gallinago gallinago* 11"
Fairly numerous but declining in East. In peat bogs, wet
grasslands, occasionally salt marshes. Most active at dusk,
◄dawn. ● Chunky with long bill; long, pointed wings. Boldly
patterned upperparts with striped head, short tail with
orange near tip. ♪ *Scaip,* rasping flight call.

Buff-breasted Sandpiper *Tryngites subruficollis* 8½"
Once abundant; shot to scarcity in 19th century, has not
recovered. Usually in flocks in spring migration on short-
grass fields; some migrate along coasts. Tame. ● Buff face,
underparts; white underwing. Head larger; neck, tail shorter
◄than in upland. ♪ *Tik-tik,* thin, sharp call; seldom heard.

Ruff *Philomachus pugnax* ♂12" ♀10" Eurasian. Annual
coastal migrant, mostly juvs. similar to buff-breasted. A few
winter in CA. ● Short, tapered bill. Distinctive white rump
spots in all plumages. Legs greenish to bright orange. Male
larger than female with variably colored neck ruff in summer.

These are the sandpipers usually encountered on rocky shores in winter, when all are shades of gray. Fortunately, the very similar rock and purple sandpipers live on opposite coasts. All the others can be easily separated by plumage. Bills are also good marks on standing birds. In flight, the pattern across the mantle is diagnostic except for separating the two turnstones. The ruddy turnstone is separated from the black by its irregular breast band and orange legs.

◀ **Wandering Tattler** *Heteroscelus incanus* 11"
Fairly numerous in winter, usually single or in loose, often mixed, flocks. In summer, nests along streams above timberline. ● Slate gray above with fairly long dark bill, dull yellow legs. Unpatterned above in flight. Finely barred below in summer. ♪ Clear piping note repeated rapidly.

◀ **Surfbird** *Aphriza virgata* 10"
Fairly numerous in winter, often in small, mixed flocks; rare on beaches. Nests on alpine rocks. ● Short, thick bill; pale spot at base of lower mandible. White belly, rump, tail base, wing stripe in winter. Spotted and streaked in summer; chestnut on scapulars. ♪ Usually silent in winter.

purple sandpiper

FLYING BIRDS IN WINTER PLUMAGE

surfbird

ruddy turnstone

Purple Sandpiper

summer

winter

winter

summer

Rock Sandpiper

summer

winter

Ruddy Turnstone

◀ **Black Turnstone** *Arenaria melanocephala* 9"
Fairly numerous in winter in small flocks, often mixed.
Also seen on beaches, mudflats. Often forages in kelp.
● Short, wedge-shaped bill. Head and breast black in summer with white eyebrows, loral spots, flecking. Grayer in
winter; legs can be dull orange. Elaborate white markings
above in flight. ♪ Like ruddy's but higher-pitched, grating.

Ruddy Turnstone *Arenaria interpres* 9½"
Fairly numerous in winter and migration. Also on beaches,
◀ esp. with shells, pebbles. Inland during migration. ● Short,
wedge-shaped bill. Distinctive "calico" back and black bib in
summer. Pattern similar but duller in winter. Orange legs.
♪ *Kek-kek*, abrupt, harsh call; also low rattle.

Rock Sandpiper *Calidris ptilocnemis* 9"
Fairly numerous in winter, usually in mixed flocks. Scarce in
southern part of range. ● Drooped bill, greenish yellow at
base in winter; greenish yellow legs. White wing stripe; black
◀ center stripe on rump, tail. Rusty above in summer with black
breast patch. Grayer in winter. ♪ Usually silent in winter.

Purple

◀ **Purple Sandpiper** *Calidris maritima* 9"
Fairly numerous in winter, usually in small flocks. ● Like rock
sandpiper but lacks summer breast patch; legs and base of
bill more orange on average in winter. ♪ *Prrt-prrt*, soft call.

Rock

ROCK PIPERS

56

Mountain Plover

summer

winter

FLYING BIRDS IN WINTER PLUMAGE

black-bellied

Black-bellied Plover

winter

summer

juv.

Rocky coastal estuary

The distinctively swollen bill tip is the sure mark of a plover (this Key and Key 58). The mountain plover suggests a killdeer (Key 58) without the neck and breast stripes. Like the killdeer, it is often in fields far from water. The black-bellied plover is drab in winter, when usually seen, but in flight it flashes diagnostic black wing pits. Winter golden-plovers are richer-colored above and lack the black wing pits. Both golden-plovers occur in small numbers along the West Coast during migration and winter. In spring, the white stripe on the Pacific golden-plover extends down its side distinctively, but separating them in fall requires experience and a close look.

◀ **Mountain Plover** *Charadrius montanus* 9"
Scarce; in summer on open prairies, not mountains. Winters in flocks in open areas, often dirt fields. Dangerously declining with loss of short-grass prairie nesting lands. ● Even, sandy upperparts; long legs. In summer, white forehead bordered by black cap above. Head duller in winter, dark eye prominent on pale face. In flight shows white in wings and white-bordered tail with black subterminal band. ♪ Low, rattling notes.

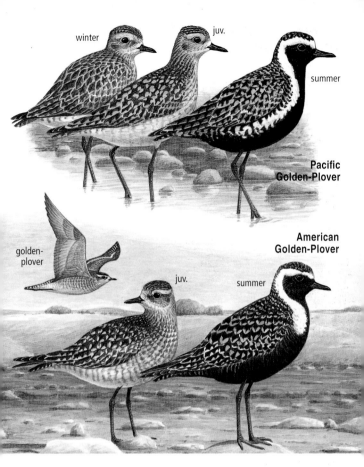

winter

juv.

summer

**Pacific
Golden-Plover**

golden-
plover

juv.

summer

**American
Golden-Plover**

◄**Black-bellied Plover** *Pluvialis squatarola* 11"
Numerous in winter and migration on coasts, salt marshes;
scarce in interior wetlands during migration. Feeds singly,
often among smaller shorebirds. Travels, roosts in small
flocks. Wary, quick to take flight. ● Black axillars, white
rump, white wing stripe. Bill larger than in golden-plover.
Bold black-and-white plumage in summer; pale gray above,
whitish below in winter. Fresh juv. shows some gold above.
♪ *Tee-oo-wee,* plaintive, whistled flight call.

◄**American Golden-Plover** *Pluvialis dominicus* 10"
Numerous in spring in pastures, plowed fields; often in large
flocks. Scarce in fall on coasts; most migrate over Atlantic.
● Dull gray axillars and underwing, barred rump. In spring,
flecked with golden yellow above, black below with white
stripe from forehead to side of breast. Juv. gray with gold
or brownish tones above, bold white eyebrow. Winter adult
paler than juv.; seldom seen in US. ♪ Like that of Pacific.

◄**Pacific Golden-Plover** *Pluvialis fulva* 10"
Rare in migration and winter along coast. Most migrate offshore to S. Pacific is. ● Slimmer than American golden-
plover; primaries in folded wing extend less distance
beyond tertials. In spring, white stripe narrower, extends
onto sides. Juv. and winter birds yellower on breast,
upperparts, eyebrow. ♪ *Queedle,* whistled flight call.

PLOVERS

57

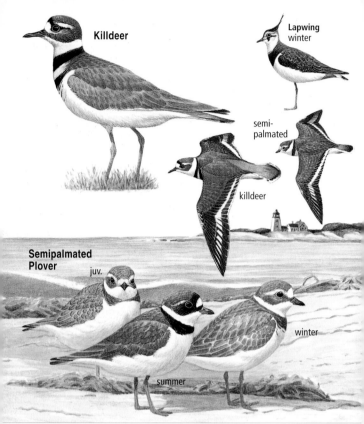

Mid-Atlantic shores

Each banded plover has one partial or complete breast band, and adult killdeers have two. Of the four small plovers, Wilson's and the semipalmated have brown backs, matching the wet sand or mud they frequent, while the piping and snowy have paler backs, blending with the dry sand they prefer. Wilson's bill is all-black and much larger than the semipalmated's. The piping plover's stubby bill, orange legs, and white rump distinguish it from the snowy.

◀**Killdeer** *Charadrius vociferus* 10"
Numerous, widespread in open areas from shores and banks to bare or short-grass fields distant from water. Sometimes in flocks, often alone or in pairs. ● Large with 2 black breast bands, orange rump, long tail, white wing stripe. Chick has single black band. ♪ *Kill-dee, dee-dee-dee*, repeated, ringing notes that usually alarm all nearby birds.

Semipalmated Plover *Charadrius semipalmatus* 7"
◀Fairly numerous in flocks or scattered along beaches, mud-flats; on lake shores, plowed fields in migration. ● Dark back, orange legs. In winter, black head markings lacking, breast band turns from black to brown, bill turns mostly black. Juv. similar to winter but wing coverts, scapulars have scaly appearance. ♪ *Chu-wee*, clear, rising whistle.

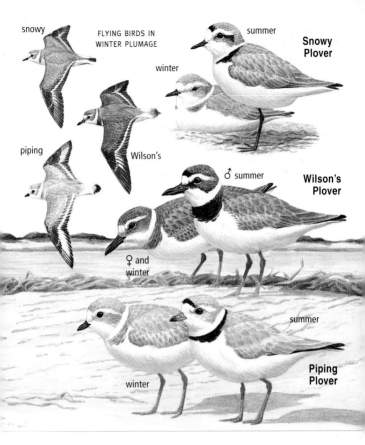

snowy

FLYING BIRDS IN
WINTER PLUMAGE

summer

**Snowy
Plover**

winter

piping

Wilson's

**Wilson's
Plover**

♂ summer

♀ and
winter

summer

winter

**Piping
Plover**

◀**Piping Plover** *Charadrius melodus* 7"
Fewer than 2,500 pairs (about 25 pairs on Great Lakes)
and declining on beaches, sand flats. Usually in pairs or
small flocks. Nesting disrupted by heavy use of beaches
by people, dogs, vehicles. Some nest areas now protected.
● Very pale gray back, white rump, stubby black bill (with
orange base in summer), orange legs. Black forehead bar
and breast band (can be broken) lacking in winter and juv.
♩♩ *Peep-lo,* clear, piping notes, given often.

◀**Wilson's Plover** *Charadrius wilsonia* 8"
Scarce and declining on ocean beaches, mudflats. Usually
alone or in pairs; fairly tame, slow-moving. ● Large black
bill. Broad black (summer male) or brown breast band; often
broken on juv. ♩ *Wheet!* Shrill, whistled alarm call; also low,
grating *quit* calls.

◀**Snowy Plover** *Charadrius alexandrinus* 6½"
Scarce, local, declining on sandy ocean beaches and sand
flats at alkali and salt ponds, where its concealing color
helps it to hide in plain sight. Usually in small flocks.
● Pale gray-brown above. Thin black bill, black legs. Black
markings on forehead, ear coverts, sides of breast in summer; absent in winter, juv. ♩ *Chu-wee,* soft, whistled call.

Lapwing (Northern) *Vanellus vanellus* 12" Eurasian. Very rare straggler in late
fall and winter along Atlantic coast south to Carolinas.

BANDED PLOVERS

Wilson's Phalarope — summer ♂ — summer ♀

winter

♀ ♂ — red-necked phalarope Key 13

juv.

summer

winter

Spotted Sandpiper

Still river backwaters

The long, needle-like bill is the best mark for Wilson's phalarope; the plumage and leg color vary. The bill is longer than in the red-necked phalarope (Key 13) and thinner than in the lesser yellowlegs (Key 53). The solitary sandpiper and often the spotted are seen on fresh water. In winter, when the spotted lacks its breast spots, its teetering walk is the initial clue. The solitary bobs its head and tail; note its white eye-ring, speckled upperparts, and streaked breast. The best mark on the pectoral sandpiper is the way its breast streaks end in a sharp line just above the white belly.

◀**Wilson's Phalarope** *Phalaropus tricolor* 9"
Numerous in West; scarce, local, but expanding range in East. In shallow wetlands; picks food from surface of water or land; often swims. Gathers at inland saltwater and alkali sites before fall migration. ● Long, thin bill. Plain wings, white rump in flight. Black stripe through eye and on neck in summer; chestnut markings, black legs. Male duller, lacks gray crown. Gray above in winter with gray eyeline, straw-yellow legs. Juv. like winter but browner above with buff feather edgings, buff wash on sides. ♪ *Wunk,* grunting call.

Spotted Sandpiper *Actitis macularia* 7½"
Numerous, widespread near water; usually alone. Teeters.

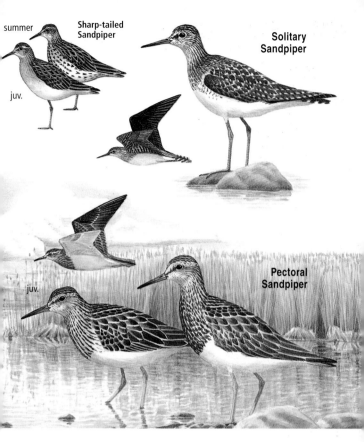

◄Flies close to water; glides on bowed, quivering wings.
 ● Spotted below in summer; orange legs and bill (with dark tip). Yellowish legs in winter; note white wedge between dark breast patch and folded wing. Juv. like winter. ♪ *Peet-weet*, shrill; last note can be absent or repeated several times.

Pectoral Sandpiper *Calidris melanotos* 8½"
Spring migration heaviest in Mississippi Valley; fairly numerous in marsh or wet meadows. Scarce, broadly distributed in fall. Often seen singly among other sandpipers. ● Heavy,
◄slightly curved bill; yellowish legs. Heavy breast streaking ends abruptly. Dark brown above with bright feather edges, faint rusty cap; duller in winter. Fresh juv. bright above with white feather edgings on sides of back; buff background to breast streaks. ♪ *Krieck*, grating flight call.

Solitary Sandpiper *Tringa solitaria* 8½"
Fairly numerous, usually alone or in pairs. Swallow-like flight. Bobs head. ● Pale eye-ring, dark rump with dark tail
◄pattern, dark bill and legs, no wing stripe. Head, neck, breast streaked in summer; back speckled white. Streaking more obscure, speckling finer, in winter. ♪ *Peet-weet*, 2 or 3 syllables given when flushed, higher than in spotted sandpiper.

Sharp-tailed Sandpiper *Calidris acuminata* 8½" Asian. Fall straggler on West Coast, usually lone juv. among pectoral sandpipers. ● Lacks sharp breast line of pectoral. Juv. has bright rufous cap, bright buff breast with streaking on sides.

PHALAROPE / SANDPIPERS

59

Dunlin

molting juv.

winter

summer

dunlin winter

Stilt Sandpiper

juv.

summer

stilt winter

winter

Arctic tundra in bloom

The dunlin, stilt sandpiper, and curlew sandpiper all have long, sturdy black bills that curve or droop at the tip. Only the dunlin has a dark rump seen in flight (white in the other two). The stilt sandpiper has long, yellowish legs, suggesting a lesser yellowlegs, (Key 53). White-rumped and Baird's sandpipers are often confused with the sandpipers on Key 61 but have longer wings, which extend beyond the tail when folded. Separating the white-rumped from Baird's is easiest in flight, when the rump color is obvious. The white-rumped's distinct call often first announces its presence.

◀**Dunlin** *Calidris alpina* 8½"
Numerous in winter in flocks on coastal beaches, tidal flats; often with sanderlings (Key 61). Feeds in characteristic hunched posture. ● Bill long, thick at base, drooped at tip. In summer, rufous above, black patch on belly (not lower breast, as in rock sandpiper, Key 56). In winter, gray-brown above with some breast streaking. Juv. begins molt to winter by fall migration. ♪ *Czeep*, grating flight call.

Stilt Sandpiper *Calidris himantopus* 8½"
Fairly numerous at interior wetlands in migration, scarce along coasts. Some winter in US, esp. at Salton Sea, CA. Feeds like, often with, dowitchers (Key 54) but more actively;

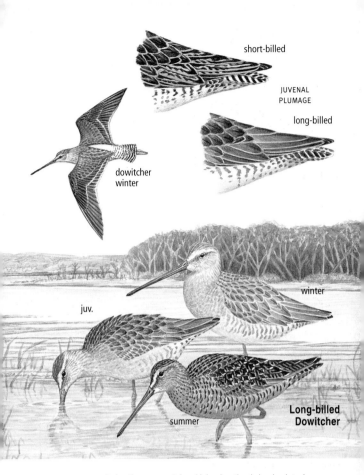

short-billed

JUVENAL
PLUMAGE

long-billed

dowitcher
winter

juv.

winter

summer

**Long-billed
Dowitcher**

◀migration on coastal and inland wetlands begins late June.
Probes in mud with stitching motion, often submerging
head. ● Reddish below in summer. Gray in winter with
white rump, lower back. ♪♪ *Tu-tu-tu*, mellow flight call.

Long-billed Dowitcher *Limnodromus scolopaceus* 11"
Numerous west of Rockies during migration and winter;
much scarcer in East. Most prefer fresh or brackish
ponds and marshes; some share saltwater habitats with
short-billed dowitcher. Fall migration starts late July, well
◀after that of short-billed. Juvs. appear in Sept., a month
after juv. short-bills. ● Much like short-billed dowitcher
(see below). Some females have longer bills than in short-
billed; males don't. ♪♪ *Keek*, thin, high-pitched flight call.

PLUMAGE DIFFERENCES IN DOWITCHERS *Winter:* Only
useful mark is barred tail, seen in flight. Width of barring
varies, but any bird whose pale bars are wider than dark
ones can be safely called a short-billed dowitcher. *Summer:* Long-billed has white
barring on uniformly red underparts, black barring on sides, spots on throat. Color
and spotting fade over summer. Most short-bills have white belly with black-
barred sides; spots extend to breast. Short-bills migrating through interior and
some in West show little or no white below and resemble long-bills, but show
spotting on breast and undertail coverts. *Juvs:* Short-billed has tiger-striped
tertials and scapulars; plain in long-billed, marked only with thin buff edge.

Upland Sandpiper

Woodcock

Shorebirds commonly seen away from water include those above and the large plovers (Key 57). Upland sandpipers are skinny-necked, small-headed, and usually seen alone. Woodcocks and snipes also forage alone; they have the heart-stopping habit of exploding unexpectedly into flight from beneath our feet. A woodcock swerves off through trees on rounded, whistling wings. A snipe zigzags away on pointed wings, usually with a raspy call. Both are chunky with long bills. Buff-breasted sandpipers are usually in flocks and are known by the striking contrast between buff underbody and white underwing.

◀**Upland Sandpiper** *Bartramia longicauda* 12"
Fairly numerous except in East, where declining due to habitat loss. Solitary, often in tall grass, where it perches on rocks and posts to see above blades. Runs in plover-like spurts. ● Small head; long, thin neck. Wings long, pointed, with conspicuous dark tips. Often holds wings extended for moment after landing, revealing barred wing linings. Long tail. ♪ *Kip-ip-ip-ip-ip*, rolling alarm call; other liquid whistles.

Curlew Sandpiper

juv.

summer

curlew
juv.

white-
rumped
juv.

Baird's
juv.

juv.

summer

White-rumped
Sandpiper

Baird's
Sandpiper

wades in deep water. ● Long, slightly drooped bill; long, greenish yellow legs; white rump. Heavily barred below in summer, rusty head markings. Drab in winter with whitish eyebrow. Juv. has buff breast; patterned upperparts suggestive of summer adult. ♪ *Querp,* soft, hoarse flight call.

Baird's Sandpiper *Calidris bairdii* 7½"
Scarce. Migrates in small numbers, stopping briefly in wet or even dry habitats. Adult migration heaviest in interior; juvs. widespread. ● Long wings; black median on tail. Buff neck, breast in spring and summer with fine breast streaks, white flanks. Gray-buff head and breast in fall, white eyebrow. Juv. buff below, scaly above. ♪ *Kreep,* soft flight call, repeated.

White-rumped Sandpiper *Calidris fuscicollis* 7½"
Scarce in spring migration except at major staging wetlands; fall migration mostly offshore south of Canada. ● White rump visible in flight; long wings. In spring and summer, has rufous tinge in crown, scapulars, ear coverts; breast streaks extend onto flanks. Juv. bright above with white eyebrow. ♪♪ *Tzeep,* high, mouse-like call.

Curlew Sandpiper *Calidris ferruginea* 8½" Eurasian. Rare but regular visitor, mainly on Atlantic Coast. ● Similar to dunlin in winter, but slimmer with unmarked white rump, longer legs that extend beyond tail in flight. Rufous color veiled with pale feather tips in spring; with wear, looks richer in early fall. Rump finely barred. Often seen in patchy molt.

Semipalmated Sandpiper summer

FLYING BIRDS IN WINTER PLUMAGE

western

Western Sandpiper summer winter

Least Sandpiper winter

juv.

summer

The sanderling is often the most abundant sandpiper on coasts and serves as a good reference. It is pale above with a broad white wing stripe. Separating the others, often lumped together as peeps, is difficult. Least sandpipers are smallest and brownest, with yellow-green (not black) legs. Western and semipalmated sandpipers are much alike; in fall, adult plumage is worn and even harder to separate, but young westerns are distinctively bright above. By October, all the semipalmateds are gone except for a few Florida stragglers.

◄**Semipalmated Sandpiper** *Calidris pusilla* 6½"
Most abundant peep in spring on Atlantic Coast, esp. at mudflats. Numerous at interior wetlands and in fall. A few migrate in West. ● Smaller, darker-backed than sanderling; much like western sandpiper. In summer, lacks side chevron marks of western, has only faint rufous markings. Winter adult nearly identical to western. Juv. has darker face, less rufous than juv. western. ♪ *Cherk*, short, 1-note flight call.

Western Sandpiper *Calidris mauri* 6½"
Numerous in West in winter, scarce in East. In flocks on estuaries, beaches, mudflats. Migration in spring heaviest along

semipalmated juv.

western juv.

least

sanderling

Sanderling

juv.

winter

summer

Pacific; more evenly distributed in fall. • Smaller, darker-backed than sanderling; like semipalmated. Bill averages longer, more tapered and drooped than semipalmated's, but variable; not a sure mark. In summer, has rufous ear coverts, crown, scapulars; black chevrons extend onto flanks. In winter, gray-brown above with whitish eyebrow, dusky wash on sides of breast. Juv. has rufous markings similar to summer adult's but clear buff-white breast. ♪ *Chir-eep,* squeaky call.

Least Sandpiper *Calidris minutilla* 6"

Numerous and widespread in winter and migration. In flocks, often mixed with western, semipalmated. Tame, often crouches when approached. • Smaller, darker than western and semipalmated with shorter, greenish yellow legs and shorter bill. In winter, has browner breast wash and upperparts than other peeps. Juv. bright above with incomplete white V on back. ♪ *Kree-eep,* thin, 2-note call.

Sanderling *Calidris alba* 8"

Abundant in winter and migration on beaches in flocks strung along water's edge, also on tidal flats; interior wetlands in migration. • Pale gray above in winter, white below; black at bend of wing, black legs. Distinctive in summer with black-spotted rufous upperparts, head, breast. Bold white wing stripe in flight. Juv. boldly checkered black and white above. ♪ *Kip,* sharp, high-pitched flight call.

ILLUSTRATOR **JOHN DAWSON**

<u>Upland</u> <u>waterbirds</u>

The dipper is inconspicuous, gray, and suggests a wren. It feeds from cascading mountain streams and is always seen along the edges. Kingfishers perch by quiet waters – even small ponds – and plunge-dive for fish, often from a hover.

◀**Dipper** (American) *Cinclus mexicanus* 7½"
Fairly numerous, solitary. Bobs. Can completely submerge to feed on aquatic life from bottom of turbulent stream, emerging a distance away. ● Plump. Gray with darker head. Juv. paler below. ♪ *Dze-eet*, given in flight, often repeated. Variable, loud, musical song.

Belted Kingfisher *Ceryle alcyon* 13"
Fairly numerous, noisy, conspicuous fisher over backwaters, marshes, ponds. Solitary except when nesting.
◀Aggressive. ● Blue-gray above with heavy bill, thick crest. Female has rusty breast band. ♪ Harsh rattle.

Green Kingfisher *Chloroceryle americana* 8½" Tropical. Fairly numerous along Rio Grande in s. TX. Scarce inland to Edwards Plateau. Rare in se. AZ.

Ringed Kingfisher *Ceryle torquata* 16" Tropical. Expanding range into lower Rio Grande Valley.

The ability to fly is the dominant feature of birds. Some, such as hummingbirds and falcons, are simply awesome in their mastery of flight. Just as impressive are the physical adaptations that make flight possible. Bones that are separate in humans are fused in birds to form a strong airframe. Organs and body tissue are arranged aerodynamically, and air sacs fill out the airframe. All unnecessary weight is eliminated: bones are hollow, reproductive organs shrink except in the breeding season, and in most females only one of the pair of ovaries and oviducts is ever functional. Even the brain cells needed for song are lost and replaced seasonally in some birds. Much of the body mass is devoted to the muscles across the breast that power the wings in flight.

Feathers are the most intriguing flight adaptation. Only birds have them, and without them birds would be flightless. Feathers grow from the skin, much like scales on a reptile. Those used for flight are flat and nearly rigid. The contour feathers covering the body are much softer and have a fluffy layer of downy feathers beneath them. Bristles and plumes are forms of feathers.

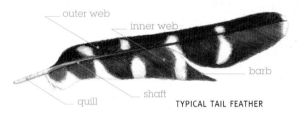

TYPICAL TAIL FEATHER

outer web
inner web
barb
quill
shaft

The outer portion of the wing, from the wrist out, provides most of the power when a bird flaps its wings. The inner portion, from the shoulder to the wrist, is held fairly steady by most birds and provides lift the same way an airplane wing does.

Feather color usually derives from pigmentation, but all blues, whites, some greens, and the iridescent sheens seen on birds such as grackles and hummingbirds are due to light reacting with the structure of a feather. The quality of iridescent colors is impossible to reproduce in pigments printed on paper.

spotted   streaked   barred   mottled

Feathers are often patterned with streaks or bars of color. A mix of colors and patterns is called mottling.

Young birds are typically in juvenal plumage when they leave the nest (fledge) during their first summer, although some, such as ducklings, fledge while they are still downy. Juveniles can look like adults, but in many species, such as the dark-eyed junco, the young are distinct until they replace all their feathers in the first fall molt. Some songbirds don't acquire adult plumage until the first spring or, as in the male painted bunting, until the second fall. Meanwhile, they wear immature plumages. Gulls can take four years, eagles five, to gain adult plumage. Once adult, most birds molt all their feathers once a year, typically in the fall. Many also have a separate molt of just their body feathers, typically in spring, which is when many male songbirds acquire their bright breeding plumages.

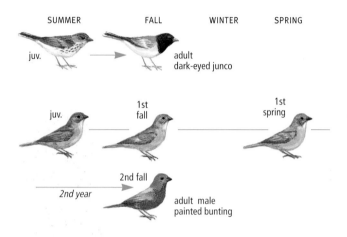

SUMMER   FALL   WINTER   SPRING

juv.

adult
dark-eyed junco

juv.

1st
fall

1st
spring

2nd fall

2nd year

adult male
painted bunting

The gradual wear of a feather can cause a change in appearance in some species similar to that produced by a molt. Birds such as the starling and rusty blackbird don't molt in spring but still have a distinctive, glossy breeding plumage. In fresh fall plumage, the white and buff spots at the tip of a starling's broad feathers give it a dull, speckled look. By spring the feather tips wear away, revealing the glossy webs below. Male starlings, like many other birds, also change bill color seasonally.

starling

FALL   WINTER   SPRING

The wing surface needed for flight is provided by the primary and secondary feathers, which are often grouped with the tail as flight feathers. Coverts overlap the bases of the flight feathers. Underwing coverts can be grouped as wing linings. Upperwing coverts are grouped with the scapulars and upper back as the mantle when all are the same color.

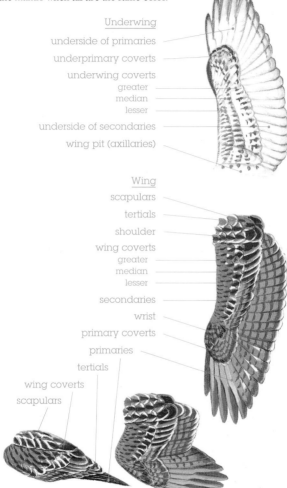

Underwing
underside of primaries
underprimary coverts
underwing coverts
greater
median
lesser
underside of secondaries
wing pit (axillaries)

Wing
scapulars
tertials
shoulder
wing coverts
greater
median
lesser
secondaries
wrist
primary coverts
primaries
tertials
wing coverts
scapulars

On the folded wing the primaries and secondaries are mostly concealed and protected by the wing coverts, scapulars, and tertials. Scapulars are arranged at the base of the wing; tertials lie inside the secondaries. Both scapulars and tertials are often especially large and prominent on ducks and shorebirds. Many songbirds show one or two wing bars on the folded wing, formed by contrasting tips on the median and greater wing coverts.

Tail feathers are not always the same color or pattern on the bottom surface as on top. When they are, the top surface of the tail can still look different from the bottom because of feather overlap. The outer tail feathers are always on the bottom when the tail is closed.

Most songbirds have blunt, rounded, or notched tails. Tail shape can be a good mark but must be noted carefully. A blunt tail when fanned can look rounded. A rounded tail tightly closed looks blunt. And a small notch can occur wherever tail feathers lie unevenly.

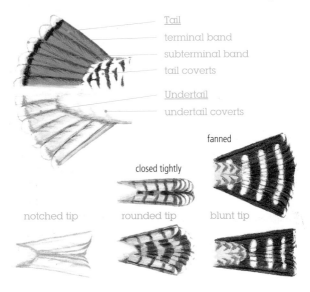

Tail
terminal band
subterminal band
tail coverts

Undertail
undertail coverts

fanned

closed tightly

notched tip   rounded tip   blunt tip

Bill length is best judged in comparison to the rest of the head. The bill of the sandpiper below is a little longer than the rest of the head. Shorter bills can be compared to the space between the base of the bill and the eye, known as the loral distance.

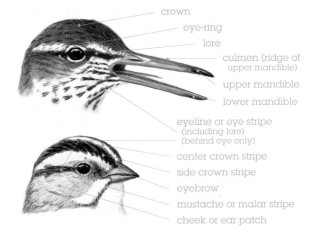

crown
eye-ring
lore
culmen (ridge of upper mandible)
upper mandible
lower mandible
eyeline or eye stripe (including lore) (behind eye only)
center crown stripe
side crown stripe
eyebrow
mustache or malar stripe
cheek or ear patch

Songbirds are more frequently heard than seen. Expert birders surveying a region find that their ears are more effective than their eyes. The voices they hear are as reliable as a plumage mark in making identifications. Indeed, a few species of birds are reliably differentiated only by their voices.

Birds produce sounds differently from mammals. Humans have a voicebox at the top of the windpipe, with cords that resonate when air flows over them. Birds have a voicebox at the base of the windpipe, with membranes that resonate with airflow. Having the weight of the voicebox close to their center of gravity, next to their lungs, is one of the adaptations that facilitate flight. Birds do not shape sound with their bills or throats. That is done by muscle pairs attached to the membranes in the voicebox. The windpipe also acts as a resonator in some species. For example, the trumpeter swan's windpipe is nearly five feet long, producing a deep, penetrating tone. A few birds, such as the wood stork and turkey vulture, have no functioning voicebox.

Birds use a variety of calls, mostly chips or whistles, to indicate alarm or to keep in contact with the flock, among other functions. Songbirds have the most complex voiceboxes, and males sing songs in spring to advertise themselves to females and to define their territory. In some species, females occasionally sing, and in a few, such as the cardinal, females sing as often as males. Songs are frequently more complex than calls and often include melodic phrases, but not in all cases. Thrushes are some of the most celebrated singers, and the mockingbird is perhaps the most persistent, singing into the night and throughout the year.

The vocal descriptions in this guide, given after a musical note (♪), are limited to the most characteristic song or call. Most songbirds produce a number of vocal variations, and there are often regional accents. Two notes (♪♪) mean that voice is particularly important in most identifications, either because a bird is secretive and seldom seen or because it looks very similar to a species with a different vocalization. Vocal information is omitted for birds whose voices play little or no role in identification.

Some vocalizations, such as the *wichity-wichity-wichity* of the common yellowthroat, can be transliterated fairly effectively; many others can't. The vocal descriptions in this guide are most useful as reminders of songs and calls you have already learned. The best way to learn songs is to identify the birds heard singing and then to imitate their songs. As you learn the songs of your local nesting species, you will become increasingly aware of the birds around you, and the unfamiliar song that indicates the presence of a rarity will quickly get your attention.

Species are keyed in this guide to make identification simple. The Keys are explained on the inside of the front and back covers. Birds are keyed by their feeding strategies and adaptations. Each species has developed its own survival strategy, and although many strategies overlap, no two species occupy identical ecological niches.

Feeding adaptations and foraging behavior are the most important points to recognize in identifying and understanding a bird. Every bird is physically adapted to its foraging style. For the beginner, the color and pattern of an unknown bird can be so striking that important points of structure and shape go unnoticed. But the structural adaptations, especially the shape and size of the bill, best reveal a bird's role in nature – its truest identity.

Among many small songbirds the only structural differences of significance are found in the shapes of their bills. If you don't immediately recognize a songbird as a sparrow, a wren, or a warbler, for example, look at its bill shape to determine whether it is a seed-crusher or a bug-eater. Seed-crushers have strong conical bills for cracking seeds. The bill can be small and adapted for grass seeds, as in many sparrows, or large enough to crush cherry pits.

The shape of a bug-eater's bill varies with the way it catches bugs. Flycatchers catch flying insects in midair (flycatch), and they have broad bills to improve their chances of success. Most bug-eaters go after slower-moving targets. They probe for insects and larvae on trees and brush, in ground litter and rock crevices. Their bills are slender and usually straight, but a few, including wrens and thrashers, have curved bills for specialized probing.

Birds are usually seen foraging. So even when the bill of a small songbird cannot be seen, its foraging behavior frequently can be noted and the bill shape inferred. A vireo methodically gathering (gleaning) insects from a limb or leaf acts differently from a sparrow collecting seeds in a weed patch. Flycatchers are often puzzling because, from the side, their broad, flat bills can look slender. Beginning bird-watchers often remain puzzled until the flycatcher actually darts out to snatch a passing insect. The experienced birder doesn't need to see any of this. The real clue, the best one, is the way a flycatcher patiently waits for a bug to pass by. Other small bug-eaters are usually in constant motion.

The best time to look for birds varies, depending on which ones you want to see. Songbirds in spring and summer become active at first light with an exuberance known as the dawn chorus. They are inactive during the heat of the day and reappear, more quietly, before sunset. Most waterbirds and aerialists remain active at midday. Shorebird activity is often set by tides: low tide is feeding time; high tide is spent roosting. Most owls, nightjars, and some rails feed at night and usually escape our notice.

Birds are found in habitats that meet their food and nesting requirements. Some birds are widespread; others have very specific habitat requirements. Learning the habitat preferences of birds enables you to find elusive species. A popular habitat, referred to as riparian, is the vegetation that lines the banks of watercourses.

Experienced birders take advantage of a principle known as edge effect, which asserts that life is most abundant where habitats intersect. They make sure to check the hedgerows between fields, the scrub margins of woodlands, and the shores of lakes or seas. While there are birds in the middle of oceans, plains, and mature forest (indeed, birds that live only there), you will see a greater number and variety at the edges. Even the minor discontinuity of a path through the countryside attracts life to its edges.

When the ancient eastern forest was still intact, there were many birds, such as the indigo bunting, that lived at its edges and in clearings, where shrubs and small trees provided a transition to open areas or watercourses. Fire also created forest edges for these species, and a succession of birds matched the succession of vegetation as a burned area regenerated. A similar succession of birds now occurs wherever cleared land – roadsides, farmland, utility line cuts – is allowed to regenerate to forest.

BIRD-WATCHING

The range maps provide a simplified picture of a bird's distribution. They also indicate the birds that can be expected in any local region. In some cases range is more than just helpful in identification: it can be the best or only way to separate similar species.

Birds are not evenly distributed over their ranges. They require suitable habitat, as described in each species account, and are typically scarcest at their range limits. Some species nest in huge, local colonies and are rare elsewhere. A generalization of overall abundance is given at the start of most species accounts. The terms abundant, numerous, fairly numerous, scarce, and rare are used to describe the relative overall abundance of a species compared with that of other similar birds. A bird may be numerous but not commonly seen because it is secretive.

Weather and food availability affect bird distribution in winter. Some birds retreat south to escape winter storms and freezing lakes. Others, whose resident population slowly creeps northward in mild winters, perish from their newly occupied range when hit by a hard winter. A few species that normally endure Arctic winters, like the snowy owl, occasionally show up in large numbers (irrupt) in the lower 48 states searching for food.

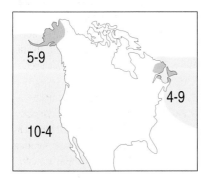

Pelagic Map

nesting range

pelagic range

1-12 months present (Jan-Dec)

Land Map

summer or nesting

winter

all year

migration (spring & fall)

- - - - extended summer range

▬ ▬ ▬ irruptive winter range

Determining bird ranges and numbers requires extraordinary efforts. Over 30,000 bird-watchers now plan Christmas holidays to participate in the Christmas Bird Count. Started in 1900 by Frank Chapman, author of the first guide to North American birds, the Christmas Bird Count began as an alternative to the then-popular Christmas practice known as the side hunt. Instead of shooting all the birds (and any other wildlife) found on Christmas Day, Chapman's idea was to count them. The National Audubon Society publishes the results, our best information on winter populations.

In 1966 the Breeding Bird Survey was organized by Chandler Robbins of the Fish and Wildlife Service to count North American nesting birds. The task requires 2,000 skilled volunteers across the continent each June. Each volunteer follows a permanent 24.5-mile route and records the birds heard singing. The data especially reveal how changes in land use have affected bird distribution. In 1989 Robbins, who also coauthored the most popular bird guide of the 20th century, used BBS data to first document the serious, continuing decline of migrant songbirds.

Also inspired by Robbins are the Breeding Bird Atlases, now completed or under way in most states. The states are subdivided into plots typically only a few miles square. Each plot is explored, and the nesting species (but not their numbers) are recorded. It took five years and 830 dedicated volunteers to complete the census of Maryland, a small state. The state atlases provide definitive nesting range information. No state has yet conducted a second census to record changes.

The Cornell Laboratory of Ornithology has been conducting both a Winter Bird Population Study and a Breeding Bird Census for more than 25 years. Each project includes an annual bird census of several hundred specific habitat plots across North America. Counts for 25 percent of the plots have been taken for at least 20 years and provide reliable data on population changes.

Bird-banding studies and the records of migrants killed in collisions with tall buildings also provide insights into the numbers and distribution of songbirds. Seabirds are being noted at sea watches operated on the West Coast by the Point Reyes Bird Observatory and at Cape May, New Jersey, by the New Jersey Audubon Society. Hawk numbers have been recorded at major hawk-watching sites for many years. There are also hundreds of special surveys each year, often involving the management of game birds or species in trouble.

Still, birds are so difficult to count scientifically that the first warnings of a species in trouble usually come from the observations of ordinary bird enthusiasts rather than from scientists. The decline in migrant songbirds was noted and discussed among local bird groups long before it was documented by ornithologists.

Many past threats to North American birds have been eliminated. We no longer routinely collect them or their eggs and nests. Hunting ducks with live decoys has ended. Hunting for market, selling either a bird's flesh for food or its feathers for fashion, ended as a result of the Audubon movement almost a century ago. Actually, much shooting had nothing to do with hunters or a market. Shooters would line ridges or shores and decimate flocks of migrating birds for the same reason they slaughtered buffalo – for the "thrill" of seeing the animals drop.

By 1918, when hunting was first regulated by the Migratory Bird Treaty Act, the population and distribution of our birds had been greatly changed by gunners. Once-abundant birds, such as the Carolina parakeet and passenger pigeon, were extinct; others, such as the whooping crane, were seriously endangered and remain so. Yet, many species, now free from persecution, have rebounded.

Habitat destruction is the continuing, persistent problem for birds. As a result of habitat loss, bird numbers now decline even as the number of bird-watchers increases. In the East over 50 percent of the original wetlands are gone, and all but tiny, scattered pockets of the ancient hardwood forest have been harvested. In the West there are few large stands of ancient forest; most that remain are on federally managed land. Commercial forests are seldom managed with concern for the needs of wildlife.

Only remnants of the grasslands that once dominated the midcontinent have survived. Many birds, from sparrows to grouse, that depended on grasslands have been unable to adapt to the agricultural lands that replaced them. One critical area is the "prairie pothole" region of the Dakotas and Montana. Many ducks nest in this region, and their numbers have been declining since the 1970s because of loss of natural habitat to agriculture. In 1994 the declines reversed, in great part because more than ten million acres of farmland had been left fallow as part of a soil bank program. All grassland species would likely recover if our agricultural practices provided sufficient habitat for them.

Migrant birds are especially at risk because they require a sustaining habitat where they nest, where they winter, and over their migration route. In some migratory species, such as the red knot, much of the population funnels through a single stopover point and depends upon its ecological health and stability.

Loss of habitat clearly means loss of the birds depending on that habitat. But the loss of a portion of forest, grassland, marsh, or scrub also has an impact on the usefulness of the habitat remaining. If an area becomes so fragmented that all of it is near an edge, it cannot sustain its normal wildlife. One reason is that small areas are easy for predators to scour. As the size of a bird-nesting area dwindles, so does the chance of nesting success, and eventually a population can no longer sustain itself. The ducks nesting in the prairie pothole region mentioned previously needed the fallow land to provide protection for their nests from foxes and crows. Songbirds that nest in fragmented forest face an even more dangerous predator, the brown-headed cowbird.

Cowbirds are nest parasites that once wandered the Great Plains with herds of buffalo and laid their eggs in the adjacent woodland nests of songbirds. A cowbird chick grows rapidly and flourishes in a songbird's nest at the expense of the songbird's own hatchlings, which usually perish. However, only nests within a hundred yards or so of a woodland edge are heavily affected, and many of the songbirds historically in contact with cowbirds developed defenses such as dumping out the cowbird egg, covering it up, or abandoning the nest and starting over. These factors once limited cowbird damage.

The clearing of the ancient forest for farms let the cowbird expand its range throughout the United States and southern Canada. Birds never before confronted with cowbird parasitism, including dozens of migrants such as the worm-eating warbler and wood thrush, are being victimized and have seriously declined. Not only are these birds defenseless against cowbirds, but the woodlands are so fragmented that many have no safe, deep forest in which to nest. Corridors cleared for roads and utility lines have been found to have the same fragmenting effect as large clearings.

It is pointless to blame the cowbird for a crisis caused by habitat modifications made by humans. We are responsible for the management of our natural heritage. "A nation behaves well," Teddy Roosevelt claimed nearly a century ago, "if the natural resources and assets which one generation turns over to the next are increased and not impaired in value." Yet few people can visit the neighborhoods or countryside of their childhood and find the natural resources improved. The debate continues over how much more we can cut, plow, fill in, dam, bulldoze, or pave.

Kirtland's Warbler   **Burrowing Owl**

The species in most serious danger have their names highlighted at the head of their species accounts. Birds highlighted in red are in greatest danger of extinction and, in most if not all cases, currently depend upon human intervention for their continued existence. Birds highlighted in yellow are either at risk of requiring human intervention if current trends continue, or they are already disappearing from a significant portion of their range.

Species evolve. When Linnaeus, in 1758, established the system of names used by science today, it was commonly presumed that all species were unchanging and that all individuals of any species descended from an original pair. Exactly one century later, Charles Darwin presented to the Linnaean Society his theory of evolution by natural selection now accepted by scientists.

Each species is a population of individuals breeding normally among themselves, not with others. Within a species, regional differences often exist. In general, color is of greatest intensity in regions of greatest rainfall, and size increases in colder areas, as in the large, dark race of the song sparrow on the Aleutian Islands. If a race becomes genetically isolated and remains so for enough time (five to ten thousand years has been theorized for birds), it can evolve into a separate species. That is, it will not normally mate with its previous conspecifics even if range overlap permits. For example, after its range had been separate for many centuries, the Florida scrub-jay was recognized as a distinct species from the western scrub-jay in 1995.

There are always differences between species, but not necessarily in appearance. Different species of wood-pewees, for instance, can be indistinguishable, but they have different songs, different ranges, and don't usually interbreed. Species that cannot safely be separated by appearance share an image in this guide.

Similar foraging strategies are sometimes adopted by species from different families. Inevitably such birds come to resemble one another, not just physically, but often in behavior as well. The process, known as convergence, reveals how deeply food gathering shapes a bird's being. Swifts and swallows are distantly related but quite similar because of the aerial feeding habits they share. The ruby-crowned kinglet and Hutton's vireo are often mistaken for each other because of similarities due to convergence.

Bird species are determined in North America by members of the American Ornithologists' Union. They decide to split and lump species as new information, such as DNA evidence, surfaces. The rufous-sided towhee, for instance, is now split into the eastern towhee and the spotted towhee. All AOU scientific names (Latin binomials) are given. A few AOU English-language names have been altered by dropping a modifier recently added by ornithologists for their purposes. Thus, birds known to scientists as the American Robin, Gray Catbird, and Northern Mockingbird are still our familiar robin, catbird, and mockingbird throughout this text. In the headline of the species account the full AOU English-language name is indicated: Robin (American). Names of regional forms and subspecies are placed in quotes.

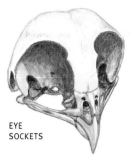

EYE
SOCKETS

Owls' eyes are so large that in some small species they nearly touch inside the head.

Nocturnal
Owls

CONSULTANT **EIRIK BLOM**
ILLUSTRATOR **HANS PEETERS**

As the hawks that patrol the skies by day head to roost, owls emerge for night operations. Owls have the same strong talons and hooked bills as hawks, plus a number of adaptations for hunting at night. Even owls weighing as little as a pound have eyes as large as a man's and with 100 times the light-gathering power. The eyeballs are fixed in their sockets, requiring an owl to turn its head to shift its gaze. Fourteen neck vertebrae (we have seven) allow the head to turn three-quarters of the way around.

An owl's hearing is so keen and focused that some can hunt in total darkness, although most prefer evening and pre-dawn hours. Fringes on the leading edges of their wings dampen noise caused by airflow. For the mice, birds, and other small animals that are the common prey of these formidable predators, death typically comes without warning, in darkness and silence. The tables are turned in daylight, when songbirds will mob a roosting owl they discover.

Because most owls roost in dense woods during the day, they are seldom seen and are best known as eerie voices in the night. Some calls are diagnostic, but owls are capable of a wide range of vocalizations. They can hoot, bark like dogs, screech like cats, whistle, and wail. Males have the deeper voices. Some owls roost communally, especially in winter. Favorite roosts can be identified by the buildup beneath them of "whitewash" and regurgitated pellets of the bones and other undigestible remains of their prey.

Eye color and markings on the facial disks surrounding the eyes are often the best visual marks among owls. Look carefully for "horns" or "ear tufts"; sometimes they are flattened. The sexes are alike, but as in hawks, females are often larger. Also like hawks, owls frequently vary in color. Screech-owls, for instance, occur in various shades of red, brown, or gray.

Habitat destruction is the single greatest threat to owls. The trees we use for our houses are the same ones they use for theirs. The plight of the spotted owl, which demands deep stands of mature forest, has focused attention on the virtual elimination of our ancient forests. However, not all owls live in forests. The loss of marshlands, grasslands, and pasture has resulted in serious declines of burrowing owls, short-eared owls, and barn owls.

Great
Horned
Owl

short-eared owl

Short-eared
Owl

"Horns" on the great horned and long-eared owls are usually obvious. The great horned is massive, much larger than the relatively slender long-eared. It can be seen at dusk or dawn, while the long-eared is strictly nocturnal. Horns on the short-eared owl are seldom visible; the bird appears round-headed. It is one of the owls most likely to be seen hunting over open areas on cloudy afternoons or at dusk. The barn owl is perhaps the most frequently seen owl. Its pale body and heart-shaped face are the most distinctive field marks; long legs are another good mark.

◄**Great Horned Owl** *Bubo virginianus* 22"
Numerous, esp. at forest edges, but widespread, adaptable; occurring in open areas, even cities. Usually nocturnal but also active at dawn, dusk. Hunts from perch, often conspicuously, and by coursing, taking prey as large as rabbits and ducks. ● Large, with wide-set horns. White throat, lacking in long-eared owl. Dark barring on underparts; may show spots on breast. Color varies primarily with latitude: ghostly pale gray in high Arctic, progressively browner to south.
♪♪ *Hoo, hoo-hoo, hoo, hoo*, deep, booming hoots.

Long-eared Owl

♀ Barn Owl

♂

Barn Owl

◄**Short-eared Owl** *Asio flammeus* 15"
Scarce in open areas, esp. marshes, grasslands, tundra. Seriously declining with habitat loss in southern portion of nesting range. Usually roosts on ground, often in groups. Takes mostly rodents, hunting like marsh hawk in low, buoyant, quartering flight. ● Straw- to rust-colored with brown mottling above, streaking below. Horns seldom seen. Dark wrist mark (also in long-eared owl). ♪ Various barks, hisses.

Barn Owl *Tyto alba* 16"
◄Fairly numerous, widespread in low, open country, esp. marshes, fields. Northern population seriously declining with habitat loss. Roosts in conifers or cavities, often communally; nests in cavities, incl. barns, nest boxes. Prefers rodents taken in low, quartering flight. ● White, heart-shaped face; dark eyes. White to cinnamon below, with small black spots; females darkest. ♪ Loud, drawn-out, rasping screech.

◄**Long-eared Owl** *Asio otus* 15"
Thought to be fairly numerous, possibly declining, but seldom seen; strictly nocturnal. Usually roosts in conifers near forest edge, often communally in winter. Perches near tree trunk in deep cover; hides by stretching to become slim, mimicking upright stub. Courses open areas in search of rodents. ● Long, closely placed ears; boldly streaked and barred underparts. ♪ Variety of shrieks, hoots, whines.

LARGE OWLS

Great Gray Owl

Barred Owl

Spotted Owl

The apparent bulk of the three owls in the genus *Strix* is largely feathers. The real mass of the great gray owl is indicated by the size of its yellow eyes. Spotted and barred owls are dark-eyed. Note the barred collar of the barred owl. Snowy owls can be pure white, but the young birds usually seen have considerable dark barring. The best field marks for the hawk owl, which hunts by day, are its long-tailed, falcon-like shape and fierce facial expression.

◄Great Gray Owl *Strix nebulosa* 27"
Scarce in boreal forest, rare in western mountains. Roosts in dense conifers. Preys on rodents from perch, both in deep woods and bordering open areas. Hunts in daylight during Arctic summers. Tame. Irruptive. ● Large, with long tail, round head, small yellow eyes in large disks. Gray with white "bow-tie" and lores. ♩♩ Slow series of deep hoots.

Spotted Owl *Strix occidentalis* 18"
◄Rare; in deep forest. Captures rodents by dropping from overhead perch; requires open understory of mature forest. Most seriously threatened in Northwest, where 90% of old-growth habitat has been cut; remaining suitable habitat

Hawk Owl

Snowy Owl

imm.

adult

mostly on public land coveted by lumber interests. Tame.
● Bulky with large round head, dark eyes. Creamy spots on
head, back, breast. ♩♫ *Hoo-hoo-hoo,* barking hoots.

◀**Barred Owl** *Strix varia* 21"
Numerous in mature deciduous woods, esp. southern
swamps. Scarce but increasing in western conifers, dis-
placing and hybridizing with spotted owl. Interior forest
perch-and-drop hunter, like spotted owl. Easily flushed.
● Bulky with large round head, dark eyes. Gray-brown with
wide barred collar, streaking on belly. ♩♫ *Who-cooks-for-
you, who-cooks-for-you-all?* Hoots, given whole or in part.

◀**Snowy Owl** *Nyctea scandiaca* 24"
Arctic. Rare and irregular, mostly imm., near US-Canadian
border in winter. Preys on lemmings, also birds, esp. waterfowl. Usually seen at rest on open ground or low perch during day. ● White, variably barred with dark brown; mature
males whitest, imm. females darkest.

◀**Hawk Owl** (Northern) *Surnia ulula* 16"
Fairly numerous at openings in boreal forest. Very rare
south of range in winter. Tame. Hunts by day, taking mostly
birds in winter, rodents in summer. Perches conspicuously.
Bobs tail frequently. Flies fast and low to the kill. ● Long,
rounded tail. Black borders to facial disks, spotted forehead.

Eastern, Western & Whiskered Screech-Owls

juv.

gray form

brown form

Flammulated Owl

Screech-owls occur in a range of colors, a score of races, and three identical-looking species, which are best separated by range and calls. They are the only small owls with ear tufts other than the flammulated owl, which has dark, not yellow, eyes. Often the ear tufts are flattened, but the facial marks and underparts are unlike those of other small round-headed owls. The burrowing owl is our only owl that roosts in a ground burrow. An adult usually guards the burrow during the day, sometimes balancing on one long leg.

eastern

whiskered

Eastern Screech-Owl *Otus asio* 8½"
Whiskered Screech-Owl *Otus trichopsis* 7½"
Western Screech-Owl *Otus kennicottii* 8½"
Numerous. Eastern screech-owl often seen in suburban woods. Whiskered screech-owl found in dense oak and pine-oak canyon woodlands. Western screech-owl most common in oak or streamside woodlands. Often freeze on perch when roosting, stretching and slimming to resemble branch stub. Aggressive. ● Ear tufts, yellow eyes. Most are gray, incl. all whiskereds. Red form common only in southeastern part of eastern screech-owl's range. Brown form scarce outside FL. Western screech-owls vary but few are bright red. Most east-

red form

Burrowing Owl

juv.

western

ern forms have pale bills (shown on red form). Whiskered screech-owl and most western forms have dark base to bill. ♪♪ Common diagnostic calls as follows. *Eastern:* long, mellow whinny, descending scale; or long, low trill. *Whiskered:* series of long and short notes, like Morse code; or series of equal notes slowing at end. *Western:* series of notes speeding up at end; or 2-part trill – short 1st burst, longer 2nd one.

Flammulated Owl *Otus flammeolus* 7"
◀ Numerous, secretive in conifers or aspen, esp. ponderosa pine; rarely below 3,000 ft. Feeds mainly on insects, often hunting from high, exposed perch. Freezes like screech-owl. ● Dark eyes; ear tufts often flattened. Plumage varies from reddish to gray, light to dark, finely mottled to coarse. Red tones on facial disk can be hard to see on dark gray birds. ♪♪ *Hoop* or *hoo-hoop,* hollow, deep-pitched call given alone or in short series.

◀ **Burrowing Owl** *Athene cunicularia* 10"
Declining seriously with loss of natural habitat and predation. Often in loose colonies in fields, prairies, deserts, esp. at prairie-dog towns, golf courses, airports. Roosts in ground burrows. Feeds mostly at dusk and dawn, favoring insects as much as rodents. ● Round head, long legs. Adult barred below; juv. lacks barring. ♪ *Coo-cooo!* Loud call given by male.

SMALL OWLS

gray extreme

Northern Pygmy-Owl

Ferruginous Pygmy-Owl

brown extreme

Saw-whet Owl

juv.

Songbirds mobbing northern pygmy-owl

These are all small, round-headed woodland owls. The tiny elf owl and the ferruginous pygmy-owl also inhabit desert saguaros. Pygmy-owls are the size of starlings. Their long tails distinguish them from elf owls. Note the much larger heads of the boreal and saw-whet owls. The boreal owl is larger than the saw-whet, but the adult is best told by the black borders on the facial disks, which give it a different expression. Young boreal owls lack the clear buff belly of young saw-whets and have a different white facial pattern.

◄**Northern Pygmy-Owl** *Glaucidium gnoma* 7"
Fairly numerous; widespread in dense, mountain woodlands, esp. pine-oak or riparian forest. Feeds mostly on rodents at dawn, dusk. Also preys on songbirds. Flies low like shrike. Bold, aggressive. ● Small round head with dark "false eye" spots on nape. Long tail with white bars. Brown to gray above with white spots; white below with heavy dark streaks. ♪♪ *Hoo*, mellow note given in short, slow series. Birds in s. AZ and s. NM give double note, *hoo-hoo;* may be separate species.

Saw-whet Owl (Northern) *Aegolius acadicus* 8"
Numerous in woodlands, esp. conifers. Often roosts low in thickets, sometimes in swampy areas. Very tame. Usually

Elf Owl

northern pygmy-owl

ferruginous pygmy-owl

Boreal Owl

juv.

hunts from low perch bordering open area; takes mostly rodents. ● Smallest owl in East. Large round head, flattened on top; white streaks on forehead. Large yellow eyes, dark bill, white Y on face. Juv. chocolate brown with buff belly. ♫♫ *Too-too-too*, long, rapid series of whistled notes.

Boreal Owl *Aegolius funereus* 10"
Numbers unknown. Secretive; in boreal forest and mature conifers, aspens of western mountains. Preys mostly on rodents; hunts from perch. Extent and size of winter irruptions to US uncertain. Very tame. ● Large round head, flattened on top; white spots on forehead. Small eyes, pale bill, dark-bordered grayish facial disks. Juv. darker below than juv. saw-whet owl, with different white face pattern. ♫♫ Trilled note, louder at end, given in long series by male.

Elf Owl *Micrathene whitneyi* 6"
Numerous but seldom seen. Widespread in desert lowlands with cavities for nesting, esp. sycamores, oaks, saguaros. Feeds on large insects, invertebrates; often near water. Declining, range contracting, esp. in CA with loss of riparian feeding and roosting habitat. ● Tiny. Round head, short tail, indistinct streaks below. ♫♫ Loud chirps and puppy-like barks given rapidly.

Ferruginous Pygmy-Owl *Glaucidium brasilianum* 7" Tropical. Rare, local, declining in lowland desert of lower Rio Grande Valley, TX and s. AZ. ● Rufous tail with dark bars. ♫♫ *Took,* explosive note repeated rapidly in long series.

SMALL OWLS

HUMMINGBIRD FOOT

feather-comb

NIGHTJAR FOOT

Toes are the only prominent part of the feet and legs of nightjars and hummingbirds.

Nocturnal
Nightjars

CONSULTANT **EIRIK BLOM**
ILLUSTRATOR **HANS PEETERS**

Nightjars feed on night-flying bugs, either by coursing or by making flycatcher-like sallies from a perch or the ground. Like swifts, swallows, and hummingbirds, they are exclusively adapted for flight and unable to walk or hop. Their tiny legs are nearly useless. On the middle toe there is an interesting adaptation, thought to be used in grooming, known as the feather-comb.

Nightjars have differing flight styles. One group, the nighthawks, is built for speed, with long, pointed wings and a tapered body. They feed like swifts, flying continuously with apparent effortlessness and often congregating where bugs abound. The remaining nightjars have shorter, more rounded wings and tails and a fluttery, moth-like flight. Even though they course low and slow, they can maneuver acrobatically to catch flying insects. They are known primarily by the nocturnal calls, for which many are also named. Because they hunt by sight, nightjars are rarely heard on really dark nights.

These birds have the unusual habit of resting during the day along the axis of a tree limb rather than across it, as other birds perch. Many also roost on open ground, where their cryptic back patterns permit them to hide in plain sight among dead leaves and ground litter. They flush unexpectedly from oncoming footsteps – not explosively, like a flock of quail, but in stealthy silence.

Nighthawks nest on the ground (a few on urban rooftops), depending on their protective coloration for concealment. East of the Great Plains, the common nighthawk has nearly disappeared as a nesting bird because its nests are so often disturbed.

COMMON NIGHTHAWK

POOR-WILL

The shape and flight style of nighthawks are different from those of other nightjars like the poor-will.

Common Nighthawk

Lesser Nighthawk

common

lesser

White wing patches distinguish nighthawks from swallows and swifts (Keys 79-81) and from other nightjars, except in southern Texas. In some lesser nighthawks the white patch is small, buff-colored, or absent. However, the best field mark separating nighthawks is the call, heard in flight. Flight style, typically more direct and closer to the ground in the lesser nighthawk, is a good initial clue.

◄**Common Nighthawk** *Chordeiles minor* 9½"
Still numerous from Great Plains westward, but scarce in East with few nesting birds. Widespread, including woodlands, plains, cities; most active at dusk, dawn. ● Gray to dark brown upperparts with white wing patches, throat, tail band. Female lacks tail band, has buff throat. Underparts white with fine dark barring. ♪♪ *Peent,* repeated nasal flight call.

Lesser Nighthawk *Chordeiles acutipennis* 8½"
Fairly numerous; declining with loss of open, arid habitat.
◄Often on posts, wires, or flying low over water at dawn, dusk.
● Like common nighthawk but smaller, with buff background to dark barring below, buff spots on inner primaries; wing patches often smaller, duskier. ♪♪ Soft, low, trilling flight call.

Antillean Nighthawk *Chordeiles gundlachii* 9½" (Not shown) Local in s. FL.
● More buff below than in common. ♪♪ *Pitty-pit-pit,* flight call.

Buff-collared Nightjar

Poor-will

♀   ♂

♂ poor-will

♀   ♂

Chuck-will's-widow

♂

Nightjars are usually identified by their nocturnal calls. Sometimes one is flushed during the day or is glimpsed in a car's headlights at night, its eyes reflecting red. All are similar, with rounded wings and tails, cryptically patterned plumage, and white partial collars (buff in some females and young). The poor-will is small and the only nightjar over much of the West. In the East, chuck-will's-widow is larger and browner than the whip-poor-will and has a brown, not black, chin. Tail patterns seldom can be seen, but they are sure marks – for sex as well as species.

◀**Poor-will** (Common) *Phalaenoptilus nuttallii* 8"
Fairly numerous in dry areas, esp. sagebrush and chaparral slopes, rural roadsides. Often flycatches from ground.
● Small, with proportionally large head. Fairly short, rounded wings and tail; broad white throat band bordered in black. Juv. has buff, not white, markings. ♪♪ *Poor-will´*, repetitious call; 1st syllable long, 2nd accented. At close range a 3rd syllable, a soft *-ip*, can be heard.

Pauraque

♂
whip-poor-will

♀   ♂
Whip-poor-will

♀   ♂

◀ **Chuck-will's-widow** *Caprimulgus carolinensis* 12"
Fairly numerous in deciduous and pine-oak woods, esp.
near fields, rivers. Range expanding in Northeast, where
sometimes occurs in pure pine woods. ● Large. Reddish
brown with brown throat, narrow white (buff in female)
throat band. ♫♪ *Chuck, will's wid´-ow,* repeated call. First
note soft, usually not heard. The 3 loud notes have whistled
quality, as in whip-poor-will, but different accent.

◀ **Whip-poor-will** *Caprimulgus vociferus* 10"
Numerous but declining. In dry, open woodlands in East,
esp. with large oaks. In wooded mountain canyons above
5,000 ft. in West. ● Grayish with black chin. Male has narrow white throat band (female, buff). ♫♪ *Whip´-poor-will´,*
repeated call. Clear whistle in East, with accent as indicated; burrier in West, with accent strongest on last syllable.

Buff-collared Nightjar *Caprimulgus ridgwayi* 9" Mexican. Rare in extreme se. AZ
and sw. NM. ● Narrow collar is white on throat, buff on nape. ♫♪ *Cu-cu-cu-cu-
cu-cukacheea,* repeated call; rising and accelerating until falling at end.

Pauraque *Nyctidromus albicollis* 11" Numerous in s. TX. ● Told from nighthawks
by rounded wings, long rounded tail; from other nightjars by white wing patches.
♫♪ *Goh-wheer´,* repeated call; 1st note soft and often repeated.

cere

gape

RED-TAILED HAWK

talons

The cere, a soft skin on the upper mandible, is often brightly colored.

Aerialists
Raptors

CONSULTANT **PETE DUNNE**
ILLUSTRATOR **HANS PEETERS**

Hawks, eagles, falcons, kites, ospreys, and vultures are birds of prey, or raptors. A typical raptor such as the abundant red-tailed hawk is an impressive and powerful bird. A strong flier, it has muscular legs, sharp talons for capturing prey, and a hooked bill for dismembering its catch. For all their power, most raptors are swift and agile – some amazingly so. This combination of strength and finesse has so deeply inspired mankind that raptors are frequently chosen as national emblems: for example, the bald eagle by the United States and the crested caracara by Mexico.

Seeing a bird of prey hunting overhead is a thrill; identifying one is a challenge that consumes many birders. Plumages on distant birds appear indistinct, and many species display confusing variations. Some birds can be so confusing that even experts debate their identification. The shape of a bird and the way it flies are often the best clues to its identification, but they too can be confusing, as apparent shape and flight style vary with circumstances. The broad, blunt wings of a red-tailed hawk soaring around one thermal can become sleek, pointed, and falcon-like as it glides to the base of another. You will gain expertise with experience and by learning the features of the various types of raptors.

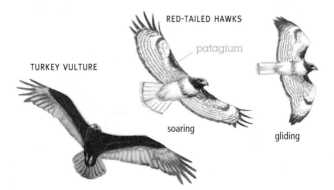

RED-TAILED HAWKS

patagium

TURKEY VULTURE

soaring

gliding

Both turkey vultures and red-tailed hawks are often seen soaring. When the red-tail glides, as it often does, its silhouette greatly changes.

COMMON FLIGHT TERMS

SOAR To fly without flapping, wings and tail fully spread to create the most surface for support. The broad wings of a buteo are ideal for soaring.

GLIDE To fly on fixed, but not fully extended, wings; primaries are closed together, wings partially bent. This causes less drag and creates more speed. The narrow wings of the osprey are adapted for efficient gliding. Less efficient gliders have to flap more to keep altitude.

STOOP To draw the wings close to the body and drop toward prey.

HOVER To flap to maintain a fixed position, often over potential prey.

KITE To maintain a fixed position by hanging in the wind.

COURSE To hunt from steady, flapping flight, either high or low, slow or fast. Peregrine falcons often hunt by high, fast coursing.

QUARTER To overfly an entire area in a methodical pattern instead of just passing through it. Northern harriers typically quarter a marsh.

Among the most distinctive raptors are New World vultures: dark birds with unfeathered heads and white or pale wing markings. Because they feed principally on carrion, they don't need the power of a hawk to subdue prey. Instead, they soar on long, broad wings, using winds and thermals as a platform from which to scan the landscape. On still, overcast days, without thermals or winds, they may remain grounded. The crested caracara is a falcon that has partially adopted the scavenging habits of vultures and has come to resemble them in some ways.

Buteos are a group of hawks that are shaped like eagles, but smaller. Both eagles and buteos are bulkier than other raptors and have long, broad wing surfaces ideal for soaring. Sometimes they seem to soar simply for enjoyment. Plumages often vary greatly within a species. There are pale and dark forms of most buteos, and many confusing intermediate color forms as well. Also, the immature plumage is different for each form, and sometimes there are distinct regional differences.

SWAINSON'S HAWKS

pale form

dark form

Dark-form buteos have red-brown to black underbodies, wing linings, and mantles. Their flight feathers are nearly identical to those on pale-form birds and are often the best marks for dark buteos.

RAPTORS

OSPREY

NORTHERN HARRIER

Buteos are extremely versatile hunters. Many species accept whatever prey the environment provides and use whatever hunting technique succeeds. The osprey, on the other hand, feeds almost exclusively on live fish. It is perhaps the most immediately recognizable bird of prey due to its unique crooked-wing flight and black wrists.

The northern harrier is the only member of its genus in North America. It is slimmer than a buteo, and its tail is relatively longer, but its hunting style is the first clue in most identifications. Northern harriers hunt over open lands, especially marshes, often no more than a few feet off the ground. They quarter with wings in a shallow V (dihedral), flapping just enough to stay airborne.

Accipiters are woodland, bird-catching hawks. They rely on surprise and a blurring burst of speed to overtake prey. Short, broad wings provide great acceleration, and slim bodies create little drag.

COOPER'S HAWK

An accipiter, like the Cooper's hawk, can chase a songbird through a maze of trees without seeming to slow down, using its long tail as a rudder to help maneuver. If a songbird does escape the initial attack, it is likely to survive the encounter, for accipiters are sprinters. They seldom engage in prolonged tail chases. Flying point to point, accipiters typically flap several quick strokes between short glides. They also regularly soar around thermals.

Kites and falcons both have long tails and long, narrow wings, but their flight styles are different. Falcons are power flyers, overtaking their largely avian prey with speed and endurance. Kites glide and wheel effortlessly, swooping down on ground prey or snatching large flying insects. When kites or falcons spread their wings and tails to soar, they resemble other soaring raptors.

MISSISSIPPI KITE
in typical gliding flight

PEREGRINE FALCON
in powered flight

Water barriers, weather fronts, thermals, and updrafts along ridges all help shape hawk migration, creating viewing sites where fascinated onlookers can count hundreds, even thousands, of hawks in a single day. Recent records at eastern viewing sites show sharp-shinned hawks are seriously declining, even as the bald eagle, peregrine falcon, and osprey recover from pesticide poisoning.

A flying raptor first appears as a speck on the horizon. The longer it takes for the speck to grow, the larger and more distant the bird. As wings become discernible you can detect the flight style and make first estimates of wing shape. Slow wing beats and even flight are the mark of a large bird. Smaller birds flap faster and get blown about more. The flight style and silhouette allow some identifications to be ventured before the first plumage mark is seen.

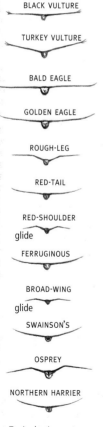

BLACK VULTURE
TURKEY VULTURE
BALD EAGLE
GOLDEN EAGLE
ROUGH-LEG
RED-TAIL
RED-SHOULDER
glide
FERRUGINOUS
BROAD-WING
glide
SWAINSON'S
OSPREY
NORTHERN HARRIER

Typical wing sets of soaring raptors.

Vultures, eagles, and dark-form buteos emerge as large, black birds. The turkey vulture's dihedral is soon visible, but it is the rocking motion that is diagnostic. Pale wing tips on the black vulture can be seen at great distances, as can the white head of an adult bald eagle. A golden eagle's head extends much less than a bald eagle's, and the heads of vultures appear tiny. In the East, the rough-legged hawk is the most likely dark-form buteo. It often flies with steady rowing strokes, but in a soar the wings angle up and flatten at the wrist.

Distant buteos are much alike; all commonly soar. When they flap, wing beats are deliberate and slow, as befits their size, usually with a glide every few beats. The wing set while soaring is helpful information. Red-tails typically soar with wings upturned in a gentle U-shape. The red tail, white chest, and belly band are also distinct at a distance. Seen head-on, a white area on the leading edge of the wings suggests an aircraft's landing lights.

Red-shouldered hawks often glide, cupping the wind with drooping wings. But it is the crescent-shaped window inside the tip of each wing that is the best distance mark. Its shape and placement are important because other hawks have translucent or white patches. The "three points of light" (base of tail and primaries of each wing) of the ferruginous hawk is its best mark from afar.

In the East, flocking buteos are usually broad-winged hawks; in the West, Swainson's. Broad-wings soar on flat wings; in a glide the wings are angled downward. Swainson's soars with wings in a dihedral and glides with wings crooked, somewhat like an osprey. Northern harriers display a distinct dihedral and frequently rock from side to side.

The flight of accipiters, kites, and falcons is treated on Keys 75-78. A gliding Mississippi kite most resembles a peregrine falcon, but the kite's tail is longer and flares at the end while a peregrine's tapers. Kites also have a very short first primary feather, a small but easily seen point.

RAPTORS

Turkey Vulture

imm.

Black Vulture

turkey vultiure

black vulture

zone-tailed hawk Key 74

A bare, unfeathered head is the mark of a confirmed carrion eater. The caracara has limited bare facial skin; it both scavenges and hunts live prey. Adult turkey vultures are easily identified by their red heads, but dark-headed young birds can be confused with black vultures. Note the shorter tail and compact body of the black vulture. Seen soaring, the two vultures (the "buzzards" of the Old West) are big, dark birds with distinctive pale patterns and small heads. Even at a distance they can normally be separated: turkey vultures float on wings held in a V; blacks on flat wings.

◀**Turkey Vulture** *Cathartes aura* L 27" W 70"
Numerous, widespread. Expanding range northward in Northeast. Soars with wings set in dihedral (more level when no wind), rocking from side to side. ● Dark, nearly black, with contrasting pale flight feathers. Long, pale tail rarely fanned. Adult has bare red head; imm. dark gray head.

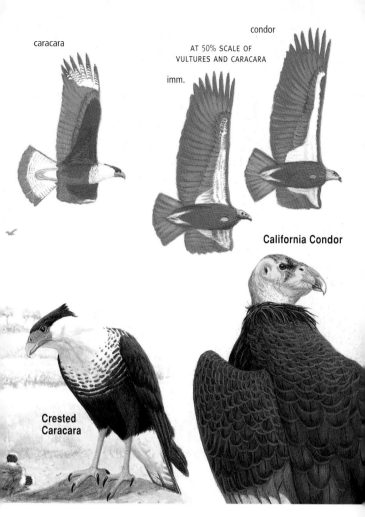

caracara

condor

AT 50% SCALE OF
VULTURES AND CARACARA

imm.

California Condor

Crested
Caracara

◀**Black Vulture** *Coragyps atratus* L 25" W 58"
Numerous, widespread. Slowly expanding range northward
in Northeast. Flies in steady soar on short, broad wings held
flat; occasional choppy flaps. ● All black except white
patches on outer primaries. Very short tail, naked gray head.

Crested Caracara *Polyborus plancus* L 24" W 50"
◀Fairly numerous in TX, AZ; scarce, seriously declining in FL
with loss of grasslands. Flight strong, direct, usually close to
ground. Often walks. ● Black crest with white neck, red or
yellow face, large bill. Imm. browner, streaked below.

California Condor *Gymnogyps californianus* L 48" W 110"
Once resided in coastal mountains from CA through OR, scavenged in nearby
coasts, foothills. In 1987 the few remaining wild birds were caught for a captive
breeding program intended to avoid extinction. Reintroduction of young birds
began in 1992 in remote sites of Los Padres National Forest, CA. Several have
perished, and success of recovery program is uncertain. Other planned release
sites include Grand Canyon. Soars with wings horizontal, deeply slotted primaries curled up at tip. ● Massive. Black with white wing linings, silver pattern
on upper secondaries. Naked red/orange head changes color with mood. Imm.
(new releases are all imms.) has dark head, white wing linings mottled dark.

bald eagle
imm.

white-bellied
form, imm.

imm.

**Bald
Eagle**

Large size, long wings, and deliberate wing beats separate eagles
from other raptors. Adult golden and bald eagles are distinctive;
but the young birds resemble each other: both have white in the
wings and tail. On young golden eagles the white never extends to
the belly or wing linings as on young bald eagles. An osprey is
somewhat eagle-like, with its white head and dark eye stripe, but
it has slimmer, gull-like wings and a bold underwing pattern.

◀**Bald Eagle** *Haliaeetus leucocephalus* L 36" W 84"
Seriously reduced by human encroachment, pesticides,
shooting; now recovering. Winter concentrations developing
widely at lakes, reservoirs. Preys largely on fish, fresh carrion. Also takes waterfowl, small mammals. Soars with wings
held flat. ● White head, neck, tail; large yellow bill. In flight,
head and tail of adults project about equally; imm. tail longer.
Imm. dark with variable white on underbody, flight feathers,
wing linings, tail. Acquires adult plumage by 4th or 5th yr.

1st yr. imm.

golden eagle

osprey

Osprey

Golden Eagle

◀**Golden Eagle** *Aquila chrysaetos* L 37" W 86"
Fairly numerous in West, scarce in East. Widespread in
winter, esp. in hilly terrain. Hunts from a perch, from a soar,
and by coursing, taking prey (usually small animals) opportunistically. Soars with wings upcurved. ● Dark body with
light "golden" highlights on crown, neck, upperwings of
mature birds. In flight, head projects much less than length
of tail. Imm. has varying amount of white at base of tail,
base of flight feathers; underbody and wing linings dark.
Amount of white decreases with maturity over 5 yrs.

◀**Osprey** *Pandion haliaetus* L 24" W 66"
Fairly numerous on coasts; expanding into interior at lakes,
reservoirs. Recovering from pesticides. Glides on crooked
wings. Dives talons-first for fish spotted from perch or while
gliding or hovering. Accepts man-made platforms or poles
for huge stick nest. ● Eagle-like breadth, gull-like shape
and buoyancy. Dark above, white below with white head,
dark eyeline and crown, dark carpal patches. Some (once
thought to be females) have "necklace" of breast streaks.
Imm. has white feather edges above, giving scalloped look.

eastern

western

eastern
imm.

"Fuertes'"
form

eastern
form

western
form

imm.
eastern

The red-tailed hawk is the most widespread and commonly seen buteo. Its plumage varies in the West, but either a red tail (pinkish from below) or a dark bar seen in flight on the leading edge of the underwing is a sure mark that is visible on most adults. A pale chest and streaked belly band are also usually present. Note that the ferruginous hawk (Key 72) has a pinkish tip to its white tail. A young red-tail has a dark bar on its underwing like an adult, but its tail is brown above and narrowly banded.

◀**Red-tailed Hawk** *Buteo jamaicensis* L 22" W 50"
Numerous, widespread, in open, perch-studded habitats. Has increased with forest fragmentation, prairie planting. Often hunts rodents from perch, but adaptable. Hovers, kites. ● Several races with pale and dark forms, intergrades, age variations. Most widespread form, common in East, has red tail with dark subterminal band, white chest

dark

Krider's

Harlan's

"Harlan's" form

dark form

Red-tailed Hawk

"Krider's" form

with dark streaking on belly, white mottling on mantle. Western birds darker above with tawny mottling and underparts; adult tails narrowly barred. Dark form (common in West) red-brown, rarely black. Adult soars with rounded wing, often angled forward at wrist; bulging outer secondaries. Note dark patagial bars. Imm. in all forms rangier, with long wings and long, brownish tail with narrow bars.

◀ **"Krider's" form** Scarce. Similar birds can be found in West.
● Whiter head and mantle than eastern form; whitish inner primaries on upperwing. White below, like ferruginous (Key 72), but has brown patagial bars. Tail white with dark band near tip, often pink tinge in adults. Imm. tail finely barred.

◀ **"Harlan's" form** Fairly numerous. Nests in conifers, winters on prairies. ● Blackish with variable white spotting, silvery flight feathers. Diagnostic adult tail is dirty white or gray at base with mottling and streaking (not barring) blending to dark terminal band. Imm. dark, tail as in other imm. red-tails.

◀ **"Fuertes'" form** Fairly numerous. ● Like eastern form but lacks belly band below and mottling above.

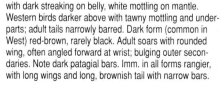

ferruginous
pale form

Swainson's
pale form

intermediate

Swainson's
Hawk

pale form

dark
form

Ferruginous
Hawk

imm.

pale
form

These hawks inhabit open land – prairie, savanna, or tundra. Pale-form ferruginous hawks are starkly white below with rusty leggings. Even rare dark-form birds have white flight feathers. Swainson's, on the other hand, has diagnostic dark flight feathers on its long, pointed wings. Rough-legged hawks vary considerably. The dark wrist patches are diagnostic and evident on all but the darkest birds. Many also have a solid dark belly band. Tails are variable, but most include a broad, dark subterminal band below.

◀**Ferruginous Hawk** *Buteo regalis* L 23" W 53"
Scarce, declining; on dry plains. Hunts from ground, wing, or perch, favoring small animals. Soars, courses, hovers, kites. ● Red-brown mantle. Large, pale, sloping head with long, yellow gape. White underparts with rusty leggings to toes. Tail white, blending to rufous-gray tip above. Soars on long wings with broad arm, tapered hand, dark "comma" at base of primaries. Rufous leggings make distinct V on white underparts. White patches in upperwings at base of

Swainson's dark form

rough-leg

dark ♂

imm.

pale ♀

Rough-legged Hawk

Swainson's pale form imm.

pale form ♂

imm.

primaries. Very rare dark-form birds have brown or red-brown bodies. Imm. lacks leggings, has dusky-tipped tail.

◀**Swainson's Hawk** *Buteo swainsoni* L 21" W 52"
Numerous; most common buteo on plains. Often feeds on insects, sometimes in loose groups on ground. Also courses low, rocking and hovering, in search of rodents. Migrates in large flocks. ● Pale-form adult white or creamy below with chestnut bib, small bill encircled by white. Dark form and intermediates scarce except CA. Soars on long, upward-reaching, tapered wings with dark flight feathers, black "comma" at base of primaries. Long, gray, banded tail. Imm. buff below and on face with dark malar stripes, chest spots.

◀**Rough-legged Hawk** *Buteo lagopus* L 22" W 56"
Locally numerous over marsh, grasslands. Favors rodents. Hovers. ● Pale form has dark carpal patches. Brown belly band; boldest in imm., can be mottled in adult male and look paler than dark-streaked breast. Subterminal band on under-side of tail lacking in imm. Some males have additional tail bands. Legs feathered to toes. Dark form scarce; blackish with silvery flight feathers. Similar to "Harlan's" form of red-tail (Key 71) but lankier. Soars on long, evenly broad wings. Imm. has white in upperwings at base of primaries.

red-shoulder

imm.

broad-wing

imm.

Red-shouldered Hawk

imm.

imm.

Broad-winged Hawk

The red-shouldered hawk is distinguished by its rufous shoulder patches and checkerboard wing pattern. Broad-wings are small buteos with oddly gentle expressions. Their best field mark is their broad tail bands. The white bands are much wider than the white bands on the red-shoulder's tail. Short-tailed hawks have either a solid black underbody and wing linings (most common) or nearly solid white ones; only the larger Swainson's (Key 72), which occasionally winters in Florida, is likely to cause confusion.

◀**Red-shouldered Hawk** *Buteo lineatus* L 19" W 40"
Fairly numerous in woodlands, esp. swamps. Seriously declining in East. Hunts from perch, often roadside in West.
● Rufous shoulder, checkered wings. Slim. Soars with wings angled forward, crescent-shaped translucent window near tip. Flight feathers barred black and white below, underbody and wing coverts rufous. Western birds darkest rufous below; southern birds palest. Imm. cream-colored below with dark-streaked breast. ♪ *Kee-ah,* loud call, repeated.

short-tail

pale
form

dark
form
imm.

Gray Hawk

Road-side Hawk

Short-tailed Hawk

pale
form

dark
form

pale form
imm.

◄Broad-winged Hawk *Buteo platypterus* L 16" W 33"
Numerous in deciduous woods. Hunts from perch, often
roadside. Tame. Large flocks in migration. ● Small, stocky.
Brown above, barred rufous below. Wings broad, short with
white linings, heavy dark trailing edge. Tail long, broad-
banded. Dark form (not shown) very rare, has same tail.
Imm. like imm. red-shouldered hawk but lacks translucent
crescent in wing; spotting concentrated on face, throat, sides.

◄Short-tailed Hawk *Buteo brachyurus* L 15" W 35"
Fewer than 500 birds in US; usually seen soaring alone with
strongly upturned outer primaries over fields and wetlands.
Often stoops at birds. ● Long, broad wings. Underbody
and wing linings either black or white. Tail broad, short, gray
below with dark bands. Dark-form imm. like adult but belly
mottled, has more tail bands. Light-form imm. resembles
imm. broad-winged hawk, but unstreaked below.

Gray Hawk *Buteo nitidus* L 17" W 35" Tropical. About 50 pairs along streams
in se. AZ, sw. NM, and lower Rio Grande Valley. ● Adult gray. Imm. brown
above, tawny below with heavy spotting; compare with imm. broad-winged
hawk. All plumages show white U-shaped rump band.

Roadside Hawk *Buteo magnirostris* L 14" W 33" Tropical. Recorded in s. TX.

Zone-tailed Hawk

Common Black-Hawk

imm.

Southwestern buteos are relatively easy to identify. Tails are the best mark for the two black hawks. The zone-tailed hawk also has slimmer wings, which it holds in a V as it mimics the flight of a turkey vulture (Key 69). Both Harris' and the white-tailed hawk have prominent rufous shoulders but are otherwise distinctive and unlikely to be confused with the red-shouldered hawk (Key 73).

◀**Zone-tailed Hawk** *Buteo albonotatus* L 20" W 51"
Scarce; in arid lands, esp. near desert watercourses. Soars and rocks like turkey vulture, wings held in distinct dihedral.
● Black with yellow cere and legs, gray lores. Slender wings, longer than in turkey vulture, with broader hand. Tail long, square-tipped, dark with gray bands, 1 continuous and 1 broken (male) or 1 continuous and 2 broken (female). Imm. has white spotting on breast; tail gray above with narrow blackish bands, white below with gray bands.

Common Black-Hawk *Buteogallus anthracinus* L 21" W 50"
About 250 pairs, declining with loss of streamside cottonwood groves. Soars on flat wings, but prefers to sit. Hunts

Harris'

white-tail

imm.

imm.

imm.

White-tailed Hawk

imm.

Harris' Hawk

‹from perch, favoring fish, frogs, snakes. ● Stout. Yellow cere, lores, legs. Short, broad wings and tail; whitish patch at base of primaries, wide white median band and narrow white tip on tail. Imm. dark above with buff eyebrow, dark malar stripe; buff below with dark splotches; tail finely banded.

Harris' Hawk *Parabuteo unicinctus* L 21" W 47"
Declining, now scarce except in TX. In mesquite brush-
‹lands, cactus desert; less commonly in woodlands. Preys opportunistically, often in family groups. Perches conspicuously. ● Chestnut shoulders, leggings, wing linings; short, paddle-shaped wings. Long black tail with prominent white base, white tip. Imm. streaked below; shows some color on shoulders, leggings, wing linings in same pattern as adult.

‹**White-tailed Hawk** *Buteo albicaudatus* L 23" W 50"
In N. America about 1,000 birds, declining over open coastal TX grasslands and semi-arid interior. Preys opportunistically, often from a soar with broad wings held in dihedral. ● Gray above with rufous shoulders; white below. Short white tail with black subterminal band. Imm. much rangier than adult; dark above and below with pale chest splotch, white on cheeks; tail gray, finely barred.

ADULTS IN TYPICAL FLIGHT; IMMS. SOARING

goshawk

imm.

Cooper's

imm.

Goshawk

imm.

Accipiters are wary forest-dwellers that often flush before being noticed, disappearing as a blur slicing through the understory. All have long, banded tails. Adults are blue-gray above and barred below; females larger. Adult goshawks have fine gray barring below, and up close the eye stripe is apparent. Adult Cooper's and sharp-shinned hawks have orange barring. Young birds are brown and streaked rather than barred below. At all ages, Cooper's and sharp-shinned hawks differ only by degree and often confound experts.

◀**Goshawk** (Northern) *Accipiter gentilis* L 21-25" W 40-46"
Scarce, except in conifers of boreal forest. Serious declines in West. Hunts from perch or coursing, favoring grouse, hare. Irrupts in winter to mid-US when northern prey scarce.
● Blue-gray above, whitish below. Black shaft streaks on breast can obscure gray barring. Black cap, eye patch; white eyebrow. Wing has broad arm, narrower hand. Tail broad with pale bands. Imm. like imm. Cooper's but with pale eye stripe, more streaking below, dirty-looking breast.

sharp-shin

imm.

sharp-shin imm. ♂

Cooper's imm. ♂

TYPICAL VARIATIONS IN SHARP-SHINNED HAWK'S TAIL

Cooper's Hawk

imm.

Sharp-shinned Hawk

imm.

◄**Cooper's Hawk** *Accipiter cooperii* L 15-18" W 30-36"
Fairly numerous and increasing. Recovering in East from
losses to insecticides, human persecution. Usually hunts for
birds and chipmunks from perch at edge of mixed or deciduous woods. ● See below.

Sharp-shinned Hawk *Accipiter striatus* L11-14" W 22-28"
Numerous in summer in woodlands. Widespread in winter,
◄more common than Cooper's, but most migrate out of US.
Declining in migration at traditional viewing sites. Hunts similarly to Cooper's, also courses. Both attack at bird feeders,
regularly colliding with picture windows. ● See below.

COOPER'S VS. SHARP-SHINNED   *Flying:* Sharpie's
smaller size, lighter weight evident in quicker wing beats,
more buoyant flight. Sharpie has broad, forward-angled
arm and small hand that gives S shape to trailing edge of wing and makes head
appear tucked in; Cooper's head appears extended. Cooper's tail rounder,
broadly white-tipped. Sharpie's tail narrowly gray-tipped, variably shaped. Imm.
Cooper's whiter below and less streaked than imm. sharpie. Cooper's migrates
alone, sharpies often in small groups. *Perched:* Cooper's head larger, squarer
with dark cap (less obvious on female). Eye looks larger, more centrally placed
in sharpie's small head, giving it startled expression. Cooper's looks fiercer.

ACCIPITERS

75

imm.

northern harrier ♀

white-tailed kite

♂

Northern Harrier

♂

♀

imm.

White-tailed Kite

The northern harrier is typically seen hunting slowly a few feet over a marsh or field. Its white rump is the easiest mark on both the gray male and the larger brown female. The kites alternately flap stiffly and glide buoyantly on long, pointed, falcon-like wings. Except for the distinctive and graceful swallow-tailed kite, they have long, square-tipped tails – black in the Mississippi, white in the white-tail. Kites regularly stray far out of their normal ranges.

◀**Northern Harrier** *Circus cyaneus* L 18-22" W 40-47"
Numerous over open lands, esp. marshes; less so in East. Usually hunts in low, slow, buoyant flight with wings in shallow V; hunts by sound as well as sight. Displays in spectacular dives and loops. ● White rump patch, owl-like facial disk in all plumages. Male gray above, white below with black wing tips. Female larger; brown above, tawny below with dark streaking. Imm. like female but washed with rufous below.

White-tailed Kite *Elanus leucurus* L 16" W 42"
Fairly numerous over open lands. Once nested east to FL and NC, now reclaiming range. Has adapted to grassy interstate borders in CA. Unlike other kites, interrupts coursing with frequent hovering. Also hunts from a perch, favoring

Mississippi kite

sub-adult

Snail Kite ♂ ♀

Hook-billed Kite ♀

♂

imm.

Swallow-tailed Kite

imm.

Mississippi Kite

rodents. ● Gray above with black shoulders, white below with black wrist patches. Imm. has brownish crown, back; rufous breast mottling; narrow, dusky, terminal tail band.

Mississippi Kite *Ictinia mississippiensis* L 15" W 36"
Increasingly numerous over open areas and forest, often in small groups. Takes ground prey, flying insects in dexterous glides. ● Pale gray head, darker mantle, black tail and wing tips. Narrow wing with short first primary, prominent white secondaries. Tail slightly flared, constantly twisted and fanned. Imm. brown above, streaked and spotted brown below; tail dark with translucent bands. 1st-yr. bird like adult but retains imm. tail and some streaking below.

Swallow-tailed Kite *Elanoides forficatus* L 23" W 48"
Fairly numerous, slowly increasing; in open forest, esp. wetlands. Once nested north to Great Lakes. Seems to float just above treetops, adjusting balance constantly. Feeds on ground prey and large insects in flight. ● Forked tail, black-and-white pattern. Imm. has fine dark streaks below, narrow white tips to flight feathers.

Snail Kite *Rostrhamus sociabilis* L 17" W 46" S. American. About 500 birds resident in s. FL. Feeds on freshwater snails subject to fluctuating water levels.

Hook-billed Kite *Chondrohierax uncinatus* L 16" W 44" Tropical. Fewer than 20 pairs in lower Rio Grande Valley. ● Color variable. Note large, long-hooked bill.

gyrfalcon imm.

prairie

Gyrfalcon

white form

gray form

imm.

Prairie Falcon

A coursing falcon flies fast and direct, without interruption. The peregrine usually courses high, attacking birds from above. Its flight style and wing shape are distinctive. Often a gleaming white breast (blushed with cinnamon in some western birds) can be seen. At close range note the dark sideburns. Prairie falcons usually course close to the ground to surprise prey; their dark underwing "struts" and pale rump and tail distinguish them from peregrines. The hunting style and color of gyrfalcons vary. They are larger and bulkier than peregrines and lack prominent facial markings.

◀**Gyrfalcon** *Falco rusticolus* L 21-24" W 52-62"
Scarce Arctic resident; rare and irregular winter visitor as far south as CA, CO, VA. Preys on small mammals, birds, esp. ptarmigan. Hunts from perch or coursing, often near ground.
● Color variable; gray tones most common. Long tail can be plain or barred. Wings pointed, but broader, wider at base than peregrine's; primaries are translucent. Lacks sideburns or "struts." Imm. dark above, heavily streaked below.

peregrine

imm.
(soaring)

**Aplomado
Falcon**

Arctic

Peregrine Falcon

Arctic
imm.

western
imm.

western

◀**Prairie Falcon** *Falco mexicanus* L 16-18" W 36-42"
Fairly numerous and widespread, esp. in arid regions. Takes
mostly ground prey from perch or by fast, low coursing.
● Pale underwing with contrasting dark wing pits. Sandy
brown above, rump and tail lighter. Narrow, dark mustache.

Peregrine Falcon *Falco peregrinus* L 17-19" W 38-43"
Once widespread and fairly numerous, esp. in East, where
it fed on passenger pigeons. Eastern breeding population
extirpated by mid-20th century, victim of pesticides. Eastern
◀reintroduction (inside dashed line) includes cities, where it
nests on bridges, buildings. Western population recovering;
Arctic fully recovered and removed from endangered list in
1994. Most migrate along coasts. ● Blue-gray above with
dark face, helmet-like sideburns. Barred below with white
breast in Arctic race (migrates on East Coast). Western
birds have cinnamon wash on breast, darker mantle; birds
of coastal rain forest darkest. Imm. brown above, buff below
with heavy streaking. Arctic imm. has blond crown, nape.

Aplomado Falcon *Falco femoralis* L 16" W 45" Cen., S. American. Once nested
in s. TX, se. AZ, sw. NM. Reintroduction began in 1993 with releases at Laguna
Atascosa NWR, TX. Nest found in TX in 1995, first US nest since 1952 in NM.

The kestrel is known by its small size (males smaller), its two black face marks, and the male's colorful plumage. Merlins aren't much bigger, but they fly with greater strength and directness. The merlin's color varies with sex and region, but all are streaked below and have a dark tail with pale bands and a whitish tip.

◄Merlin *Falco columbarius* L 10-12" W 22-25"
Fairly numerous; scarce in winter. In open areas, forest edges. Takes mostly birds or insects by coursing or from perch. Does not hover. ● Pale-banded, dark tail. Narrow white eyebrow, dark mustache. Male blue-gray above; female and imm. brown. Streaked below, darker in female. Northwestern form dark, eyebrow obscure, tail bands narrow. Plains form pale, mustache indistinct.

Kestrel (American) *Falco sparverius* L 9-11" W 20-23"
◄Numerous and widespread, including suburban areas, but decreasing in Northeast and FL. Hunts small rodents, insects, birds from a favorite perch, often wires, poles. Commonly hovers. ● White cheeks and throat with 2 black streaks. Male has blue wing coverts, red back and tail with black sub-terminal band, white tip. Female has heavily barred, reddish-brown back, tail, wing coverts.

Aerialists
Swifts and swallows

CONSULTANT **KIMBALL GARRETT**
ILLUSTRATOR **ANDREW VALLELY**

Swifts and swallows have tiny bills but wide gapes for collecting insects in flight, which, weather permitting, is how they spend most daylight hours. Swifts fly continuously, leaving the skies only to roost. Even such chores as drinking and collecting twigs for nests are performed in flight. Some species are thought to mate in midair. Swallows, while strong fliers, are often seen perched, their tiny feet tightly grasping a wire or small limb.

Although swifts and swallows are not closely related, they are quite similar because they have adapted to the same method of feeding. However, swifts are built for greater speed than swallows. The wrist is closer to the body, and they have much longer, narrower primaries, which bow slightly when they glide. Their flight is fast and erratic, with rapid, shallow wing beats that create a unique twinkling effect, especially in the smaller species. Swallows fly more slowly and gracefully. Both swifts and swallows can be seen at great distances and can often be recognized by their shape or flight style as well as by their calls, which are given in flight and carry for some distance.

All species require cavities for nesting. Some build their own hollows out of mud on protected vertical surfaces or overhangs.

Hollow gourds for nesting were provided for the purple martin, our largest swallow, by Native Americans, who valued it for devouring insects, as did the European settlers who followed. Now martins, chimney swifts, and many swallows nest in man-made cavities ranging from birdhouses to buildings, culverts, bridges, and chimneys. The steep walls of gravel pits and vertical highway and railroad cuts are also popular nest sites. The cave swallow is the latest to accept man-made structures, beginning in the mid-1900s. Its numbers and range are now increasing, as in other species that have adapted.

Swifts roost on vertical surfaces.

Because they feed on insects, swifts and swallows are only summer visitors to the northern states and Canada. They arrive mostly in small flocks in spring and are usually seen feeding in flocks in the summer. During fall migration flocks can be huge, numbering in the thousands at favored roosting sites.

White-throated Swift

Black Swift

Swifts can be distinguished from swallows by their flying style and shape, as described in the introduction. The chimney swift is usually the only swift in the East. It is difficult to separate from Vaux's swift except by range. Both have a tapered, tailless look that has been aptly compared to a flying cigar. The two larger swifts have notched tails and are not likely to be confused with each other. Nighthawks (Key 67) are sometimes confused with swifts.

◀**White-throated Swift** *Aeronautes saxatalis* 6½"
Fairly numerous but very local. Nests on rock cliffs in mountains, desert canyons, coasts. Ranges into nearby valleys, flatlands. Perhaps fastest-flying N. American bird, estimates of over 200 mph. ● Long, notched tail often carried in point. White breast, side patches, tips of secondaries. Violet-green swallow (Key 81) has similar white side patches but is all white below. ♪ *Jee-jee-je-ee-ee-ee*, shrill call.

Black Swift *Cypseloides niger* 7"
Scarce, local; nests in small colonies on wet cliffs, cave

common nighthawk
Key 67

White-collared Swift

Vaux's Swift

Chimney Swift

walls, either coastal or behind mountain waterfalls. Also irregular or isolated nesting colonies elsewhere in West. Often forages in flocks far from nest; soars high. ● Black with long, slightly forked tail. Silvery forehead markings usually not visible. Narrower wings than in purple martin (Key 80). ♪ *Pic-pic-pic*, given softly near nest site.

Chimney Swift *Chaetura pelagica* 5¼"
Numerous in flocks over most habitats: open, wooded, or developed. Expanding range in West; a few summer in s. CA. Roosts and nests in chimneys, air shafts; rarely in hollow trees, which are no longer common in eastern forest. Small spines on tail used for support when roosting. ● Sooty brown; paler on throat, upper breast. Long, narrow, slightly bowed wings; tailless appearance. ♪ Loud, rapid chips.

Vaux's Swift *Chaetura vauxi* 4¾"
Fairly numerous in flocks, esp. over woodlands. Still a forest-dweller, rarely uses chimneys. ● Like chimney swift but slightly smaller; paler on throat, rump. ♪ Rapid, high chips and trilling; higher, more insect-like than in chimney swift.

White-collared Swift *Streptoprocne zonaris* 8½" Tropical. Several widespread coastal records. ● Huge swift.

SWIFTS

79

Purple Martin

♂

♀

Barn Swallow

The purple martin is our largest swallow and the only one in which the sexes differ strongly: females are duller and grayer. The forked "swallow tail" of the barn swallow is an easy mark, although less pronounced in young birds. Cliff and cave swallows both have nearly square tails and buff rump patches. The best mark for the cliff swallow is its dark throat. The cave swallow has a buff throat and collar, which make its dark cap conspicuous.

◀**Purple Martin** *Progne subis* 8"
Fairly numerous but declining, esp. in West, due to nest competition from starlings, house sparrows. At birdhouses in East, esp. near water; open woodland, burns, towns in West; saguaros in Southwest. Glides in circles, flapping intermittently. ● Large with broad wings. Male blue-black. Female and imm. duller above, gray below with gray collar. **Cuban Martin** (*P. cryptoleuca*) recorded in s. FL; not separable in field by sight. ♪ *Tew, tew,* rich call; song a liquid gurgling.

barn | juv. barn

juv. cliff | cliff

cave

♂ martin ♀

juv.

Cave Swallow

Cliff Swallow

◀**Barn Swallow** *Hirundo rustica* 6¾"
Abundant in pairs or small colonies. Nests nearly exclusively on man-made structures. ● Deeply forked tail. Deep blue above, orange-buff below with chestnut throat. Juv. and some races paler below than shown. Juv. has shorter tail. ♪ *Sleep, sleep,* liquid alarm call.

Cliff Swallow *Hirundo pyrrhonota* 5½"
Abundant in West, fairly numerous in East. Widespread in open country, over water. Longer glides than other swallows, ◀with steep, rising finish. Gourd-shape mud nest on cliffs, banks, similar man-made surfaces. ● Nearly square tail with buff rump, dark throat patch. Forehead white (buff in Southwest). Juv. duller, with less distinctly patterned head. ♪ *Churrr* and *syew,* soft call notes; also grating calls.

Cave Swallow *Hirundo fulva* 5½"
Once scarce, now fairly numerous and wider ranging as nesting colonies adapt to bridges and culverts in addition ◀to original caves. Flight like cliff swallow's. ● Like cliff swallow but with buff throat and collar, cinnamon forehead, dark cap. Juv. duller. ♪ *Weet,* clear flight call.

SWALLOWS

80

Tree Swallow

juv.

Violet-green Swallow

juv.

Both the tree swallow and the violet-green swallow have flashing white underparts and green or blue upperparts. Note how the white on the underparts of the violet-green extends onto the rump and face. The erratic, bat-like flight of the little bank swallow makes the dark breast band hard to see except when the bird is perched, but the flight itself is diagnostic. Young tree swallows and violet-green swallows have only faint breast bands. The rough-winged is the only brown-backed swallow with a dusky throat; the rest have white throats.

◄**Tree Swallow** *Tachycineta bicolor* 5¾"
Abundant and expanding range; in pairs or loose colonies, esp. around still water. Large flocks along coast in migration. Nests in tree holes, birdhouses. Alternately flaps and glides in circular flight, rising while flapping. Eats berries in fall, winter when insects unavailable. ● Glossy blue-green above, greener in fall; females duller. Clear white below. Juv. brown above (can show some blue-green), often with dusky band across breast. ♪ *Kleet* or *cheet*, twittering flight call.

Bahama Swallow

violet-green

tree

juv. tree

bank

rough-winged

Bank Swallow

Rough-winged Swallow

◄Violet-green Swallow *Tachycineta thalassina* 5¼"
Numerous along coasts and in mountains, where it nests in tree hollows, birdhouses, or rock crevices. Usually in small colonies. ● Similar to tree swallow, but white extends high onto rump and over eye. Green back contrasts with purplish rump; female duller. Juv. gray-brown above, often with dusky wash across breast. ♪ *Twee-chee*, and chipping calls.

Bank Swallow *Riparia riparia* 5¼"
Numerous but local, in colonies. Originally nested in holes ◄dug in steep riverbanks; now also in railroad and highway cuts, gravel pits near water. Flight bat-like, shallow and fluttery. ● Brown above, slightly paler on rump. White below with brown breast band. ♪ *Brtt*, dry flight call.

Rough-winged Swallow (Northern) *Stelgidopteryx serripennis* 5½"
Fairly numerous, widespread singly or in small groups. Nests in existing cavities in vertical or overhanging riverbanks, bridges, culverts; sometimes in bank swallow ◄colonies. Flight stronger, more direct, strokes deeper than in bank swallow. ● Brown above, white below with dusky throat and upper breast. ♪ Like bank swallow's but harsher.

Bahama Swallow *Tachycineta cyaneoviridis* 5¾" W. Indian. Recorded on FL Keys. ● Like tree swallow but deeply forked tail.

SWALLOWS

Hummingbirds

CONSULTANT **NANCY L. NEWFIELD**
ILLUSTRATOR **F. P. BENNETT**

Ruby-throated hummingbird at wild columbine.

A hummingbird's world centers on flowers. Cardinal flowers and some columbines are examples of plants that have evolved with hummers – blossoms and birds creating each other over time through the process of natural selection. The plants rely on hummers for pollination and provide nectar and tiny insects in exchange. The hummer's adaptations for extracting nectar are striking, especially its mastery of flight. It hovers while probing flowers with its long bill and can dart in any direction – even backwards and upside down.

Not only is the anatomy of the hummingbird shaped by flowers, but so is its social life. Upon locating a patch of blossoms, a hummer claims ownership, defending it from other hummers even when not actively feeding. Its possessiveness results in such belligerence that a male will accept a female into his territory only long enough to mate. The male's brilliant gorget (throat) and crown patch are displayed as a threat to all others.

Hummingbirds readily visit gardens and feeders. The popularity of feeders is allowing some species, such as Anna's, to expand their range and numbers. Also hummers are overwintering on the Gulf Coast in ever greater numbers. Most are rufous or black-chinned hummingbirds, but many species are recorded each year.

Males can be identified by the colorful metallic glints that flash from their gorgets and crowns when light strikes from an advantageous angle. The shape of the gorget can also be informative. Females and young birds are difficult to separate in the field; some are impossible. Females can show a few iridescent feathers on their throats. Often, however, they can be grouped only according to whether or not they show buff to rusty sides and tail markings.

Most often a hummer's gorget appears flat black; the brilliant, jewel-like reflections are seen only at favorable angles.

♀ broad-tailed
Key 83

**Rufous
Hummingbird**

♂

♀ rufous &
Allen's

**Allen's
Hummingbird**

♂

♀ calliope
Key 83

The green back and crown of the male Allen's hummingbird distinguish it from the male rufous hummingbird. Female and young of both species are best identified by range and can be confused with female broad-tailed and calliope hummingbirds. All have buff or rusty sides, not the gray or greenish sides of the females on Key 83.

◀**Rufous Hummingbird** *Selasphorus rufus* 3¾"
Fairly numerous, widespread from mountain meadows to lowland gardens. ● Male has orange-red gorget; rufous back, tail, sides; some have green flecks on backs; a few can be as green as Allen's. Female has rusty sides and undertail coverts (sometimes dull, buff when worn), as in female broad-tailed and calliope, but female broad-tailed bulky with full tail, distinct tail pattern; female calliope's tail is shorter (folded wing extends only to its tip) and shows little rufous color. ♪ *Chip*, given loudly; chatter.

◀**Allen's Hummingbird** *Selasphorus sasin* 3¾"
Fairly numerous in coastal foothills. ● Like rufous hummer except male has green back. ♪ Similar to that of rufous.

Males have distinctive gorgets. Look for the violet throat on the black-chinned, as the gorgets of other hummers can often appear black. Female and young calliope and broad-tailed hummers (Key 82) have buff sides, not gray or greenish as in the females on this Key. The female ruby-throated and black-chinned are very similar but have separate ranges. The female Anna's is bulkier with grayer underparts, while Costa's female is small with a faint mask.

◀**Ruby-throated Hummingbird** *Archilochus colubris* 3¾"
Fairly numerous, but declining. Only widespread hummer in East. ● Male has ruby gorget and dark, deeply notched tail. Female and imm. lack gorget, may show fine throat spots; body is slender, tail rounded with white corners. ♪ *Tchew*, given softly.

Black-chinned Hummingbird *Archilochus alexandri* 3¾"
◀Fairly numerous and widespread, esp. at lower elevations. Western counterpart of ruby-throated. Pumps tail rapidly while hovering to feed. ● Male has black chin, violet throat. Female and imm. slightly longer wings and longer bills than ruby-throated. ♪ *Tchew*, given softly.

Costa's ♀

Anna's ♀

Costa's
Hummingbird

♂

Calliope
Humming-
bird

♂

♂

Anna's
Hummingbird

◄**Broad-tailed Hummingbird** *Selasphorus platycercus* 4"
Fairly numerous in Rocky Mountains; frequents flowers in
forest glades. Male's wings make loud trill except briefly
after late summer molt. ● Deep bluish green above; large
tail. Male has rose-red gorget. Female and imm., see comparison with female rufous (Key 82). ♪ *Chirp*, given sharply.

Calliope Hummingbird *Stellula calliope* 3¼"
◄Fairly numerous; in alpine meadows and subalpine forest
clearings, esp. near streams. ● Small with short bill and
tail. Male has purple-red gorget with long plumes that can
be flared. Female and imm., see comparison with female
rufous (Key 82). ♪ *Tik*, given very softly.

Anna's Hummingbird *Calypte anna* 4"
Fairly numerous and widespread from lowland gardens to
◄mountains and, esp. in winter, deserts. ● Large, bulky.
Male has rose-red crown, flared gorget. Female and imm.
dirty gray below, often with red patch near center of throat.
♪ *Tzip*, given sharply, or explosive *tzip, tzip, tzip*.

Costa's Hummingbird *Calypte costae* 3½"
Fairly numerous in arid areas, chaparral. Typically flies
in high arc between stands of flowers. ● Male has violet
crown, flared gorget. Female and imm. usually clean-
◄throated with short tail, faint mask. ♪ *Tik*, high-pitched.

Blue-throated
Hummingbird ♀

♂

Magnificent Hummingbird

♀

♂

Violet-crowned
Hummingbird

♀

♂

Plain-capped
Starthroat

Lucifer
Hummingbird

A number of tropical hummingbirds have strayed into the southern US, and a few regularly nest there. Most are seen either in the mountains of southeastern Arizona and southwestern New Mexico or in the Big Bend area of Texas, but sightings are increasingly widespread.

Blue-throated Hummingbird *Lampornis clemenciae* 5" Numerous near canyon streams, feeders in AZ, NM, TX. ● Large with white eyebrow, whisker stripe. Big, blackish tail with white corners. Male has blue gorget. ♪ *Seek,* high-pitched, loud.

Magnificent Hummingbird *Eugenes fulgens* 5¼" Fairly numerous in AZ mountains; rare in NM, TX. ● Large with long bill, flat head, big tail. Male dark overall with purple crown, green throat. Female similar to female blue-throated; note greenish tail with small gray corners. ♪ *Chirp,* loud and musical.

Violet-crowned Hummingbird *Amazilia violiceps* 4½" Scarce in AZ, NM. ● Red bill with black tip. Pure white below, violet crown. Female's crown duller.

Plain-capped Starthroat *Heliomaster constantii* 5" Recorded in AZ. ● Long bill, small red gorget bordered by white stripe, white flank spots.

Broad-billed Hummingbird ♀

White-eared Hummingbird

♀ ♂

Buff-bellied Hummingbird

Berylline Hummingbird

Green Violet-ear

♀ ♂

♀ ♂

Cuban Emerald

Bahama Woodstar

Lucifer Hummingbird *Calothorax lucifer* 3½" Scarce and local in TX at agave plants. Rare but annual in AZ, NM. • Curved bill. Male has flared purple gorget; deeply forked black tail usually held closed, appearing pointed.

Broad-billed Hummingbird *Cynanthus latirostris* 3¾" Numerous in AZ, NM; scarce in TX. • Red bill, dark tip. Male dark green (can look black); blue throat, breast. Female duller above, gray below; small gray tail corners. ♪ *Jedit,* given loudly.

White-eared Hummingbird *Hylocharis leucotis* 3¾" Annual in AZ. • Red bill, black tip. Broad white stripe behind eye, bordered below in black. Male has purple forehead and chin. ♪ *Chik,* repeated loudly.

Buff-bellied Hummingbird *Amazilia yucatanensis* 4½" Fairly numerous in lower Rio Grande delta, TX. • Red bill, black tip. Back and foreparts green, belly buff.

Berylline Hummingbird *Amazilia beryllina* 4¼" Rare visitor in AZ. • Red on base of lower mandible. Green extends farther down front, less down back than in buff-bellied hummingbird; belly darker; wings and tail chestnut. Female duller below.

Green Violet-ear *Colibri thalassinus* 4¾" Recorded in TX. • Green overall with violet patches on face and breast; tail bluish. Female duller.

Bahama Woodstar *Calliphlox evelynae* 3½" W. Indian. Females and imm. recorded in s. FL. • Female has rusty base of outer tail feathers, buff tips.

Cuban Emerald *Chlorostibon ricordii* 4½" W. Indian. Recorded in s. FL. • Forked black tail. Male green below, female grayish.

crop

glandular
stomach

gizzard

intestine

Food is held in the crop, chemically digested in the glandular stomach, and pulverized in the gizzard.

Ground-walkers

CONSULTANT **EIRIK BLOM**
ILLUSTRATOR **HANS PEETERS**

In North America two groups of birds forage primarily by walking on the ground, browsing on seeds, grains, buds, or other vegetation: doves and gallinaceous birds, which include pheasants, turkeys, grouse, and quail. The greater roadrunner also qualifies as a ground-walker, although it might better be classed alone as a ground-runner since it runs down small animals.

The lifestyle of the ground-walkers has resulted in a distinctive fleshy body with strong legs and a muscular breast. The breast development is needed to power the broad, paddle-like wings. It takes much breast muscle to accelerate a large grouse into rapid flight so as to escape a predator's surprise attack. Some species, like the pigeons and some grouse, are also capable of sustained flight (and have dark breast flesh instead of white).

As everyone learns as a child, birds don't have teeth. If they did, the center of gravity of most would be shifted so far forward that they couldn't fly. In order to digest grains or other hard foods, ground-walkers grind them in a gizzard, near the bird's center of gravity. Grit (small pebbles or sand) is swallowed to aid the process, which is powerful enough to pulverize glass. Ground-walkers also have a storage pouch in the digestive channel known as a crop, which allows them to feed in a hurry and digest at their leisure. Hawks, owls, and many other birds also have gizzards and crops.

Many of the ground-walkers are raised domestically, including the various chickens, all decended from the red jungle fowl of Asia. Many others are hunted as game birds. Gallinaceous birds have responded to predation by coming to quick maturity and by raising large broods. Their populations support a wide range of wildlife, including owls and hawks. Even in areas that are heavily hunted, most game bird losses are to other wildlife.

Except during the nesting season, most gallinaceous birds live in coveys. The human intruder who unexpectedly flushes a covey is in for a heart-racing surprise. Birds burst into flight, their short wings beating rapidly and loudly. The flights are low, fast, and usually end in the nearest cover. Such flight is usually a last resort; most birds prefer to escape by running or to remain undetected by freezing. The notable exceptions are the blue grouse and the spruce grouse, which have both earned the name "fool hen" because of the ease with which they can be approached.

Males of many species have elaborate and impressive courtship displays similar to the well-known displays of tom turkeys. Some gather at traditional sites, called leks, to display for the females. Booming sounds produced by special air sacs or by wing-beating accompany the strutting displays.

Eye combs enlarge and become vivid during display.

Pigeons and doves (the only difference is in the name) walk on short legs with heads bobbing characteristically back and forth. They do not run from danger as the gallinaceous birds often do, but are capable of swift, sustained flight. When not feeding,

they are often seen perched high on wires or in trees. Some, like the band-tailed pigeon, feed in trees as well, but most North American pigeons use their short legs to scamper on the ground for food. Their diet is similar to that of the gallinaceous birds and so is their digestive system. Their crops are even more highly developed and produce "milk" during the nesting season.

Doves feed their squabs milk from their crops.

The significance of these birds as game has had great impact on their ranges and populations. The passenger pigeon and "heath hen" became extinct due at least partly to unregulated hunting in the 19th century. Others, like the band-tailed pigeon and the wild turkey, barely survived that period. Wild turkeys have been reintroduced over much of their historical range and far beyond. Exotic game birds have also been introduced, but of 70 different exotics released, only the ring-necked pheasant, gray partridge, and chukar have established themselves widely.

Human impact on their habitat also greatly affects many of these birds. While city pigeons (rock doves) and mourning doves spread with us wherever we settle, prairie grouse are disappearing with the grasslands. Croplands, mostly of wheat and corn used for feeding cattle, now stretch from the Mississippi to the Rockies. States in the heart of the prairie, like Iowa, retain less than one percent of their native grassland, which is why prairie-chickens have been absent from Iowa since 1984. Overgrazing by livestock has destroyed much habitat and resulted in a continuous decline in the numbers of scaled quail and "Attwater's prairie-chicken."

display
(western form)

Himalayan
Snowcock

Wild Turkey

♂

♀

Wild turkeys are dark with a mostly bronze iridescence. They are slimmer than their domesticated cousins. Male pheasants are also iridescent, but the color varies; note the long tail. The female's tail is shorter, although still a very good mark. The fabled greater roadrunner of the Southwest is indeed comic — racing and then stopping abruptly, looking about and pumping its tail.

◀**Wild Turkey** *Meleagris gallopavo* 48"
Once numerous in open woodlands of South and East, then extirpated or hunted to scarcity in most areas. Now widely established, fairly numerous; managed as game bird in all 48 adjacent states. Roosts in trees. Shy. ● Large with bronze sheen, naked head. Male larger, brighter, with colorful wattles, more prominent beard (breast plume). Some western males have white-tipped tails. ♩ Gobbling.

Plain Chachalaca

Greater
Roadrunner

Ring-necked Pheasant

♀   ♂

◀**Ring-necked Pheasant** *Phasianus colchicus* 32"
Introduced from Asia. Numbers fluctuate; declining in East.
On grasslands, grainfields, nearby brush and woodland
edges. Takes waste grain when available. Alone or in small
groups, often a male with harem. Very wary. ● Long, pointed
tail. Males iridescent, but colors variable; most common form
shown. Others can lack neck ring, have white wings or green
bodies; red eye patch always present. Female smaller, mottled brown. Old females become male-like.

◀**Greater Roadrunner** *Geococcyx californianus* 24"
Fairly numerous, usually in pairs, in brush, grass, open
woods, esp. arid brush. Runs down small animals. ● Large
bill, crest; long tail often cocked. ♪ Dove-like cooing.

Himalayan Snowcock *Tetraogallus himalayensis* 28" Asian. Introduced and
established in Ruby Mtns., NV, and Wallowa Mtns., OR.

Plain Chachalaca *Ortalis vetula* 22" Tropical. Locally common in flocks in lower
Rio Grande Valley. Introduced on Sapelo I., GA. Walks, but primarily arboreal.

Sharp-tailed Grouse

display

Sage Grouse

♂

♀

♀

Sage grouse displaying on a lek

The sage grouse is a pheasant-sized bird of the western sagebrush. Males have a distinctive black throat and bib and a large white ruff. Females resemble female pheasants, but they are seldom confused because habitats differ and the sage grouse has a black belly. Sharp-tailed grouse and prairie-chickens are more often confused with each other. The sharp-tailed is scaled below, not barred, and has a pointed tail with much white in it. Prairie-chickens have dark, rounded tails and are told from each other by range. Males of all species return each year to the same areas, or leks, to court mates.

historical range

◀**Sharp-tailed Grouse** *Tympanuchus phasianellus* 17"
Fairly numerous and widespread in open areas from northern bogs and woodland margins to grass plains and sagebrush. Local. Shy. Roosts under snow in winter; feeds in trees on twigs and buds. ● Tail pointed with white sides, white spots in wings. Mottled above, scalloped and spotted below; northern birds darker. Displaying males have yellow combs, purple air sacs.

greater
prairie-chicken

lesser prairie-chicken

display

sharp-tailed

prairie-chickens

♀   ♂

historical
range

historical range

◀Sage Grouse *Centrocercus urophasianus* 28"
Scarce, declining; in flocks in sagebrush. Sage provides cover and principal food. Wary. ● Large, with black belly, pointed tail. In flight, white wing linings contrast sharply with darker body. Male is twice bulk of female, has black throat and bib, white ruff. Displaying male has yellow air sacs.

Greater Prairie-Chicken *Tympanuchus cupido* 17"
◀Declining with loss of tall-grass prairie. Eastern race, the "heath hen," is extinct. Gulf Coast race, "Attwater's prairie-chicken," is endangered from predation and risks inherent in a small, isolated population; only 68 birds recorded in 1995, down from nearly 500 in 1990. Most widespread race now extirpated from Canada and much of former US range, but common enough to support hunting in several states. ● Boldly barred above and below. Male has black tail, long blackish neck plumes, yellow-orange air sacs (seen in courtship). Female has shorter plumes, barred tail.

◀Lesser Prairie-Chicken *Tympanuchus pallidicinctus* 16"
Scarce, local in shorter grassland habitat than greater prairie-chicken. ● Slightly smaller and paler than greater prairie-chicken; air sacs smaller, rounder, darker.

PRAIRIE GROUSE

86

Ruffed Grouse

gray form

red form

display

ruffed

♀ spruce

♂

♀

Spruce Grouse

A barred tail with a dark band near the tip is a reliable mark for ruffed grouse of either color. Tails and tail bands are less consistent in spruce and blue grouse, with sexes and regional forms having different features, but the gray underparts of both sexes of the blue grouse are always distinct from the black underparts of the male spruce grouse or the barred underparts of the female. Coastal blue grouse have yellow air sacs and are sometimes called "sooty grouse." Spruce grouse in the Rockies have white-tipped uppertail coverts and are often called "Franklin's grouse."

◀**Ruffed Grouse** *Bonasa umbellus* 17"
Fairly numerous but cyclical. Usually alone in open deciduous or mixed woods, nearby fields. Shy, but in winter feeds openly on twigs and buds in tops of trees, esp. aspen, poplar. Roosts under snow. ● Broad, dark subterminal band on finely barred gray (northern) or reddish (southern) tail. Band broken in center on females, young males. Dark erectile feathers on neck most prominent in male.

spruce grouse display

"Franklin's grouse"

blue grouse display

interior form

coastal form "sooty grouse"

♀ blue

Blue Grouse

♀

♂

◀**Spruce Grouse** *Dendragapus canadensis* 16"
Numerous in Arctic, scarcer to south; in conifers, esp. near burns. Alone or in small flocks. Feeds on needles in winter; usually seen in trees. In summer often browses on ground. Very tame. ● Small. Male has black throat and upper breast, crimson combs, dark tail with rufous terminal band. Female mottled gray to reddish brown above and on upper breast, barred black and white below; tail brown, variably barred rufous or tipped with white. "Franklin's grouse" lacks rufous tail band, has white tips on uppertail coverts.

coastal form, "sooty grouse," west of line

◀**Blue Grouse** *Dendragapus obscurus* 20"
Fairly numerous, alone or in small flocks. Winters in conifer thickets, feeding on needles. In open forest, alpine clearings, or grassland in summer, taking berries, buds, leaves, insects. Very tame. ● Male sooty gray (slightly paler in birds of interior). Yellow comb; red or orange at peak breeding. Female mottled gray-brown above and on upper breast (grayer in interior form); gray below. Dark gray tail; pale terminal band often broken with barring on center feathers in female, can be lacking or indistinct on birds of northern Rockies. Air sac dark in interior form, yellow in coastal form. ♪ Series of low hoots.

Gray Partridge

juv.

Gray Partridge

willow ptarmigan
Key 167

spring ♂

White-tailed Ptarmigan

♀

summer ♂

In winter white-tailed ptarmigan are easy to identify – the plumage is completely white. But in spring they begin a molting sequence that alters their appearance almost continuously throughout summer and fall. At all times the wings and tail remain white, although long uppertail coverts can conceal the tail. The willow and rock ptarmigan (Key 167) have black tails. The gray partridge and chukar are introduced species that suggest our native quail with their bold, distinctive plumage patterns and flocking habits. Shapes are also similar, but quail are smaller.

◄**Gray Partridge** *Perdix perdix* 13"
Introduced European game bird; widely established. Fairly numerous in coveys on grassland, farmland but shy, local. Feeds heavily in stubble fields in winter. ● Tan to orange face, gray breast, chestnut belly patch (often U-shaped). Female often has smaller, duller face patch; can lack belly patch. Shows chestnut in outer tail feathers in flight. Juv. brown with dark streaks, spots. ♪♪ *Keé-uk*, hoarse call.

Chukar

juv.

white-tailed ptarmigan

late fall
(molting to winter)

◄**White-tailed Ptarmigan** *Lagopus leucurus* 12"
Fairly numerous in North; scarce south of Canada. Small
population introduced and established in high Sierras, CA.
In summer above timberline on alpine meadows, slopes,
and near snowfields. At sheltered basins in winter, often
well below timberline. Browses on ground vegetation. Often
roosts under snow in winter. Unwary, but well camouflaged.
● White in winter, with black bill and eye, orange to crimson
eye combs; feet and toes heavily feathered; sexes alike. In
spring male's upperparts are heavily barred with brown and
with finer bars of buff and black; underparts remain white.
Female molts later than male, is blacker above with fine
yellow barring, and has barred underparts. In summer both
sexes molt again, males first, to finely patterned, cinnamon-
tinged upperparts that soon fade in bright alpine sun.

◄**Chukar** *Alectoris chukar* 14"
Introduced European partridge. Fairly numerous but local in
coveys on open, arid mountains. Wary. ● Whitish throat
and cheek, outlined in black. Red bill, legs. Flanks barred
black and white. In flight shows chestnut in tail. Juv. brown
with barring and spotting, pink legs. ♪ *Chuck*, given in loud,
rapid, staccato series.

"masked" race

Bobwhite

huddling for warmth

Scaled Quail

California Quail

♂ ♀

California and Gambel's are the only quail that are likely to be confused. Both have handsome, curved head plumes and similar head patterns, but their belly markings are distinctive. Ranges of the two species are also largely separate. Except when nesting, quail live in coveys, scampering warily in or near ground cover. They will flush, but only when they can't run from danger. Males call in spring and summer and are more easily heard than seen.

◀**Bobwhite** (Northern) *Colinus virginianus* 10"
Numerous in tall grass, brush, open woodlands, farmlands. Seriously declining in most of East. Introduced in Northwest. Absent from northern range after severe winters. "Masked bobwhite" extirpated from AZ about 1900 due to cattle grazing; reintroduction from Mexico being attempted in se. AZ. ● Reddish brown with white throat and eyebrow on male, buff on female. "Masked bobwhite" has black face, throat; white eyeline. ♪♪ *Bob-white*, whistled.

◀**Scaled Quail** *Callipepla squamata* 10"
Fairly numerous, declining; in arid scrub, nearby grasslands. Introduced in WA, NV. ● White-tipped crest, buff on female. Scaled breast and belly. Male in s. TX has chestnut belly patch as in California quail. ♪♪ *Pe-cos*, repeated, nasal call.

hiding by "freezing"

♀ ♂

Montezuma Quail

Mountain Quail

Gambel's Quail

◄**California Quail** *Callipepla californica* 10"
Numerous, widespread from wet coastal brush to dry chaparral, suburban parks and gardens. Roosts in trees or brush.
● Male has black plume, bold head pattern, scaled belly.
Female and young birds have shorter plumes, lack distinct
head pattern of males. Some coastal birds browner than
shown. ♫ *Chi-ca-go,* loud call.

◄**Gambel's Quail** *Callipepla gambelii* 11"
Numerous in desert scrub, nearby open woodland, esp.
near water. ● Like California but unscaled belly; male has
black, not buff, forehead and black spot on pale belly.
♫ *Chi-ca-go-go,* higher than in California, usually 4 notes.

Mountain Quail *Oreortyx pictus* 11"
Numerous in summer on mountain slopes to 10,000 ft.;
◄lower altitudes in winter. In dense brush, esp. regrowth after
fire, logging. ● Long head plumes (2 appear as 1). Chestnut
throat and flanks with black-and-white markings. Female a
bit duller, shorter plumes. ♫ *Kee-ark,* loud, whistled call.

Montezuma Quail *Cyrtonyx montezumae* 9"
Scarce on pine-oak slopes with grass undergrowth; to
9,000 ft. Often digs for bulbs, tubers. Freezes in crouch
◄rather than running from danger. ● Male has clown-like
face markings, rounded brown crest, very short tail. Female
mottled brown with traces of male's face pattern. ♫ Soft
whinny; also mellow hoot.

QUAIL

89

Band-tailed Pigeon

Mourning Dove

White-winged Dove

At first glance, band-tailed pigeons resemble some of our darker city pigeons, or rock doves. But note the gray terminal band on the tail and the yellow legs and base of the bill. The mourning dove's best mark is its pointed tail. White wing patches mark the white-winged dove. There is much variety in rock dove plumage due to its history of being selectively bred for exotic variations. The ancestral form, still commonly seen, is in the foreground.

◀**Band-tailed Pigeon** *Columba fasciata* 14"
Numerous in woodlands, esp. oak (coastal) or pine (inland); usually in flocks. Shy, but adapting to parks, suburbs. Declining in Northwest. Often feeds in trees, taking seeds, fruit, acorns. ● Gray tail band, yellow feet, black-tipped yellow bill. White collar may be absent on female, imm. Distant flocks distinguished from rock doves by uniform appearance. ♪ *Whoo-whooo,* low cooing.

◀**Mourning Dove** *Zenaida macroura* 12"
Widespread except in Arctic and closed forest. Abundant and increasing near farms, suburbs. Seen singly, in pairs, or in flocks. Flight swift, darting, with whistling sound. ● Tapered tail shows white edges in flight. Female slightly duller, juv. dullest. ♪ *Woo-oó, woo-woo-woo,* mournful call.

◀**White-winged Dove** *Zenaida asiatica* 12"
Numerous, widespread from cactus desert to suburbs, esp.

Red-billed Pigeon

White-crowned Pigeon

White-tipped Dove

Eurasian Collared Dove

Spotted Dove

Zenaida Dove

typical color variations

Rock Dove

mesquite brush; alone or in flocks, often with mourning doves. Feeds frequently on cactus fruit. Introduced in FL.
● White patches in wings and tail. Female slightly duller.
♪ *Who-cooks-for-you?* Cooing, repeated with variations.

◀**Rock Dove** *Columba livia* 12"
The abundant pigeon of cities and farms, feeding on handouts, spillage. Native to rocky cliffs of Eurasia. Has been domesticated for over 5,000 yrs., introduced nearly worldwide. ● Ancestral form gray with dark foreparts, black tail band and wing stripes, white rump. ♪ Soft cooing.

Red-billed Pigeon *Columba flavirostris* 14" Tropical. Scarce in summer, rare in winter on branches in woods along lower Rio Grande. ● Often appears all dark.

White-crowned Pigeon *Columba leucocephala* 13" Caribbean. Scarce, declining in FL Keys, nearby mainland. ● Crown gray in female, lacking in imm.

White-tipped Dove *Leptotila verreauxi* 12" Tropical. Locally numerous in brushy woods along lower Rio Grande. Shy. ● White corners on blunt tail.

Eurasian Collared Dove *Streptopelia decaocto* 11" Eurasian. Established in FL in 1980s, now spreading into Southeast. Ringed turtle-doves, popular cage birds, are similar and escapes can be found. ● Black collar. ♪ *Coo-coó-coo*, plain, loud cooing, unlike rolling or bubbling cooing of the ringed turtle-dove.

Spotted Dove *Streptopelia chinensis* 12" Asian. Introduced in 1900s, now numerous in coastal CA from Santa Barbara to San Diego. ● Lacks wing markings of mourning dove, tail more rounded. Spotted neck lacking in imm.

Zenaida Dove *Zenaida aurita* 10" Caribbean. Once nested on FL Keys, now seldom recorded. ● Similar to mourning dove but blunt tail, white-tipped secondaries.

The Inca dove is about the same body size as the common ground-dove but has a much longer tail with white edgings. Also note the scaly-looking upperparts of the Inca dove. Both birds fly swiftly, flashing bright rufous wings.

◀**Inca Dove** *Columbina inca* 8"
Fairly numerous in parks, suburbs, farmlands; less so in desert scrub. Tame. ● Gray with scaled breast and back. Long, white-edged tail; rufous primaries. Sexes nearly alike, but male has pink blush on chest. ♪ *Coo-coo*, mournful 2-syllable call given repeatedly.

◀**Common Ground-Dove** *Columbina passerina* 6½"
Fairly numerous but local, seriously declining; in open or brushy areas, esp. farmlands, roadsides. Secretive in wild, but usually tame near civilization. ● Plain gray back, scaled breast. Short tail, rufous primaries. Red bill, black tip. Male pink below, bluish crown; female duller. ♪ *Coo-oo*, repeated call, rising in pitch at end.

Ruddy Ground-Dove *Columbina talpacoti* 7" Tropical. Recorded near Mexican border from CA to TX. ● Lacks scaling on breast.

Key West Quail-Dove *Geotrygon chrysia* 12" W. Indian. Several recent records; all in extreme s. FL.

Ruddy Quail-Dove *Geotrygon montana* 9½" Tropical. Several records on FL Keys, Dry Tortugas; one on extreme s. mainland FL.

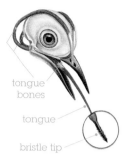

tongue
bones

tongue

bristle tip

The long tongue is supported by bones that extend over the skull and attach in the nostril.

Tree-climbers

CONSULTANT **KIMBALL GARRETT**
ILLUSTRATOR **DOUG PRATT**

Woodpeckers, nuthatches, and creepers all climb trees and search for bugs in the bark. Woodpeckers use their heavy, sharp bills to hammer and chisel beneath the bark, but it takes more than a sharp bill to succeed. Powerful neck muscles drive the blows, and a thick but spongy skull helps absorb the shock, protecting the brain. The long tongue is often used to probe for grubs in deep tunnels. Woodpeckers have sharp, curved claws for clinging to a tree, and most have feet in which two toes point forward and two back, unlike the more typical three-forward/one-back arrangement. The central pair of tail feathers is stiff and used to prop up the bird as it hammers.

Few woodpeckers depend solely on the insects they can collect from trees. Many also flycatch, consume fruits and seeds, or store nuts for winter. Some show up for suet at feeders. Flickers (which are woodpeckers) often forage on the ground for ants. Sapsuckers (also woodpeckers) drill pits in trees and then return to feed on the sap wells and any insects they have attracted.

Some woodpeckers travel in small flocks; most are seen singly or in pairs. Plumage patterns are usually complex and distinctive, with males often showing more red than females. "Drumming," resonant blows to the trunk of a tree, substitutes for song in most woodpeckers, although most also have many vocalizations.

Most woodpeckers rise with several wing beats, then fall with their wings briefly closed.

Nuthatches and creepers are smaller, more compact tree-climbers than woodpeckers. Nuthatches have such long toes that they can creep headfirst down a tree trunk. They probe in bark furrows and hammer with their strong, sharp bills. The brown creeper circles up a tree, probing with its slender, curved bill.

The loss of our ancient forests has greatly affected birds that depended on them. The ivory-billed woodpecker is extinct, and the red-cockaded is endangered; both species require mature or dying trees. Others, such as the downy woodpecker and northern flicker, have adapted well to orchards and shade trees.

Pileated Woodpecker

♀

♂

"red-shafted"

The pileated woodpecker, with its dramatic red crest, is the stereotypical woodpecker, and quite unlike any other bird. Flickers, on the other hand, often feed on the ground and may not even be recognized as woodpeckers. They flash white rumps and bright color in their wings and tail when they take flight. Each of the flickers has a similar pattern but a different combination of colors. Males have a black or red mustache that females lack.

◀**Pileated Woodpecker** *Dryocopus pileatus* 17"
Fairly numerous, widespread in forests. Most common in Southeast. Declined seriously, esp. in East, with logging of mature primeval forest. Has increased as 2nd-growth forest has matured. Favors carpenter ants; also takes other insects, acorns, fruit. ● Large red crest, black back, white neck stripe and underwing. Female lacks red mustache and forehead. Imm. grayer; red areas are orange. ♪ *Wuk-wuk-wuk-wuk*, loud, ringing call; rising and falling in pitch.

Gilded Flicker

"yellow-shafted"

♂

"yellow-shafted"
form

♀

Northern Flicker

♂

"red-shafted"
form

"yellow-shafted"

"red-shafted"

Northern Flicker *Colaptes auratus* 12"
Numerous, widespread in open woods. Feeds heavily on ants from ground; also feeds in trees like other woodpeckers. Once separated by open plains, forms now meet and interbreed because of extensive tree planting. Birds combining features of both forms (intergrades) occur well beyond zone of contact. • Both forms have brown backs with black barring, white rumps, spotted underparts with black breast crescents. Yellow-shafted form shows yellow in wings and undertail in flight; crown is gray with red nape patch; male has black mustache. Red-shafted form has salmon in wings and undertail; crown is brown with no nape patch; male has red mustache. ♪ *Wik-wik-wik-wik*, ringing call; higher than in pileated woodpecker. Also loud *Kleeer!*

Gilded Flicker *Colaptes chrysoides* 12"
Scarce in cactus desert and nearby riparian woodlands. Feeds like northern flicker. Hybridizes with northern flicker. • Much like red-shafted form of northern flicker but with yellow in wings. More black in tail than in northern, larger breast patch. ♪ Slightly higher than in northern flicker.

Downy and hairy woodpeckers are both usually recognized by their white backs. It can be difficult to estimate the overall size of an individual, but the difference in bill size is always easy to judge. Males have red patches on their hind crowns. Male three-toed and black-backed woodpeckers have yellow crowns and are separated from one another by their back colors. Even the darkest form of the three-toed shows some white on the back. The female three-toed is a bit like a female hairy woodpecker, but the back and face patterns differ, and the hairy lacks barred sides.

◀**Downy Woodpecker** *Picoides pubescens* 7"
Numerous, widespread from forests to suburbs. Active, tame. Enjoys suet at feeders in winter. Usually alone or in pairs; sometimes with mixed flocks of small birds in winter.
● Small size, small bill, white back. Females lack red hind-crown patch. Western forms may have very few white spots in wings and/or pale brownish gray replacing white on underparts, face. Most forms show black bars on white outer tail feathers. Juv. has reddish crown patch. ♪ *Pik*, given evenly; softer than in hairy woodpecker; also, descending whinny.

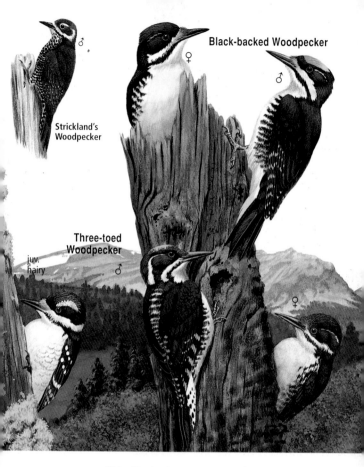

Black-backed Woodpecker ♀

Black-backed Woodpecker ♂

Strickland's
Woodpecker ♂

Three-toed
Woodpecker

juv.
hairy

♂

♀

◀**Hairy Woodpecker** *Picoides villosus* 9"
Fairly numerous; scarcer in backyards than downy woodpecker. Shy. ● White back, large bill. Sex, age, regional
variations similar to downy's. Outer tail feathers usually clear
white, but some forms show black spotting on outer tails,
sides, backs. ♪ *Peek!* Given sharply, sometimes in series.

Three-toed Woodpecker *Picoides tridactylus* 9"
Scarce. Forages by stripping bark from newly dead conifers
for insects, larvae. Wanders erratically in search of trees
◀killed by flood, fire, insect attack; can be numerous at such
sites. Tame. ● Black and white with barred sides. Back can
be solid white or variably barred black and white. Male has
yellow cap. Imm. also shows yellow cap; imm. female's disappears gradually. ♪ *Kik,* suggests downy woodpecker's call.

Black-backed Woodpecker *Picoides arcticus* 9½"
Scarce. Black-backed more common in East, three-toed in
West. Habits like three-toed's. ● Similar to three-toed, but
◀has solid black back, smaller white line behind eye. Both
species have three toes. ♪ *Kyik,* sharp, distinctive call.

Strickland's Woodpecker *Picoides stricklandi* 7½" Mexican.
Fairly numerous in oak or pine-oak forest of se. AZ. Shy.
● Brown; female lacks red on nape. ♪ Like call of hairy
woodpecker; also, *jee-jee-jee,* given in series.

White-headed Woodpecker

juv.

♀

♂

Acorn
Woodpecker

♀

♂

The red-headed is the only woodpecker in the East with a solid red head. The white-headed is the only woodpecker on the continent with a white head – or, more accurately, a white face, crown, and throat. The head pattern of the acorn woodpecker is more complicated, but the whitish eye-rings on a dark background give it a unique clown-like aspect. Lewis' woodpecker is also distinctive, lacking the characteristic crisp patterns of other woodpeckers. Its glossy back, gray collar, and straight, crow-like flight further distinguish it.

◀**White-headed Woodpecker** *Picoides albolarvatus* 9"
Fairly numerous, but shy, inconspicuous. Scarce in northern portion of range. In mountain conifers, esp. ponderosa, Jeffrey, sugar pines. Bores into pine cones and excavates seeds; probes tree bark for insects. ● Black with white head, white wing patches. Female lacks red on hind crown. Juv. duller black with variable red crown patch.
♪ *Peek-it!* Given sharply.

Red-headed
Woodpecker

juv.

♂

juv.

Lewis'
Woodpecker

◀**Red-headed Woodpecker** *Melanerpes erythrocephalus* 9"
Once numerous, now much scarcer over most of range due
to competition with starling for nest holes; rare in Northeast.
Widespread in open woods, scattered trees incl. suburbs.
Feeds in trees and on ground; often flycatches. ● Red
head; white wing patches, rump, underparts. Juv. brown
with white rump; dark bars on wing patches. Brown head
becomes red over 1st winter. ♪ *Kweeer,* given loudly.

◀**Acorn Woodpecker** *Melanerpes formicivorus* 9"
Numerous in oak, pine-oak woods; also parks, suburbs.
Usually in small, noisy groups. Drills holes in trunks, limbs
of selected trees for winter storage of acorns. ● Black-and-
white face with red crown and nape on male, red nape on
female. Throat yellowish. White rump and patches in primaries obvious in flight. ♪ *Ya-kup, ya-kup,* given harshly.

◀**Lewis' Woodpecker** *Melanerpes lewis* 11"
Scarce, local, seriously declining with loss of nest holes to
starling. In mountain conifers in summer, esp. ponderosa
pine. Winters in oaks, nut trees; often in flocks. Flycatches
heavily. Straight flight. ● Greenish black with gray collar, red
face, pink breast. Juv. lacks collar; patchy below, with brown
head and upperparts. ♪ *Churr,* given in series, in summer.

Gila Woodpecker ♀

Red-bellied Woodpecker ♂

♂

♀

♂

Golden-fronted Woodpecker ♀

Black-and-white barring extends over the back *and* wings of these woodpeckers. For the most part, the three larger species have separate ranges and so do the three smaller ones. Head patterns are the best field marks where ranges overlap, although Nuttall's woodpecker must be compared carefully with the ladder-backed.

◀**Gila Woodpecker** *Melanerpes uropygialis* 9"
Scarce, noisy, conspicuous. Widespread from cactus deserts and woodlands to city parks. Habits like red-bellied woodpecker's. ● Tan head and underparts; male has round red cap. Wing patches like red-bellied's. ♪ Like red-bellied's.

◀**Golden-fronted Woodpecker** *Melanerpes aurifrons* 9½"
Scarce, noisy, conspicuous. In woodlands, orchards, suburbs. Habits like red-bellied woodpecker's. ● Gold on nape and above bill; male has round red cap. Wing patches like red-bellied's, but lower rump unbarred. ♪ Like red-bellied's.

Red-bellied Woodpecker *Melanerpes carolinus* 9"
Numerous, noisy, conspicuous. Widespread in wooded areas incl. parks, suburbs. Forages in trees and on ground;

Red-cockaded
Woodpecker

Ladder-
backed
Woodpecker

♀

♂

♀

Nuttall's
Woodpecker

♂

◀ often flycatches. ● Red nape, extending over top of head in
male. White wing patches, uppertail coverts. Red wash on
lower belly hard to see. ♪ *Churr,* soft, rolling call.

Ladder-backed Woodpecker *Picoides scalaris* 7"
Numerous, widespread in desert cactus, brush, woods,
towns. Forages in trees, shrubs, cactus, on ground. ● Off-
white face, underparts; narrow black cheek stripe, black side
◀ spots; male has red cap. No wing patch. ♪ *Pik!* Sharp call.

Nuttall's Woodpecker *Picoides nuttallii* 7½"
Fairly numerous, esp. in chaparral, oak, streamside trees.
● Like ladder-backed woodpecker but brighter white with
larger black area on cheek, upper back; male has black
◀ forehead. ♪ *Pid-it,* and rolling *prrt-prrrrr,* call.

Red-cockaded Woodpecker *Picoides borealis* 8½"
Rare, local, declining in open stands of pine. In small, vocal
colonies. Mature pines, usually with heartwood softened by
fungus, used for nest cavities but seldom present in com-
◀mercial forest. Birds drill into nest trees causing resin to flow
around nest cavity for security. ● Black head with large
white cheek, spotted sides. Tiny red cockade of male hard to
see. Juv. duller, variable red on crown. ♪ *Shripp,* raspy call.

Williamson's Sapsucker ♀ ♂

imm.

Yellow-bellied Sapsucker ♀ ♂

Sapsuckers have white rumps and, with the exception of the female Williamson's, distinctive white patches on their shoulders – not in the primaries, as in other woodpeckers. The female Williamson's is largely brown, like many young woodpeckers, but note her yellow belly and extensive brown barring. The other sapsuckers have separate ranges. The red nape is the best mark distinguishing red-naped from yellow-bellied sapsuckers. Red-breasted sapsuckers have an entirely red head, brightest in their northern range. Sapsuckers are wary. All drum with a distinctive broken rhythm: *brrrrrrp-rrp-rrp.*

◀**Williamson's Sapsucker** *Sphyrapicus thyroideus* 9"
Fairly numerous in summer in mountain conifers, aspens. In pine, pine-oak woods at lower elevations in winter.
● Both sexes have yellow belly, white rump. Male jet black with white face stripes, red throat (white in imm.). Female has brown head, brown barring on back, wings, sides, breast. Barring on breast often merges into large black spot.
♪ *Cheeur,* nasal, often in series.

southern form

juv.

Red-breasted Sapsucker

northern form

♀

Red-naped Sapsucker

♂

◀**Yellow-bellied Sapsucker** *Sphyrapicus varius* 8½"
Fairly numerous in summer in mixed forest, esp. with aspens. In open woods, suburbs, in winter. ● Red forehead, black-and-white face, yellowish belly. Male has red throat (female, white) framed in black. Yellowish-tinged back heavily barred with black but less than in red-naped sapsucker. Imm. remains brownish through 1st winter; has same white rump, shoulder patches as adult. ♪ *Cheer,* given nasally.

Red-naped Sapsucker *Sphyrapicus nuchalis* 8½"
◀Fairly numerous. Habitat like that of yellow-bellied sapsucker, but most are in mountains in summer. ● Similar to yellow-bellied. Red nape patch in both sexes. Male has red throat; female, red with white chin. Red on male's throat breaks black frame, spills onto white sides of neck. Back darker than in yellow-bellied, less pale color. Juv. like imm. yellow-bellied but attains adult plumage by 1st fall. ♪ Like yellow-bellied's.

◀**Red-breasted Sapsucker** *Sphyrapicus ruber* 8½"
Fairly numerous. Habitat like yellow-bellied sapsucker's. ● Red head, chest; lacking sharp outline of red-headed woodpecker (Key 94). Yellow belly. Juv. browner. Southern form has longer mustache; paler head, underparts, back spots. The two forms meet in s. OR. ♪ Like yellow-bellied's.

black-and-white warbler
Key 133

White-breasted Nuthatch

♀

♂

♂

Red-breasted Nuthatch

Nuthatches are the only tree-climbers so agile that they can creep *down* a tree trunk. Presumably they find morsels that upward-climbers miss. The smaller nuthatches also feed frequently on insects at the tips of small branches and on seeds from pine cones. All nuthatches can be very tame, and all are compact, with stubby tails and blue-gray backs. The white-breasted nuthatch has a rufous tinge on its lower parts but much less than the red-breasted has. Pygmy and brown-headed nuthatches are very similar but have different ranges and cap colors. Brown creepers blend so well into a background of bark that they are usually first noticed when they fly from one tree trunk to another. In winter, nuthatches and creepers are often seen feeding with mixed flocks of small songbirds.

◀**White-breasted Nuthatch** *Sitta carolinensis* 6"
Numerous and widespread in large trees from forest to sub-urbs, esp. mature, open, deciduous forest. Usually paired, sometimes in mixed flocks. Feeds heavily on insects; also takes seeds, nuts, suet from feeders in winter. ● Black cap (grayish in some females), white face and underparts. Variable rusty tinge on sides and undertail coverts.
♪ *Yank*, nasal call; rapid *eh-eh-eh-eh* in western interior.

Pygmy Nuthatch

Brown-headed Nuthatch

Brown Creeper

◀**Red-breasted Nuthatch** *Sitta canadensis* 4½"
Numerous in conifers. Pries seeds from cones, also takes insects from bark. Irrupts south in large numbers in winters when cone crop fails. ● Black crown, white eyebrow, black eyeline, rusty underparts; female paler. ♪ *Nyak, nyak*, higher-pitched, more nasal than in white-breasted nuthatch.

Brown-headed Nuthatch *Sitta pusilla* 4½"
◀Fairly numerous but local in open pine or mixed pine and deciduous forest. In small flocks except when nesting. Feeds like pygmy nuthatch. ● Like pygmy but slightly larger with brown cap. ♪ Twittering notes, more nasal than in pygmy.

Brown Creeper *Certhia americana* 5"
◀Fairly numerous but irregular in winter. Often overlooked; can appear on trunk of any tree, esp. mature ones. Flies from top of one trunk to base of another and spirals upward, probing for insects. Usually alone, sometimes in pairs; often in mixed flocks in winter. ● Cryptic pattern of brown, black, and white above; dull white below. Curved bill; long, stiff tail. ♪ *Tssit*, high, hissing note; song a seesaw series of high, thin notes.

Pygmy Nuthatch *Sitta pygmaea* 4¼"
◀Fairly numerous but local in mountain pine forest, esp. ponderosa pines. In small, twittering flocks; often in tops of pines except when nesting. Feeds on pine seeds, insects. ● Gray-brown cap, pale nape spot, dark eyeline. White below with creamy wash on breast. ♪ *Ti-di*, repeated high, piping notes.

NUTHATCHES / CREEPER

Bristles at the base of the bill help flycatchers capture bugs.

Flycatching bills

CONSULTANT **KENN KAUFMAN**
ILLUSTRATOR **JOHN DAWSON**

Flycatchers, waxwings, and shrikes all catch flying bugs in summer, and their broad bills make them especially proficient at it. The bills of flycatchers and waxwings are broad at the base, usually quite flat, and have a tiny hook at the tip. Shrikes have stouter, more strongly hooked bills for tackling larger prey, such as the songbirds and rodents they depend on for food in winter. Most flycatchers migrate to the tropics in fall, when the northern insect population collapses, but shrikes and waxwings winter in North America, where waxwings wander in flocks searching for fruit and berries.

Because flycatching is a solitary pursuit, flycatchers are usually seen singly, often at a favored spot where insects abound, such as beside a stream. They typically sit erect and still on an exposed perch, although some flick their wings or tails nervously while waiting for a passing insect. After darting out to capture a bug, they often return to their original perch to repeat the process. The solitary, motionless waiting is their best mark, because their broad bills are not obvious from the side. Many warblers and other small perchers flycatch occasionally – some quite often – but they seldom sit patiently and erect as true flycatchers do. Flycatchers also have large heads that seem even larger when they raise their crown feathers, as they do regularly.

Some flycatchers have benefited from human activities. On the treeless plains, kingbirds now use wires as perches. Phoebes nest on bridges and other man-made structures. But many of the larger flycatchers are beginning to decline as humans increasingly win the chemical war against the insects that birds feed their young.

EASTERN PHOEBE

WOOD-PEWEE

EMPIDONAX FLYCATCHER

Three different groups of small flycatchers are often confused. Tail-pumping is the best mark for the plain eastern phoebe. Wood-pewees have wing bars; empids have wing bars, and most have distinct eye-rings.

Northern Shrike

imm.

Loggerhead Shrike

shrike

juv.

mockingbird
Key 111

Often confused with a mockingbird, a shrike has different wing patches and a larger head, with a black mask and hooked bill. The shrikes' ranges overlap only in winter, when a few northern shrikes – mostly distinctive brownish young – visit loggerhead areas. Both shrikes are wary but hunt from open perches. They often store prey by impaling it on thorns, earning the nickname "butcher-birds."

◀**Northern Shrike** *Lanius excubitor* 10"
Scarce, unpredictable winter visitor from Arctic. Prefers open conifers in summer, esp. near bogs. ● Larger than loggerhead shrike with longer, more distinctly hooked bill; narrow black mask does not extend across forehead. Faint barring below. Imm. paler, more heavily barred, brownish until 1st spring. ♪ *Chek*, grating call, often repeated.

Loggerhead Shrike *Lanius ludovicianus* 9"
Seriously declining, becoming scarce; in open areas, esp.
◀rangeland. Flight as in northern shrike; low and undulating, swooping up to perch at end. ● Bill shorter than in northern shrike; mask extends across forehead. Juv. paler; fine barring disappears before 1st winter. ♪ Like northern's.

Phainopepla

♀ ♂

Great Kiskadee

Cedar Waxwing

Bohemian Waxwing

juv.

Although not a true waxwing, the phainopepla is closely related, with a similar crest and sleek plumage. Waxwings are so fastidiously smooth that marks such as crests and the yellow-tipped tail are hardly needed. Note the Bohemian waxwing's distinctive white wing stripe, rusty undertail coverts, and gray belly. Adult scissortailed flycatchers are unmistakable; young birds are best told by the contrast of the black wings and tail with the pale body.

◀**Phainopepla** *Phainopepla nitens* 7½"
Scarce, sometimes in small flocks, in various open habitats. Perches conspicuously. Flycatches in summer; also feeds heavily on berries, esp. mistletoe. ● Male glossy black with prominent crest; white wing patch seen in flight. Female and imm. gray with pale wing patch. ♪ *Wurp*, low, liquid call.

◀**Cedar Waxwing** *Bombycilla cedrorum* 7"
Numerous. Wanders in flocks most of year searching for fruit, berries, sap, flower petals. Feeds heavily on insects in summer. Tame. ● Sleek, brownish, crested. Yellow-tipped tail, black mask, white undertail coverts. Juv. streaked below. ♪ *Sssee-seee*, high-pitched, lisping call.

Sulphur-bellied Flycatcher

Rose-throated Becard

♂

♀

Fork-tailed Flycatcher

juv.

Scissor-tailed Flycatcher

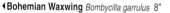

◄**Bohemian Waxwing** *Bombycilla garrulus* 8"
Numerous, but less so than cedar waxwing. Irrupts east in some winters. Habits as in cedar; a few sometimes flock with cedars. ● Larger than cedar waxwing with yellow-and-white wing markings, rusty undertail coverts. Juv. like juv. cedar but with wing markings of adult Bohemian, rusty undertail coverts. ♪ *Sreee*, repeated call; buzzier than in cedar.

Scissor-tailed Flycatcher *Tyrannus forficatus* 14"
Fairly numerous on plains, perching conspicuously. Tame.
◄Migrates in flocks. ● Pale gray or whitish with long, forked tail. Bright pink wing pits; pink wing linings, sides, lower underparts. Female duller, shorter tail. Juv. dullest, shortest tail, brownish back. ♪ *Kek*, given sharply.

Great Kiskadee *Pitangus sulphuratus* 10" Tropical. Numerous in s. TX. Catches insects, also fishes like kingfisher. ♪ *Kiss-me-dear!* Loud call; much noisy chatter.

Sulphur-bellied Flycatcher *Myiodynastes luteiventris* 8½" Tropical. Fairly numerous in se. AZ. Shy. ♪♪ *Squeez-zee!* Loud, high-pitched call. **Variegated Flycatcher** (*Empidonomus varius*) smaller with much smaller bill; several records in East.

Fork-tailed Flycatcher *Tyrannus savana* 15" Tropical. Rare in US, but wanders even to eastern Canada. ● Imm. lacks long tail but otherwise resembles adult.

Rose-throated Becard *Pachyramphus aglaiae* 7" Tropical. Rare, local along streams in summer in se. AZ lowlands, even rarer in lower Rio Grande Valley.

Eastern Kingbird

Gray Kingbird

The eastern kingbird is the only songbird in the East with a white-tipped tail. Gray kingbirds, which share the eastern's range in Florida, have plain tails, larger bills, and are grayer above. Tails are good marks for kingbirds in the West as well. Western and Cassin's kingbirds have black, square-tipped tails, which distinguish them from the flycatchers on Key 101 with rufous patches in their tails. The western kingbird's tail has narrow white edges; Cassin's has an obscure, dusky tip. Most kingbirds have hidden red crown patches.

◄**Eastern Kingbird** *Tyrannus tyrannus* 8½"
Numerous, conspicuous, in open areas, woodland edges; expanding westward, declining in East. Noisy, territorial, aggressive. ● Blue-black above with black on crown, side of face. White below with pale gray wash on breast. Tail black with white terminal band. Imm. has darker wash on breast.
♪ *Tzeet* or *kip*, given harshly, usually in a sputtering series.

◄**Gray Kingbird** *Tyrannus dominicensis* 9"
Numerous in FL Keys, esp. on wires. Local in mainland coastal mangroves. ● Gray above with dark ear patch; whitish below. Bill black, heavy; tail slightly notched.
♪ *Pe-chéer-ry*, given shrilly.

Couch's & Tropical
Kingbirds

Thick-billed
Kingbird

Cassin's Kingbird

Western Kingbird

◀Western Kingbird *Tyrannus verticalis* 9"
Numerous, widespread in open country. ● White outer webs on outer feathers of black, square-tipped tail can be worn or missing. Head, breast, back paler than in Cassin's, making greater contrast with dark wings and ear patch, less contrast with white throat. ♪ *Kip,* sharp call.

Cassin's Kingbird *Tyrannus vociferans* 9"
◀Fairly numerous in high open lands, woodland edges; CA birds in open coastal woodlands, grassy foothills. Usually noisier than western kingbird. ● Tail broader than in western kingbird, with dusky tip. Darker upperparts contrast more with well-defined white chin, less with dark ear patch than in western kingbird. ♪ *Che-bew,* rough, nasal call.

Couch's Kingbird *Tyrannus couchii* 9" Tropical. Fairly numerous, nesting in lower Rio Grande Valley. ● Like western but has notched, dusky tail, longer bill, darker ear patch; yellow extends onto breast. ♪♪ *Kip,* like western's; also *ka-breeer.*

Tropical Kingbird *Tyrannus melancholicus* 9" Tropical. Rare, local in summer in se. AZ lowlands, often along streams. Even rarer in s. TX. ● Almost identical to Couch's. ♪♪ Thin trills and twittering notes, differing from Couch's.

Thick-billed Kingbird *Tyrannus crassirostris* 9½" Tropical. Scarce in summer in se. AZ lowlands. ● Brown above with large black bill. ♪ *Puareet,* given loudly.

Loggerhead Kingbird *Tyrannus caudifasciatus* 9" (Not shown) W. Indian. Several records in s. FL. ● Like thick-billed kingbird. Some show pale tail tip.

KINGBIRDS

Ash-throated Flycatcher

brown-crested

great crested

ash-throated

UNDERSIDE OF TAILS

Great Crested Flycatcher

Myiarchus flycatcher

The flycatchers in the genus *Myiarchus* flash rufous in their wings. In the East, the great crested is the only *Myiarchus*. Over much of the West, the same is true for the ash-throated flycatcher. Both show rufous in their tails as well as wings. In the Southwest, where the closely related brown-crested and dusky-capped flycatchers are also possibilities, voice is the best mark. Pewees are drab, but the olive-sided flycatcher (a pewee group member) has a snappy vest formed by its dark sides and white breast. Greater pewees lack the vested look. Ranges and calls separate the small wood-pewees.

◀**Ash-throated Flycatcher** *Myiarchus cinerascens* 8"
Fairly numerous, widespread in open woodlands, saguaros.
● Smaller, paler than great crested flycatcher with much less contrast below; bill smaller, all dark. Rufous patch in tail does not extend to tip except on juv. ♪♪ *Prrt,* burry call; also *ka-dick* or *ka-wheer,* 2nd syllable accented.

Great Crested Flycatcher *Myiarchus crinitus* 8½"
◀Fairly numerous, widespread; noisy in open woodlands, shade trees; often unseen in canopy. ● Gray throat and breast, yellow lower underparts. Brown above with rufous in primaries and on entire inner web of tail feathers (narrow dark outer web). Lower mandible pale or horn-colored at base. Juv. paler below, redder tail than in adult.
♪♪ *Wheeep!* Loud, piercing call; also a rough *berg, berg.*

Dusky-capped Flycatcher

alder flycatcher
Key 103

Eastern & Western Wood-Pewees

Olive-sided Flycatcher

Greater Pewee

◄**Greater Pewee** *Contopus pertinax* 8"
Fairly numerous in high pine and pine-oak forest. ● Stout.
Olive-gray with slight crest, faint wing bars, orange lower
mandible. ♪ *Ho-say ma-ri-a,* whistled song; *pip-pip,* call.

Olive-sided Flycatcher *Contopus borealis* 7½"
◄Fairly numerous in northern and mountain conifers. Often
flycatches repeatedly from dead snag. ● Stout with large
head, short tail, faint wing bars. Vested look. Bill can show
orange at base of lower mandible. White tufts on back often
hidden. Imm. browner. ♪ *Whoops-three-beers,* whistled.

Eastern Wood-Pewee *Contopus sordidulus* 6"
Western Wood-Pewee *Contopus virens* 6"
Both species numerous, widespread in woods, often high
◄in canopy. ● Olive-gray above, grayish white below. White
wing bars, buff in imm. ♪♪ *Pheeer,* wheezy call (western).
Pee-wee or *pee-a-wee,* given plaintively (eastern).

overlap
↓
eastern

Brown-crested Flycatcher *Myiarchus tyrannulus* 9" (Not shown)
Fairly numerous, noisy; in saguaros, dry woodlands. ● Size
as in great crested, color as in ash-throated. Bill black. Dark
outer edge on tail extends onto inner web. ♪♪ *Whit,* call.

western

Dusky-capped Flycatcher *Myiarchus tuberculifer* 7" Tropical.
Fairly numerous in se. AZ canyons, esp. streamside. Often
gleans foliage while hovering. ● Like ash-throated but
smaller; rufous in wings, brown tail. ♪♪ *Pee-ur,* whistled.

brown-crested

La Sagra's Flycatcher *Myiarchus sagrae* 7½" (Not shown) W. Indian. Nearly
annual in s. FL. ● Like ash-throated, but often whitish below. ♪♪ *Oo-ee,* shrill.

Eastern Phoebe

juv.

♂ **Vermilion Flycatcher** ♀

imm. ♂

Tail-pumping is a good mark for these flycatchers, especially for separating the eastern phoebe from pewees (Key 101) and empids (Key 103). A male vermilion flycatcher is so bright that its tail-pumping is unimportant, but it is a helpful mark in the plainer females and young birds. Black phoebes look something like juncos, but their behavior is all flycatcher. Say's phoebe can suggest a female vermilion, but note Say's larger size, gray throat, and unstreaked underparts. All these flycatchers are tame and conspicuous, with an affinity for water or human habitation, or both.

◀**Eastern Phoebe** *Sayornis phoebe* 7"
Numerous, widespread; often nests under bridges, eaves. Some return each spring to same nest site. Has increased, expanded range since adapting to man-made nest sites.
● Gray-brown above, darkest on head, wings, tail; dull white below. In fall, briefly shows yellow wash below, olive tones above. Bill all-black. Juv. yellowish below, buff wing bars.
♪ *Fee-bee*, repeated, alternately rising and falling in pitch.

gray flycatcher
Key 103

Say's Phoebe

Black Phoebe

vermilion flycatcher juv.

◀**Vermilion Flycatcher** *Pyrocephalus rubinus* 6"
Fairly numerous along wooded stream edges and on agricultural lands near water. Often drops to ground to feed, quickly returning to a low perch. ● Adult male bright red with black upperparts, wings, tail. 1st- and 2nd-spring males slightly paler, more yellowish. Female and imm. whitish below with light streaking, gray-brown above, usually with distinct face mask. Belly and undertail coverts variable; females yellowish to salmon pink, imm. males brighter pink, juv. can show no color. ♪ *Pitsk,* given sharply.

◀**Black Phoebe** *Sayornis nigricans* 7"
Fairly numerous, widespread from woodlands to towns. Usually nests and remains resident near water. Often fly-catches from low perch, capturing insects close to ground. ● Black with white belly, undertail coverts, tail edge. Juv. browner with tawny wing bars. ♪ *Tsip,* given sharply.

◀**Say's Phoebe** *Sayornis saya* 7½"
Fairly numerous in open, arid habitat, often near buildings and stock tanks. Will perch on boulder when fence or bush not available. Active, tame. ● Gray-brown with contrasting black tail and tawny underparts. Juv. browner with tawny wing bars. ♪ *Pee-ur,* given plaintively.

Empidonax Flycatchers

typical fresh fall plumage

ruby-crowned kinglet Key 143

typical worn summer plumage

LOWER MANDIBLES AS SEEN FROM BELOW

PLUMAGES AS SEEN IN SPRING MIGRATION

Buff-breasted Flycatcher

Least Flycatcher

Pacific-slope & Cordilleran Flycatchers

A small, drab flycatcher with two whitish wing bars and a white eye-ring is a member of the genus *Empidonax*. Science currently recognizes 11 species, distinguished by differences in voice, nesting habits, and habitat. Unfortunately, empids usually sing only at the nesting grounds, and migrants can appear in any habitat, making species identification impossible at times. Most species are so alike in plumage that their color varies more due to molt and wear than from one species to another. Few birders can identify more than their local nesting species plus the gray flycatcher, which has a diagnostic tail-pumping behavior, and the buff-breasted flycatcher, which is smaller and distinctively browner than other empids.

To gain familiarity with nesting empids, first identify them by song and then study them minutely, using your field glasses almost like a microscope. Note the shape and prominence of the eye-

beardless-
tyrannulet
Key 142

least flycatcher's wing
in worn plumage

short primary
extension

Acadian flycatcher's
wing in fresh plumage

long primary
extension

**Hammond's
Flycatcher**

**Dusky
Flycatcher**

**Gray
Flycatcher**

**Yellow-bellied
Flycatcher**

**Acadian
Flycatcher**

**Alder & Willow
Flycatchers**

ring, the exact shade of the throat, the size and shape of the bill, and the color of the lower mandible. The primary extension – the distance the primaries extend beyond the rest of the wing – can be a useful mark, and it doesn't change appreciably with wear.

Plumage condition must be determined before body colors and wing bars have any meaning. Molts occur at different times for different species, and fresh or worn plumage, by itself, can be a good clue for migrating birds. Birds in fresh plumage look clean, their backs are rich in subtle tones, wing bars are broad and buff, and bellies are washed in yellow. With wear (or in strong, direct light) the plumage loses its radiance, upperparts become dull, and underparts lose even a hint of color.

A strong case must be made for any empid identification. *Probably* and *maybe* are important qualifiers for most sightings.

EMPIDONAX

◀ Hammond's Flycatcher *Empidonax hammondii* 5¼"

Numerous, usually in upper story of mature coniferous or mixed (esp. with aspens) forest; often at high altitude. Habitat partially overlaps those of dusky and Pacific-slope flycatchers. ● Small, straight-sided bill can be all dark below, usually dull pink or yellow at base. Eye-ring thicker behind eye. Long wings with long primary extension, short tail. Adults acquire full fresh plumage (juvs., fresh body plumage) before fall migration. Some, not all, have fresh body plumage in spring. When fresh, note gray head and throat contrasting with olive back. Belly can be bright yellow; gray on breast often extends to sides. Buff fall wing bars fade to white by spring. ♫ *Chi-pit...brrk...grrip!* Dry, rapid, double note followed by 2 rough, low-pitched notes, 2nd one rising. Can be given in any order or separately. Call a sharp *peep.*

◀ Dusky Flycatcher *Empidonax oberholseri* 5½"

Fairly numerous in brushy areas, esp. openings or edges of conifers, aspens. Usually below 2,000 ft. in North. Habitat partially overlaps those of Hammond's and gray flycatchers. ● Bill slightly longer than in Hammond's, more extensively pale below. Primary extension shorter than in Hammond's, tail a bit longer. Lores can be pale, giving spectacled look. Plumage color resembles that of Hammond's except in fall, when dusky migrates in worn plumage and molts on winter grounds. ♫ *Chirp...ggrreep...pweet.* Three notes as in Hammond's, but 1st note not distinctly 2-parted; 2nd rises at finish, 3rd uniquely clear and high-pitched. Call a dry *whit.*

◀ Gray Flycatcher *Empidonax wrightii* 5½"

Fairly numerous in semiarid lands, esp. sagebrush, piñon-juniper; less so in open pines, where it shares habitat with dusky flycatcher. Best known by habit of dipping tail down slowly, then quickly raising it. ● Fairly long, narrow, straight-sided bill; pale pink below with small dark tip. Short primary extension; long tail. Same molting pattern as dusky, but color paler than in dusky or Hammond's; eye-ring shows less contrast with pale face; throat nearly white. ♪ *Chu-wip...teeah.* Clear 2-syllable note, often repeated, followed by a high, thin note, often omitted. Call like dusky's.

◀ Buff-breasted Flycatcher *Empidonax fulvifrons* 5"

Scarce and local in open pine woods of se. AZ mountains. Shares habitat with cordilleran flycatcher. ● Tiny, brownish, with short tail, little or no peak to head. Eye-ring often pointed at rear. Whitish below with buff wash on breast sometimes disappearing by summer. Plumage usually pale and worn, but molts to fresh plumage just before fall migration. ♪ *Chee-bit,* 2nd note can be lower or higher, often followed by soft notes or a trill. Call a very short *pt.*

◀ Least Flycatcher *Empidonax minimus* 5¼"

Fairly numerous, widespread, but declining; in deciduous and mixed woods incl. parks, suburbs. Shares habitat with alder, willow, and Acadian flycatchers. ● Small with fairly large, nearly round head. Smallest-billed eastern species; orange-yellow lower mandible, darker at tip. Prominent, even eye-ring. Short primary extension. Fresh body plumage in spring migration, but can be incomplete, patchy-looking. Fall adults migrate early in pale, worn plumage. Juvs. follow with fresh body plumage, buff wing bars. ♫ *Che-beck´.* Call a thin *pit.*

Pacific-slope Flycatcher *Empidonax difficilis* 5½"

Fairly numerous in moist, shaded forests. Habitat overlaps

those of Hammond's and cordilleran flycatchers. ● Bill long, wide, convex-edged; yellow-orange to pinkish below. ◄Almond-shaped eye-ring, pointed behind eye, usually narrow or broken at top. Short primary extension, fairly long tail. Greener above, yellower below than other western empids. Distinctive yellow throat can be worn gray by fall migration. Molt occurs on winter grounds. ♪♪ *Tseweep…pttsik…tsip.* Like cordilleran's; variable but higher, squeakier than in other western empids. Call of male a rising, slurred note, *peweat!*

◄**Cordilleran Flycatcher** *Empidonax occidentalis* 5½"
Fairly numerous in mountain forests, esp. shady canyons. Habitat overlaps those of Hammond's and Pacific-slope flycatchers. ● Inseparable from Pacific-slope except by call note of male; separation of ranges not well understood. Both once known as "western flycatcher," a name still useful in identification. ♪♪ Male's call more strongly 2-noted, *pit-peet,* than in Pacific-slope male. Both females' calls a thin *tseet.*

◄**Yellow-bellied Flycatcher** *Empidonax flaviventris* 5½"
Fairly numerous in boreal conifers, esp. wet areas, bogs. Habitat does not overlap those of others. ● Much like "western" but range barely overlaps; eye-ring typically narrow, round. Juv. Acadian is only other eastern empid regularly showing yellow on throat. Fresh plumage of spring becomes dull by fall, can lack yellow throat. Adults molt on winter grounds. Juvs. migrate in fresh body plumage. ♪♪ *Che-bunk,* given evenly. Calls varied, musical, incl. a whistled *per-wee.*

◄**Acadian Flycatcher** *Empidonax virescens* 5¾"
Fairly numerous in mature deciduous forests, esp. bottomlands, swamps. Expanding range in Northeast. Only breeding empid in southern lowlands, but shares some habitats with least flycatcher. ● Large with large bill, long wings, long primary extension. Lower mandible pinkish yellow. Eye-ring usually narrow; can be faint as in alder and willow flycatchers. Fresh plumage in spring and fall migrations: greenish above from head to rump with buff wing bars. Faint yellow belly, faint olive breast, white throat. Adults worn, whitish below in midsummer. Juvs. bright: green above with buff edges on body feathers creating scalloped effect; yellow wash below often extends to throat. ♪♪ *Peet-sah,* given forcefully. Call a loud *peek!* like 1st note of song.

◄**Alder Flycatcher** *Empidonax alnorum* 5¾"
Fairly numerous in deciduous thickets, esp. wet areas with alder or willow trees. Habitat overlaps those of willow and least flycatchers. ● Large with large bill, long primary extension. Lower mandible yellowish pink, sometimes with dusky tip. Eye-ring narrow; can be conspicuous, but usually nearly absent. Spring migration in fairly fresh plumage; olive-gray above with gray on face and breast band contrasting with white throat (a very few may have yellow hints on throat); pale yellow belly. Adult plumage drab by fall migration; juv. only slightly brighter. Molts on winter grounds. ♪♪ *Rrree-bee´-a,* buzzy, 3rd note often inaudible. Call a flat *kep.*

◄**Willow Flycatcher** *Empidonax traillii* 5¾"
Fairly numerous, widespread in deciduous woods, thickets. Rare, declining in CA and Southwest. Habitat overlaps those of alder and least flycatchers. ● Like alder flycatcher (once lumped with alder as "Traill's flycatcher"). ♪♪ *Fitz´-be-yew,* buzzy as in alder but accent on 1st note, final notes often run together. Call a thick *whit!*

EMPIDONAX

Curved bills

CONSULTANT **EIRIK BLOM**
ILLUSTRATOR **JOHN DAWSON**

The cactus wren, like all wrens, has a curved bill.

A curved bill is the perfect foraging tool for three groups of birds. Wrens use their curved bills to probe for insects and spiders in weedy tangles, low branches, bark, and rock crevices. Thrashers use their bills like a hoe or rake, digging in the ground and raking through leaf litter for insects and other small creatures. Cuckoos favor hairy caterpillars and are common in woodlands at caterpillar outbreaks. Presumably a curved bill aids them in gleaning prey from anywhere on a round limb.

Birds of these three groups share other traits as well. None flock and most are secretive, seldom straying far from cover. Even the common suburban house wren and brown thrasher demand adequate cover. Because most are so retiring, they are frequently identified by voice. All are dedicated singers, and some sing year-round. Wrens have big, energetic voices for their small size, and female wrens occasionally sing also. They typically scold intruders furiously from the security of their thickets. Wrens are as inquisitive as they are bellicose, and bird calls or simple squeaking noises often coax them into view.

Brown thrashers fly fast, low, and straight from one thicket to another.

Thrashers are known for rich, varied songs that sometimes mimic those of other birds. Cuckoos' songs, on the other hand, are repetitive and monotonous. Thrashers and cuckoos are most often seen darting between patches of cover. Some western thrashers run for cover, but most species fly close to the ground. Cuckoos fly higher, but just as directly, from one stand of trees to another.

There is no significant sexual or seasonal variation in the plumage of the curved-bill birds, and young birds resemble adults.

Mangrove Cuckoo

juv.

Yellow-billed Cuckoo

yellow-billed

juv.

Black-billed Cuckoo

The cuckoos are elongated birds with long, spotted tails. The two widespread species are named for their bill color, but the large white tail spots and bright rufous primaries of the yellow-billed cuckoo are more easily seen. The red eye-ring of the black-billed cuckoo is a good mark for adults. Both species feed heavily on caterpillars and are often concealed by foliage.

◄**Yellow-billed Cuckoo** *Coccyzus americanus* 12"
Rare in West, seriously declining with loss of riparian habitat. Fairly numerous in East in dense thickets and 2nd-growth woodlands. ● Yellow on lower mandible, 6 long white tail spots, rufous primaries. Juv. has less distinct tail spots, may lack yellow on bill. ♪♪ *Kakakakaka-kow-kow-kow–kowp–kowp–kowp*, guttural call; starting fast, slowing at end.

◄**Black-billed Cuckoo** *Coccyzus erythropthalmus* 12"
Scarce. More northerly than yellow-billed, usually at higher elevations where ranges overlap. ● Black bill, small white spots on gray undertail, red eye-ring. Juv. has light eye-ring; may show some buff below and lack tail spots. ♪♪ *Cu-cu-cu* or *cu-cu-cu-cu*, repeated monotonously.

Mangrove Cuckoo *Coccyzus minor* 12" Rare, local in coastal mangroves of sw. FL. ● Buff belly, black ear patch. ♪♪ *Gawk*, guttural note; repeated in long, lazy series.

California Thrasher

Crissal Thrasher

Le Conte's Thrasher

California and crissal thrashers are much alike, with plain breasts and deeply curved bills. Luckily, ranges barely overlap. Le Conte's is much paler, with a contrasting blackish tail. Bendire's and the curve-billed thrasher have breast spots, although often obscure. Those on the curve-billed are usually large, mostly rounded, and often merge so that the breast looks mottled. Bendire's spots are small, pointed, and form fine streaks. The sure mark is Bendire's shorter, straighter bill with a pale base to the lower mandible.

◄**California Thrasher** *Toxostoma redivivum* 12"
Fairly numerous in brush, esp. chaparral. Runs; seldom flies. ● Long, curved bill. Chocolate-brown above with faint white eyebrow, flecks on ear. Tawny undertail coverts.
♪ Typical thrasher song: loud, long with clear and guttural notes, mimicked phrases; often repeated.

Crissal Thrasher *Toxostoma crissale* 12"
Numerous at lower elevations in thick desert vegetation, esp. streamside thickets, mesquite. ● Like California, but

mockingbird Key 111

juv.

Bendire's Thrasher

juv.

Curve-billed Thrasher

grayer above, paler eye, duskier malar stripe. Chestnut undertail coverts. ♪ More musical song than California's.

Le Conte's Thrasher *Toxostoma lecontei* 11"
Scarce, local in desert with thin vegetation, esp. saltbush, creosote bush. Runs rapidly, tail erect. ● Very pale with contrasting blackish tail. Long, curved bill. ♪ Typical song, see California. Calls include low, rising *ti-wup!* and *whit!*

Curve-billed Thrasher *Toxostoma curvirostre* 11"
Numerous; most common arid-land thrasher. Widespread, esp. in cactus, thorn scrub, suburbs. Flies, perches openly. Movements jerky and stiff compared to Bendire's. ● Long, black curved bill. Breast spots and white tail tips fade with wear. Can have thin white wing bars in Southwest. Juv. (Mar-July) has short bill like Bendire's but lacks pale base. ♪ Typical thrasher song. Common call a sharp *whit-wheet!*

Bendire's Thrasher *Toxostoma bendirei* 10"
Fairly numerous in open areas with scattered brush, cholla cactus. In winter, scarce and local in saltbush flats, suburbs, farmlands. ● Lower mandible straight, with pale base. Arrowhead-shaped breast spots. ♪♪ Song a continuous warble without guttural interruptions. Seldom calls.

Long-billed Thrasher

spotted thrushes
Key 119

**Brown
Thrasher**

juv.

Sage Thrasher

The widespread brown thrasher must be carefully compared with
the long-billed thrasher in Texas. Elsewhere its rufous upperparts
and heavily streaked underparts are distinctive. The sage thrasher,
the only other heavily streaked thrasher, is gray-brown and
shaped more like a robin than a thrasher. The cactus wren is so
large that the only identification problem is recognizing it as a
wren. The two smaller wrens are drawn to scale with those on Key
107. The white throat of the canyon wren contrasts sharply with
the darker body, while the black and buff tail bands of the rock
wren are obvious when the bird fans its tail, as it does constantly.

◀**Long-billed Thrasher** *Toxostoma longirostre* 12"
Numerous in mesquite thickets, bottomlands. Habits like
brown thrasher's. ● Like brown thrasher but darker back
and slightly grayer sides of face; bill longer, heavier, all-
black; eyes orange. ♪ Song like brown thrasher's.

◀**Brown Thrasher** *Toxostoma rufum* 12"
Numerous but declining. Widespread, skulks in underbrush,
esp. hedgerows. Sings from open perch. ● Bright rufous

Canyon Wren

Rock Wren

SCALE X 1.5
(TO MATCH KEY 107)

Cactus Wren

above, streaked with brown below; yellow eyes in adult.
♪ Song a long series of phrases, each paired or tripled.

◀**Sage Thrasher** *Oreoscoptes montanus* 8½"
Numerous in brushy growth, esp. sagebrush. Flicks tail
sideways. ● Gray-brown above, streaked below; white tail
corners. White wing bars quickly wear off. Juv. streaked
above. ♪ Musical series like mockingbird's.

◀**Cactus Wren** *Campylorhynchus brunneicapillus* 8½"
Fairly numerous but declining; in cactus desert. Feeds and
behaves much like thrashers. ● Streaked back and underparts, barred wings and tail, rufous crown, white eye stripe.
♪ *Chur-chur-chur*, low monotone series, given year-round.

◀**Rock Wren** *Salpinctes obsoletus* 6"
Fairly numerous in open, semi-arid, rocky areas, esp. cliff
faces, talus slopes. Bobs and calls as it forages. ● Buff and
black terminal tail bands, cinnamon rump, fine breast streaks.
Compare with Bewick's wren (Key 107). ♪ Song a series of
repeated couplets plus tinkling notes. Call a buzzy *tick-ear*.

◀**Canyon Wren** *Catherpes mexicanus* 5¾"
Fairly numerous but wary in shaded, rocky canyons. Bobs
like rock wren. ● Long bill, flat head. White throat and
breast contrast with dark belly, upperparts. ♪♪ Sweet
notes, slowing as they cascade down. Call a shrill *beet!*

THRASHERS / WRENS

106

Winter Wren

House Wren

Bewick's Wren

western

eastern

Both the house and winter wrens are small, nondescript birds with barring over much of their plumage. The winter wren is smaller and darker with a stubbier tail. Bewick's and Carolina wrens have prominent white eyebrows and long, fan-like tails. Bewick's constantly flicks its tail, flashing white tips. Note the buff underparts of the Carolina. The marsh wren also has a distinct white eyebrow, but its tail is short and its back is streaked, as in the sedge wren. Streaking extends onto the crown in the shorter-billed sedge wren. Both marsh and sedge wrens are skulkers and hard to see. Their habitats are different but often adjacent. Listen for their songs.

◀**Winter Wren** *Troglodytes troglodytes* 4"
Scarce; in cool, dense undergrowth of conifers in summer, esp. along streams and in boreal bogs. More widespread in migration and winter, entering parks, gardens. Very vocal, active, but furtive, hard to see. ● Tiny with very short tail. Flanks barred black and white. Indistinct whitish eyebrow.
♪ Song an energetic series of musical trills and warbles.

House Wren *Troglodytes aedon* 4¾"
◀Numerous. Originally in brush and undergrowth of woodlands; now common in suburbs, around farms. ● Brown to grayish brown, paler below with fine barring on flanks.
♪ Song a persistent, rapid chatter, rising then falling in pitch.

Marsh Wren

brown creeper
Key 97

Sedge Wren

Carolina Wren

◄**Bewick's Wren** *Thryomanes bewickii* 5¼"
Numerous in West. Once numerous over most of East, now
rare, facing extirpation east of the Mississippi. Widespread in
brush and undergrowth from woodlands to arid scrub; at
abandoned farmlands in East. Flicks and fans tail. ● White
eyebrow and tail tips; gray underparts. Western form duller.
♪ Song cheerful and musical, similar to that of song sparrow.

◄**Carolina Wren** *Thryothorus ludovicianus* 5½"
Numerous and widespread in brush and heavy undergrowth
from forests to parks, gardens; esp. in moist or swampy
areas. Declines in colder areas after severe winters.
● Rufous above, buff below, with white throat and eyebrow.
♪ *Tea-kettle, tea-kettle, tea-kettle;* loud, repetitious song.

◄**Sedge Wren** *Cistothorus platensis* 4½"
Scarce, local, declining. Now rarely breeds in southern part
of summer range. In wet meadows with scattered shrubs
and at freshwater marsh edges, often loosely colonial.
Shuns deep marsh and heavy cattails. ● Tiny, with short
bill. Streaked back and crown, with indistinct pale eyebrow.
Buff below. ♪♪ Song is 1-3 harsh notes followed by slow,
buzzy trill; often given at night.

◄**Marsh Wren** *Cistothorus palustris* 5"
Numerous. Favors tall marsh vegetation – cattails, sedges,
rushes – in fresh or brackish water. Nests in colonies.
● Blackish crown, white eyebrow on dark back.
Long bill. ♪ Song a reedy, guttural series of notes ending in
rasping chatter; often given on bright nights. Western birds
(may be separate species) have more complicated repertoire.

WRENS

107

Straight bills

CONSULTANT **EIRIK BLOM**
ILLUSTRATOR **JOHN DAWSON**

The bills of crows and most other corvids have bristle-like feathers at the base, covering the nostrils.

Most large birds with straight, elongated bills are omnivorous, feasting on whatever food is available. Their bills are slender enough to pry and probe, blunt enough to hammer, large and strong enough to rip and tear. Crows, ravens, and magpies scavenge if possible and have been victims of poisoned carcasses set out for coyotes. Many jays favor acorns, pine seeds, or other mast, which they bury for winter feeding. Seeds not recovered are an important component of forest regeneration.

All the birds in this section except for grackles and the mockingbird are closely related and known as corvids. They are long-lived and very intelligent, much wiser to man than others. They quickly learn the range of a gun and avoid humans where persecuted, as they routinely have been. Where left alone, many inhabit farmlands and suburbs. Some become bold and aggressive, chasing smaller species from feeders.

The intelligence of corvids has resulted in high social development. Flock members defend and contribute to their community by doing such tasks as serving sentry duty, assisting in raising the young, cooperating in food gathering, and mobbing intruders. They communicate with numerous vocalizations and can produce a wide range of sounds. Flocks range from small, loose bands of blue jays to "crows' congresses" (so called because of the crow's expressive vocalizing) in the tens of thousands. This clannish behavior has helped maintain numerous, similar-looking regional races in some species. Among crows, and jays in the genus *Aphelocoma*, there are birds classified as distinct species that are nearly identical.

Grackles, larger cousins of the blackbirds and orioles, feed omnivorously like the corvids and also live in noisy, conspicuous, and highly social flocks. Unlike the corvids, in which the sexes look alike, dull female grackles bear little resemblance to their much larger, iridescent mates.

Where man disrupts the environment, corvids typically increase. Disruption favors generalists, like most corvids, that are capable of adapting to changing habitats and sources of food. Their success comes at the expense of birds that are specialized and have their habitats destroyed.

Yellow-billed Magpie

Black-billed Magpie

The magpie's streaming, dark green, iridescent tail is as striking and diagnostic as its black-and-white plumage pattern. The two magpies are distinguished by range and bill color; the yellow-billed is found west of the Sierra Nevada; the black-billed, elsewhere.

◀**Yellow-billed Magpie** *Pica nuttalli* 17"
Fairly numerous in small flocks on agricultural and residential lands, nearby foothills. ● Slender with long, graduated tail; white wing patches; yellow bill and eye patch. Juv. has shorter tail, dark bill, lacks eye patch. ♪ *Mahg?* High, whining call. Also series of loud *chuck* or *wah* notes.

◀**Black-billed Magpie** *Pica pica* 19"
Numerous, widespread in small, noisy flocks over farmlands, open woodlands; esp. thickets, groves along watercourses. Occasionally wanders as far as East Coast. Can be shy or tame. ● Like yellow-billed but slightly larger and with black bill, no eye patch. ♪ As in yellow-billed.

common raven

Jackdaw

Chihuahuan raven

Common Raven

The common raven is much larger than a crow, with a heavier bill, longer, wedge-shaped tail, and shaggy-looking, pointed throat feathers. Voices and flight are also distinct. Crows usually fly straight with steady rowing strokes; ravens are raptor-like masters of the air and often soar. The Chihuahuan raven is near the size of a small common raven or a large crow and difficult to separate by eye.

◀**Common Raven** *Corvus corax* 24"
Numerous, widespread, from deserts to Arctic. Scarce but increasing in Appalachians. Typically in flocks except in nesting season. ● Large, with heavy bill, shaggy neck, wedge-shaped tail. ♪ *C-r-ock,* hoarse, low-pitched call, often with other higher notes.

Chihuahuan Raven *Corvus cryptoleucus* 19"
Fairly numerous in open grasslands, esp. yucca flats. Often in large flocks in winter at farms, dumps. ● Because of size ◀variations, usually told from common raven by range, flocking habits. Base of neck feathers white (gray in common); rarely visible. ♪ Like common's croak but slightly higher.

American, Fish & Northwestern
Crows

crow

Chihuahuan
Raven

◀**American Crow** *Corvus brachyrhynchos* 17"
Abundant and widespread except in deserts, mature forest,
Arctic. Has increased with settlements and is common near
them. Feeds singly or in flocks, heavily on grains in winter.
Sometimes roosts in huge flocks. ● Black overall, blunt
tail. ♪ *Caw* or *Cah*, loud call; singly or in series.

Fish Crow *Corvus ossifragus* 15"
Numerous on coast; also along rivers and at dumps, esp.
in winter. Often scavenges, preys on eggs and young in
◀heronries. ● Like American crow. ♪♪ *Eh-eh,* nasal, dou-
ble-noted call is diagnostic. (Juv. American crow makes
similar-sounding single-note call.)

Northwestern Crow *Corvus caurinus* 16"
Fairly numerous coastal scavenger. Widely, but not officially,
considered race of American crow. ● Not separable in field
◀from American crow. ♪ As in American crow.

Jackdaw (Eurasian) *Corvus monedula* 13" Eurasian. Records
in Northeast now suspected of being escapes.

Tamaulipas Crow *Corvus imparatus* 14" (Not shown) Mexican.
Since 1968, regular in winter near Brownsville, TX; esp. at
dump. ● Like American crow but slightly smaller; lower voice.

Blue Jay

Steller's Jay

juv.

Pinyon Jay

Not all jays are blue, but these are. The blue jay, with its striking crest, is the only jay in most of the East. Its western counterpart, Steller's jay, is much darker and is the only other jay with a crest. The pinyon jay is told by its overall blue plumage and short tail. The remaining birds, in the genus *Apbelocoma,* are much alike but have separate ranges for the most part. The intensity of their blues and grays varies regionally. The Mexican jay lacks the white throat and blue-gray breast band of other *Apbelocoma* species.

◄**Blue Jay** *Cyanocitta cristata* 11"
Numerous, expanding range in West. Originally in oak and pine forest, feeding on mast. Now also in suburban shade trees. Noisy, bold, usually in small, loose flocks except when nesting. ● Blue above with crest, white markings in wings and tail; dull gray below with black necklace. ♪ Varied raucous calls; often mimics other birds.

◄**Steller's Jay** *Cyanocitta stelleri* 11"
Numerous in small flocks in mountain and coastal conifers; pine-oak woods in Southwest. Feeds on mast. Bold. ● Dark blue with black or blackish brown head, foreparts. Streaks on eyebrow, chin, crest vary regionally from blue to white, often absent. ♪ Varied raucous notes, often in triplets.

Mexican Jay

Western & Island
Scrub-Jays

juv.

Florida Scrub-Jay

Pinyon Jay *Gymnorhinus cyanocephalus* 10"
Numerous in piñon-juniper highlands, also ponderosa pine in CA; farmlands, suburbs in winter. Often in large flocks. Shape, behavior, flight like small crow's. ● Sky blue, darkest on head. Gray throat with fine blue streaks. Long, spike-like bill, short tail. Imm. grayer. ♪ *Cah-ah,* piercing flight call.

Florida Scrub-Jay *Aphelocoma coerulescens* 11"
Fewer than 10,000 birds; in scrub oak habitat rapidly disappearing to development. Sometimes in groups. ● Eyebrow, forehead whiter than in western scrub-jay. ♪ As in western.

Western Scrub-Jay *Aphelocoma californica* 11"
Island Scrub-Jay *Aphelocoma insularis* 11"
Island scrub-jay only on Santa Cruz I., CA. Western scrub-jay numerous in brushy areas, esp. scrub oaks; also parks, suburbs. Often takes mast from ground. Can be shy. ● Slim, with long tail. Blue above with gray-brown back patch. White throat with blue-gray streaks and necklace, white eyebrow. Island scrub-jay and some western scrub-jays darker than shown; some interior birds paler. Juv. grayer than adult. ♪ Various harsh notes, often given in series.

Mexican Jay *Aphelocoma ultramarina* 11"
Scarce; in small flocks in pine-oak canyons. Behaves like a scrub-jay. ● Stouter with shorter tail, less color contrast than in scrub-jay. Lacks white on throat or eyebrow. Juv. of AZ race has yellow bill. ♪ *Wink?* Flight call, repeated.

Brown Jay

sage thrasher
Key 106

northern flicker
Key 92

Green Jay

Clark's Nutcracker

Some jays are gray, and so is the mockingbird. Clark's nutcracker (which is a jay) and the mockingbird have distinctive wing and tail markings, while the gray jay is a fluffy gray bird whose best mark is its contrasting nape, which varies regionally. Clark's nutcracker and the gray jay have both earned the name "camp robber" for their boldness. Mockingbirds are closely related to thrashers (Keys 105-6), as can be seen in their juvenal plumage. Adult mockers are celebrated vocalists and mimics.

◄**Clark's Nutcracker** *Nucifraga columbiana* 12"
Numerous. Wanders in small flocks among conifers near timberline. Occupies lowland winter range only in years pine seed crop fails. Noisy, tame, bold. Flies like a crow; often walks like one. ● Gray with unique black-and-white wing and tail pattern; long, pointed bill. Juv. similar but browner, duller. ♪ *Kra-a-a*, hoarse, drawn-out call.

Gray Jay *Perisoreus canadensis* 11"
Numerous in small flocks in conifers, esp. spruce. Tame,

juv.

Mockingbird

loggerhead
shrike
Key 98

Mockingbird

Gray Jay

juv.

bold. Feeds opportunistically, caching food for winter. Flight straight with rapid wing beats, level glides. ● Gray, crestless, small bill. Extent and shade of dark nape vary. Juv. sooty gray, usually with white mustache streak. ♪ Usually silent, but can give variety of notes, esp. soft chatter, whistles.

Mockingbird (Northern) *Mimus polyglottos* 10"
Numerous, conspicuous, widespread in open land, suburbs. Most common in South, but increasing and expanding range in North. Alert, active. Aggressively defends breeding territory, attacking animals, humans. Feeds on insects; fruit; usually alone or in pairs. ● Gray above. White patches in dark tail and wings conspicuous in flight. Juv. browner with spotted breast. ♪ Original and mimicked phrases repeated tirelessly by both sexes, even at night by unmated males.

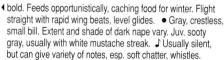

Brown Jay *Cyanocorax morio* 16" Tropical. Rare; in noisy flocks in brush, woodlands along lower Rio Grande. ● Large. Yellow or variegated bill for 1st yr.

Green Jay *Cyanocorax yncas* 10" Tropical. Locally numerous in streamside woods along lower Rio Grande, nearby farms and towns.

Bahama Mockingbird *Mimus gundlachii* 11" (Not shown) Caribbean. Nearly annual in s. FL. ● Like mocker but lacks white wing patches, has white tail tip.

juv.

♀

Common Grackle

♂

Great-tailed Grackle

♂

The metallic sheen of male grackles is usually evident, and even in poor light their size and large, keel-shaped tails are obvious. Females are duller and smaller – surprisingly different from the shiny black males. Flocks are easily recognized as grackles, even at a distance, by the distinctive contrast between the sexes. Female common grackles are not much larger than the similar blackbirds (Key 114) but have flatter foreheads and, in adults, longer tails. Great-tailed and boat-tailed grackles are large and similar but have separate ranges except for a small overlap on the Gulf Coast.

◀**Common Grackle** *Quiscalus quiscula* ♂12" ♀10"
Abundant, widespread in flocks, esp. in marshes, farmlands, rural areas. Often with blackbirds, starlings. Has adapted to civilization and prospered. ● Slender with sloping forehead; bright yellow eyes; long, pointed bill; long, scooped or keel-shaped tail. Iridescence variable. Males in West and North have bronze sheen on body, purple on head. In South and along eastern seaboard, overall purple

ani
Key 144

♂

Boat-tailed Grackle

♀ boat-tailed

♀ great-tailed

sheen. Female smaller, duller, with some sheen on upperparts. Juv. dingy brown, brown eyes. ♪ *Chuck,* loud call.

◀**Great-tailed Grackle** *Quiscalus mexicanus* ♂18" ♀15"
Numerous and expanding in marshes, arid grasslands, esp.
around settlements. Feeds in noisy flocks. Can be bold.
● Male black with purple iridescence, long keel-shaped tail.
Crown flatter than in boat-tailed grackle. Female smaller,
brown with slight sheen above. Pale brown breast, throat,
eyebrow – very pale in parts of CA, AZ. Both sexes have
yellow eyes, female paler. Juv. like female but dark-eyed,
faintly streaked below. Imm. male resembles adult by mid-
fall but lacks gloss, has dark eyes. Eyes turn yellow over
1st winter. ♪ Variety of whistles, clucks, cackles, hisses.

◀**Boat-tailed Grackle** *Quiscalus major* ♂16" ♀14"
Numerous in coastal marshes, shores. In FL also at inland
waters, farmlands, prairies. Behaves like great-tailed
grackle. Where ranges overlap boat-tailed usually in coastal
marshes, great-tailed inland. ● Like great-tailed but male
has blue iridescence, female lacks any sheen. Eyes variable: yellow in East, usually brown in LA, TX coast, where
range overlaps with great-tailed. Juv. not separable from
juv. great-tailed. ♪ Not as wildly varied as great-tailed's.

Blackbird-size
Straight bills

CONSULTANT **EIRIK BLOM**
ILLUSTRATOR **HANS PEETERS**

The songs of many of the birds in this section are loud and beautiful.

This is a diverse group of birds. They all share a diet that is heavy on bugs and other small creatures, and many also forage often on fruit and berries. A few, especially those that overwinter, also consume quantities of seed. Most belong to three families – the icterids, tanagers, and thrushes – but there are a number of exceptions, the best known of which is the starling, abundant in cities and suburbs.

The starling was introduced in New York late in the 19th century. It rapidly colonized the continent in our wake, often at the expense of other cavity nesters. Lewis' woodpecker, the acorn woodpecker, the purple martin, and all bluebirds have suffered serious declines as a result of competition with the starling for nesting holes. The starling most resembles some of the icterids and is grouped with them at the beginning of this section.

The remaining exceptions (grouped at the end of this section) are the horned lark and pipits, which dwell on the ground in fields, and the catbird and chat, which are brush-loving species. The horned lark is marked similarly to a meadowlark. Pipits are streaked like sparrows but have slender, not conical, bills. Catbirds are often seen flying in a beeline from one patch of cover to another, like the thrashers, to which they are related. Male chats are sometimes heard singing while hovering with legs dangling. The songs of both the chat and the catbird include a variety of unmusical noises mixed with whistled and warbled phrases.

The icterids include blackbirds, meadowlarks, orioles, and cowbirds – species that might not at first seem closely related. But note the long, sharply pointed bill on all but cowbirds. Cowbirds are treated here rather than with the conically billed birds, because they are most easily confused with their straight-billed relatives, especially blackbirds. Grackles are also icterids and have the characteristic sharply pointed bill. Because of their large size, however, grackles are shown in the preceding section of jay-size birds with straight bills.

Many blackbirds are associated with marshes, where they nest and roost, although their foraging is usually done on the ground in nearby fields. They nest in colonies that can number in the hundreds of thousands, but each male maintains his own small

MEADOWLARK

BALTIMORE ORIOLE

RUSTY BLACKBIRD

BROWN-HEADED COWBIRD

Most icterids have fairly straight, evenly tapered bills. The prominent exceptions are the cowbirds, which have conical, finch-like bills.

territory. In some species that territory can include more than one nesting female. In fall and winter, starlings often flock with blackbirds. Unlike orioles, which disappear from most of North America in winter, blackbirds and meadowlarks remain, foraging heavily on seeds and grains.

Orioles forage in trees and shrubbery. Although brightly colored, orioles are typically concealed by foliage, so the male's songs are often the first clue to the bird's presence. In some species, such as the hooded oriole, a yearling bird is sometimes seen with a nesting pair, assisting them at the nest. Young male orioles can be confusing because most are in transition from their female-like juvenal plumage to the bright adult male plumage.

Tanagers, like orioles, nest and frequently feed high in the canopy of mature trees and are usually heard before being seen. Males will sing tirelessly without changing perches. The plumage of female tanagers resembles that of female orioles, but tanagers don't have the long-tailed, slim-bodied look of the orioles, and their bills are distinctively "swollen," approaching conical. They glean insects from the canopy foliage and also flycatch to varying degrees, but often they just sit. They seldom seem nervous or impatient. By winter all have returned to the tropics.

The thrushes include Townsend's solitaire, bluebirds, and the robin. Townsend's solitaire frequents high, exposed perches and does a lot of flycatching. It has the slim form and erect posture of a flycatcher instead of the plump body of the other thrushes. Bluebirds, as symbols of good cheer, have been familiar to most of us since childhood. They do some flycatching, but most often they perch a few feet above the ground and flutter down to capture crawling bugs. The other thrushes (all, except the robin and veery, with "thrush" in their names) are birds of the forest understory, foraging through leaf litter and grass in search of insects and earthworms. Most venture onto the lower limbs of trees and shrubs, especially for berries in fall. They tend to be shy, but their beautiful songs ring through the woods.

Freshwater marsh

The starling is chunky and has a shorter tail and longer bill than the blackbirds, with which it can be confused. Red-winged blackbirds are widely known by the male's orange-red shoulder patches, although often only the yellowish lower border is visible. The shoulder patches of the tricolored blackbird are a deeper red, but again, often only the distinctive white border is visible. Females of both species are smaller than males and suggest large streaked sparrows. Female yellow-headed blackbirds are not as dramatically marked as males but show some yellow.

◀**Starling** (European) *Sturnus vulgaris* 8"
Eurasian species, introduced and now abundant in N. America. Bold. Has proliferated at expense of other cavity nesters like bluebirds, woodpeckers. In flocks when not nesting, sometimes large flocks mixed with blackbirds, grackles.
● White feather tips conceal glossy black plumage in fall, gradually wear away over winter; brown bill becomes yellow. Juv. gray-brown. ♪ Calls include imitations of other birds.

Red-winged Blackbird *Agelaius phoeniceus* 8¾"
Nests abundantly in large fields and marshes, esp. among

cattails. Forages in nearby open areas, esp. farmland. Flocks can be huge and often mixed, except when nesting. Aggressive. ● Male has orange-red shoulder with narrow yellow to whitish lower edge (lacking in "bicolored" race of CA). Female and imm. brown, heavily streaked below. Adult female often reddish on face or shoulder; imm. can have yellow wash on breast. Imm. male acquires adult plumage gradually by 2nd fall. ♪ *Conk-ca-ree*, liquid song; call a low *chack*.

Tricolored Blackbird *Agelaius tricolor* 8½"
◄ Local. Flocks must be large and densely occupy a freshwater marsh before they will nest. Flocks forage at nearby fields, farms; sexes often separate when not nesting. ● Male has dark red shoulder patch with wide white edge (can be buffy in fall). Female darker, esp. on belly, than most female red-wings and seldom shows red on shoulder, but not reliably separated in field. Imm. male acquires adult plumage gradually by 2nd fall. ♪ Nasal, raspy, unlike that of red-wing.

◄ **Yellow-headed Blackbird** *Xanthocephalus xanthocephalus* 9½"
Numerous, local, declining; in flocks in freshwater marshes. Feeds at nearby fields, farms; often in mixed flocks when not nesting. ● Male has yellow hood, white wing patch. Female smaller, brown, with yellow throat and breast. Imm. like female; male acquires adult plumage by 1st spring. ♪ Song a choking, scraping noise made with much apparent effort.

♀ common grackle
Key 112

♂

♀

Brewer's Blackbird

Brown-headed Cowbird

molting fall juv.

♀

♂

The plumages of the rusty blackbird and Brewer's blackbird can resemble each other and that of the common grackle (Key 112). Grackles are larger than either blackbird, with longer, wedge-shaped tails; males are glossier. Rusty and Brewer's blackbirds have different habitats and largely separate ranges. Although both can be found in the Southeast in winter, then the rusty blackbird is distinctively "rusty." Cowbirds have shorter, thicker bills than the blackbirds, with which they often flock. While the brown-headed cowbird is aptly named, the bronzed cowbird does not look bronze. The red eye color is the bronzed cowbird's best mark.

◄**Brewer's Blackbird** *Euphagus cyanocephalus* 9"
Abundant, widespread except in deep forest, hot desert. Has extended range to East. In flocks, often mixed.
● Smaller-headed than rusty blackbird with slightly shorter bill. Male glossy black; green sheen on body and purple sheen on head visible in good light; pale yellow eye. Female and juv. brown with dark eye. Fall birds can show some pale barring but much less than in rusty blackbird and never on wings. ♪ *K-sheik*, creaky song; call a metallic *check*.

summer

winter

Shiny Cowbird

Rusty Blackbird

♂

♀

Bronzed
Cowbird

◀**Brown-headed Cowbird** *Molothrus ater* 7½"
Abundant, increasing in West; often in mixed flocks with
blackbirds. Once known as "buffalo bird," now attends livestock, inhabits fields, farmlands. Deposits eggs in other
species' nests; host bird raises cowbird chicks, often at
expense of own young. ● Short, wide, nearly conical bill;
short tail. Male glossy black with brown head. Female gray-
brown; juv. similar but distinctly streaked below.

Bronzed Cowbird *Molothrus aeneus* 8¾"
◀Fairly numerous, expanding range. Habits, habitat similar to
brown-headed cowbird's. ● Red eyes, can be dull in winter.
Bill longer than in brown-headed. Male glossy black. Female
smaller, gray-brown, can be flat black. Juv. gray-brown.

◀**Rusty Blackbird** *Euphagus carolinus* 9"
Numerous in bogs, wetlands. Flocks with other blackbirds
after nesting but rare in open fields. Often wades, feeding
on aquatic life. ● Longer bill with more acute point than in
Brewer's blackbird. Yellow eyes (brown in juv). Broad, rusty
tips of fresh fall feathers wear away over winter to reveal flat
black summer plumage. Male seldom shows gloss; female
can be dark gray. ♪ Similar to that of Brewer's.

Shiny Cowbird *Molothrus bonariensis* 8½" S. American invader recorded throughout South but still rare. Reached FL in 1985. ● Brown eye. Violet gloss on male.

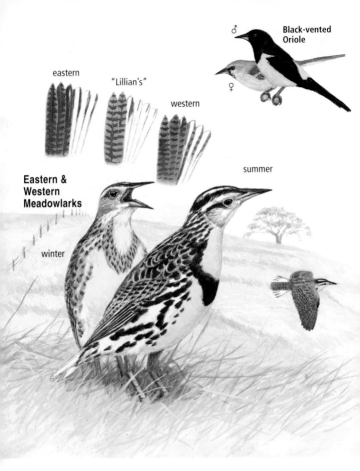

eastern

"Lillian's"

western

Black-vented Oriole
♂
♀

summer

Eastern & Western Meadowlarks

winter

The meadowlark (with its familiar black V on a yellow breast) is actually two or perhaps three species, best separated by song and range. Three male orioles have entirely black heads, but their body colors differ: chestnut in the orchard oriole, yellow in Scott's oriole, and bright orange in the Baltimore oriole (next Key). Female and young orioles, including those on the next Key, are much alike. Songs and calls are helpful in identifying orioles, as the birds are often in dense foliage.

◄**Eastern Meadowlark** *Sturnella magna* 9½"
Numerous in fields, meadows; showing dramatic declines in northern part of range. Walks. Often seen singing from roadside poles, wires. Flies quail-like, with rapid strokes interrupted by short glides. In flocks in fall, winter. ● Black V on yellow breast, blackish head stripes, sharply pointed bill, short tail with white outer tail feathers. Dusky feather edges of fresh plumage in fall obscure chest and head ◄pattern; edges wear away over winter. Brightness varies regionally, with "Lillian's meadowlark" in Southwest paler, duller than image shown; more white in tail. ♪♪ *See-you, see-yeer*, whistled song; call a raspy, *dzzrt*.

"Lillian's"

Audubon's Oriole

1st spring ♂

Orchard Oriole

♀

♂

Scott's Oriole

fall imm.

♀

♂

◀**Western Meadowlark** *Sturnella neglecta* 9½"
Numerous. Habits like eastern meadowlark's. Hybrids occur where ranges overlap. ● Browner than most eastern meadowlarks, face darker, but field identification by plumage nearly impossible. Yellow extends slightly farther onto face than in eastern but usually obscured in winter. ♪♪ Rich, flute-like song, accelerating at end; call a low, throaty *chuck*.

◀**Scott's Oriole** *Icterus parisorum* 9"
Fairly numerous in semi-arid lands, esp. canyons, yucca stands. ● Male yellow and black with white wing bar, yellow shoulder. Yellow extends onto long black tail. Female, imm. duller than female hooded oriole (Key 116); back streaked. Imm. lacks throat spots; male acquires adult plumage by 2nd fall. ♪ Loud, varied, whistled song; call a sharp *chuck*.

◀**Orchard Oriole** *Icterus spurius* 7¼"
Numerous, expanding range; in open woods, shade trees. ● Male chestnut and black. Female and imm. olive above, yellow to yellow-green below, lacking orange tones of female Baltimore oriole (Key 116). Imm. male shows black bib by 1st spring. ♪ Rich, varied song; call a soft *chuck*.

Audubon's Oriole *Icterus graduacauda* 9½" Tropical. Scarce, shy in dense woods of s. TX; usually in pairs. ● Like Scott's but yellow-green back; female duller.

Black-vented Oriole *Icterus wagleri* 9½" Mexican. Several records in Southwest.

Baltimore Oriole ♂

♀

1st spring ♂

1st spring ♂

♀

♂

Bullock's Oriole

Each male oriole has a distinctive plumage pattern; note especially the different wing bars and tail markings. Females and young birds are duller and much alike. Compare them with female orioles on the previous Key and female tanagers on the next. Most young male orioles begin to acquire their black adult markings by the first fall. When they return in spring, the process is well along, but it is not complete until the second fall.

◄Baltimore Oriole *Icterus galbula* 9"
Numerous in open deciduous woods, shade trees in parks, suburbs. Distinctive, large, hanging nest. ● Male orange with black hood extending onto back, black wings, black tail with large orange corners. Female and imm. usually richer in color than female Bullock's but can be as pale above and below. Imm. male shows orange splotches by 1st spring.
♪ Song of variable rich, whistled notes; call a whistled *hoo-li.*

Bullock's Oriole *Icterus bullockii* 9"
Numerous western counterpart of Baltimore oriole, with hybrids where ranges overlap. ● Male has large white wing patch as well as distinctive orange-and-black pattern.

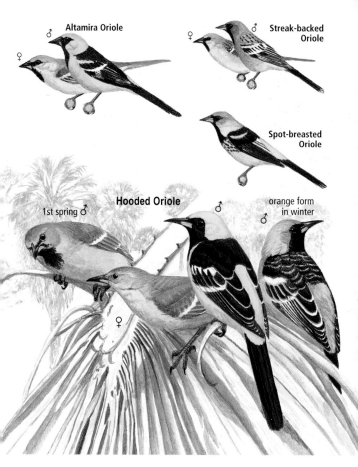

Altamira Oriole ♂ ♀

Streak-backed Oriole ♂ ♀

Spot-breasted Oriole

Hooded Oriole

1st spring ♂

♀

♂

orange form in winter

♂

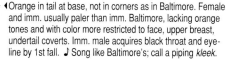

◄Orange in tail at base, not in corners as in Baltimore. Female and imm. usually paler than imm. Baltimore, lacking orange tones and with color more restricted to face, upper breast, undertail coverts. Imm. male acquires black throat and eye-line by 1st fall. ♪ Song like Baltimore's; call a piping *kleek*.

Hooded Oriole *Icterus cucullatus* 8"
Fairly numerous, in treetops and low growth; often hidden
◄in tall palms. Range has expanded with ornamental growth and a few now winter in US. ● Adult's bill more curved than in other orioles. Male yellow over most of US, more orange in TX; has buff bars (not streaks) on black back in winter. Female and imm. yellow-green below, including belly; can be inseparable from imm. orchard oriole (Key 115). Imm. male has dark bib and lores by 1st spring. ♪ Songs more warbled, less whistled, than in other orioles; call a high, rising *eeet!*

Altamira Oriole *Icterus gularis* 10" Tropical. Once rare, now fairly numerous in extreme s. TX. ● Larger than hooded oriole, heavier bill, yellow-orange shoulder patch. Imm. yellow, adult by 2nd fall. ♪ Low, raspy call notes.

Streak-backed Oriole *Icterus pustulatus* 8" Mexican. Rare but increasing in se. AZ, s. CA. ● Imm. female lacks black throat, may lack back streaks.

Spot-breasted Oriole *Icterus pectoralis* 9½" Tropical. Only oriole in se. FL in summer. Introduced in 1950s, now fairly numerous, esp. in ornamental growth. ● Female slightly duller. Imm. yellower, may lack spots on breast.

ORIOLES

116

Scarlet Tanager — spring ♂, fall molt ♂, ♀
Stripe-headed Tanager — ♂, ♀
Summer Tanager — ♂, 1st yr. ♂, ♀

Though male tanagers are bright and distinctive in summer, they are typically located by voice, as they are relatively inactive and often hidden in foliage. Females have an olive and greenish yellow plumage similar to that of female orioles (Keys 115-116). Note that tanagers are more compact than orioles, with distinctively swollen bills, not sharply pointed ones. All but the western tanager lack the wing bars obvious on most orioles. Female tanagers and first-year males can be confusing but are identifiable.

◀ **Scarlet Tanager** *Piranga olivacea* 7"
Fairly numerous, usually in canopy of mature mixed and deciduous forests, shade trees. ● Spring male scarlet and black; yellow-orange and brown in 1st spring, can show yellow wing bars. Male patchy in fall molt; retains black wings, tail. Female and imm. greenish above, pale yellow below; darker wings, smaller bill than in female summer tanager.
♪♪ Song of raspy, robin-like phrases; call a hoarse *chip-burr.*

Summer Tanager *Piranga rubra* 7½"
Numerous in pine-oak woods of South, cottonwoods and willows of Southwest. ● Male bright red by 3rd summer,

duller in 2nd summer. 1st-summer male and some females show uneven washes of red (not distinct patches). Female and imm. warmer yellow below than female scarlet tanager; wings often reddish. ♪♪ Song less raspy than in scarlet tanager; call a staccato *pit-i-tuck*, up to 5 notes.

Hepatic Tanager *Piranga flava* 8"
Fairly numerous in mountain forest, esp. pine-oak. ● Gray cheek patch and dark bill in all plumages. Male bright red by 3rd summer. Female and imm. gray above, yellow below; males brighter in 1st summer, red by 2nd summer but often with patches of yellow. ♪♪ Song robin-like; call a low *chuck*.

Western Tanager *Piranga ludoviciana* 7"
Numerous in open forest, esp. in canopy of conifers. ● Male has black back, tail, and wings, with yellow shoulder, whitish wing bar; red face in summer. Fall male has yellow face, like female, but retains black wings. Female and imm. have dark wings, narrow wing bars; grayish back contrasts with yellower nape and rump; underparts pale to bright yellow. ♪♪ Song of robin-like notes; call a slurred *pit-u-rick*.

Stripe-headed Tanager *Spindalis zena* 7" W. Indian. Handful of s. FL records.
● Female greenish, wing pattern similar to male's.

Flame-colored Tanager *Piranga bidentata* 7" Mexican. Several records in se. AZ.
● Wing bars, streaked back; female greenish yellow.

Except for Townsend's solitaire, these thrushes are often seen in parks or gardens. The buff wing patches and white tail feathers on Townsend's solitaire are prominent in flight; the white eye-ring is always conspicuous. The male varied thrush has a distinctive black breast band and orange eye stripe; females can be mistaken for robins if the orange wing bars and eye stripe are overlooked. Wood thrushes resemble the spotted thrushes on the next Key but are larger, with a reddish crown and back and bolder spotting below.

◄Townsend's Solitaire *Myadestes townsendi* 8¾"
Fairly numerous, alone or in small groups in open mountain conifer forests. Perches upright, sometimes behaves like typical flycatcher but closely related to thrushes. Winters at lower elevations, feeding extensively on juniper berries.
● Slender with long tail, stubby bill. Gray with white eye-ring, buff wing patch, white outer tail feathers. Juv. heavily spotted. ♪ Fluty, thrush-like notes given in melodious warble.

Varied Thrush

♂

♀

juv.

juv.

Wood Thrush

◀**Robin** (American) *Turdus migratorius* 10"
Abundant backyard species. Also in moist woodlands,
where it is much shier and often brighter. ● Red breast,
black head with split white eye-ring, yellow bill. Female
browner above, duller below. Juv. heavily spotted.
♪ *Cheerily, cheery, cheery-o,* varied short phrases.

Wood Thrush *Hylocichla mustelina* 8"
Numerous in shady deciduous woodlands, esp. in moist
areas, swamps. Only spotted thrush common in parks, back-
◀yards. ● Plump. Rusty head and back, browner rump and
tail. Extensive large black spots below (not streaks as in
brown thrasher, Key 106). White eye-ring, streaked cheek.
♪♪ *Eee-o-lay,* 3-5 slow, flute-like notes often ending in trill.

Varied Thrush *Ixoreus naevius* 9½"
◀Fairly numerous but shy in moist coniferous forests at
all elevations. Feeds in trees more often than robins.
● Male blue-gray above, orange below with black breast
band. Female duller, breast band gray or lacking. Orange
eye stripe and wing bars in all plumages. Juv. like female
but paler, with dark scaling on breast. ♪ Slow series of
notes, each trilled on different pitch.

The most distinctive spotted thrush is the wood thrush on the previous Key. Note its bold black spots and rusty head and back. Hermit thrushes are brightest on the rump and tail. The others don't show much contrast in the upperparts, and the shade of each varies regionally. The veery has the least spotting and a dull eye-ring at best. Swainson's thrush has buff spectacles and buff on its face and breast. The gray-cheeked and Bicknell's thrushes are inseparable in the field, with gray cheeks and incomplete eye-rings.

◀**Veery** *Catharus fuscescens* 7¼"
Fairly numerous in underbrush of deciduous and mixed woods, esp. wet areas. ● Tawny brown above; shade varies regionally. Spots on throat and upper breast often indistinct. May show pale eye-ring. ♪♪ *Vee-ur,* given in series of 4-5 cascading, flute-like notes for which the bird is named.

Hermit Thrush *Catharus guttatus* 7"
◀Numerous, widespread in underbrush of mixed and coniferous forests. Only spotted thrush to habitually pump tail.
● Reddish rump and tail contrast with gray-brown to olive-brown back. Complete thin white eye-ring. ♪♪ A phrase of clear, flute-like notes repeated in series on different pitches and with some variation; distinctive call a soft *chuck.*

Clay-colored Robin

Fieldfare

Rufous-backed Robin

Gray-cheeked & Bicknell's Thrushes

Swainson's Thrush

◀**Swainson's Thrush** *Catharus ustulatus* 7"
Numerous in underbrush of cool boreal or mountain forests, esp. moist areas. ● Buff spectacles, malar area, throat, and upper breast. (Other species can show some buff on face and breast but lack bold spectacles.) Olive-brown above in East, reddish brown in West. ♪♪ Ascending series of flute-like notes; often sings in migration.

Gray-cheeked Thrush *Catharus minimus* 7¼"
Bicknell's Thrush *Catharus bicknelli* 7¼"

gray-cheeked

◀Gray-cheeked thrush fairly numerous in migration; nests in boreal forests, often scrub spruce, as distant as Siberia. Bicknell's thrush rare; nests in cool mountain forests. ● Both have gray cheek, inconspicuous eye-ring. Can show pale buff on malar area and breast. ♪♪ Descending *wee-o, wee-a, wee-o,* rising at end with, *chi-wee-wee;* often sing in migration.

Aztec Thrush *Ridgwayia pinicola* 9" Mexican. Recorded in se. AZ; Big Bend, TX. ● Female browner, heavily streaked.

Bicknell's

Clay-colored Robin *Turdus grayi* 9" Mexican. Several records in s. TX. Has nested in TX.

Fieldfare *Turdus pilaris* 10" Eurasian. Several records in eastern Canada and northeastern US.

Rufous-backed Robin *Turdus rufopalliatus* 9¼" Mexican. Rare in winter near US-Mexico border.

SPOTTED THRUSHES

119

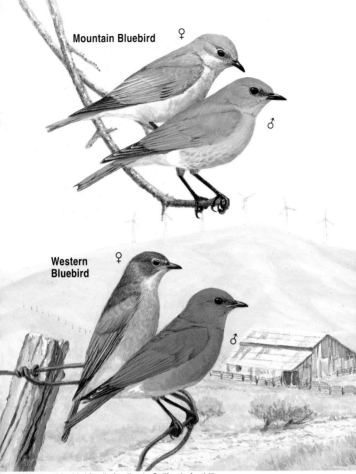

Mountain Bluebird ♀

♂

Western Bluebird ♀

♂

Western bluebird family feeding in California foothills

Male mountain bluebirds are truly blue, but blue in the females is limited to the rump and flashes in the wings and tail. Eastern and western bluebirds both have rusty breasts. The western male has a blue throat (pale gray in the female) and a dirty gray belly. In eastern bluebirds the rust on the breast extends to the throat and sides of the neck and the belly is white. Young bluebirds are heavily spotted when first seen foraging with their families. Bluebirds suffered serious declines due to competition for nest cavities with starlings and house sparrows, two introduced species. They are now recovering, partly with the aid of nest boxes.

◀**Mountain Bluebird** *Sialia currucoides* 7¼"
Fairly numerous but still threatened by competition for nest cavities. In summer, in open areas from foothills to treeline. Flycatches but more often perches or hovers over open ground, flutters down to capture ground insects. In flocks in open lowlands in winter, where it also feeds on fruits, berries. ● Less hunched than other bluebirds; longer

lazuli bunting
Key 149

Eastern Bluebird

♀

juv.

♂

wings, legs, bill. Male sky blue with white lower belly and undertail coverts. Female gray with blue in wings, rump, and tail; may show rusty blush on breast. Juv. spotted like eastern bluebird. ♪ *Terrr,* low call.

◀**Western Bluebird** *Sialia mexicana* 7"
Numerous; widespread except in deep forest, open areas lacking nest hole sites. Flutters from perch to ground to capture insects; sometimes flycatches or hovers like mountain bluebird. ● Upright but hunched posture. Male has deep blue hood and upperparts with rusty breast, gray belly and undertail coverts. Rusty patch on back variable, sometimes absent. Female duller with gray head, throat. Juv. spotted like eastern bluebird. ♪ *Phew,* soft call. Song a short warble.

◀**Eastern Bluebird** *Sialia sialis* 7"
Numerous, but numbers in some areas dependent on nest boxes. Widespread, wherever there are nest boxes or scattered trees with holes for nesting. Forages like western bluebird. ● Upright, hunched posture like western bluebird. Male deep blue above with rusty throat, breast, sides of neck; white belly. Southwestern males paler. Female duller with white or grayish white sometimes evident on chin. ♪ *Chur-li,* rich call note. Song a short warble.

Sprague's Pipit

American pipit

American Pipit

fall

spring

East shore, San Francisco Bay

Pipits are patterned like sparrows, but unlike the little, chunky, conically billed sparrows that hop about, pipits are larger, slender-bodied, slender-billed, and walk or run. Both pipits have brown tails with white margins, but only the American pipit pumps its tail. The best plumage marks for the horned lark are the black areas on its face and breast; its "horns" are often not visible. Like the pipits, the horned lark has white margins on its tail. In winter, flocks of American pipits and larks can be seen searching open, nearly barren spaces for tiny windblown seeds. When flushed, they and Sprague's pipit all give clear, diagnostic flight calls.

◀**Sprague's Pipit** *Anthus spragueii* 6½"
Scarce; hidden in short-grass prairie. In flocks in winter. Has declined greatly with plowing of prairies. Quickly returns to cover when flushed. On nesting grounds, male sings while flying in great arcs. ● Heavily scalloped and streaked back, pale legs. Faint streaks on breast, none on flanks. Blank-looking face. ♪♪ *Tweep*, given loudly in flight, often doubled.

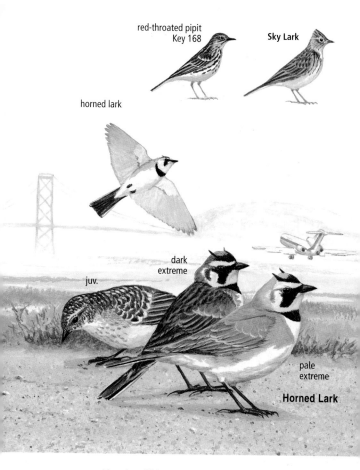

red-throated pipit
Key 168

Sky Lark

horned lark

juv.

dark
extreme

pale
extreme

Horned Lark

◀**American Pipit** *Anthus rubescens* 6½"
Numerous in summer on Arctic tundra and mountain meadows, snowbanks. Flocks in winter in open areas: beaches,
fields, golf courses, even parking lots. Pumps tail while
walking and bobs head like dove. ● Dark legs (except for
a few birds in fall). White margins on brown tail. In summer,
buff below with fine breast streaks, grayish above with little
or no streaking. In fall, heavily streaked below incl. flanks,
dark brown above with some blurry streaking. ♪♪ *Chip-it*,
sharp, thin flight call, and higher *tsee-tseet*.

◀**Horned Lark** *Eremophila alpestris* 7½"
Abundant in open areas with little or no vegetation: dirt or
short-grass fields, shores, gravel. Winters in flocks, often
mixed with longspurs (Key 154), snow buntings (Key 153).
● All forms have black face and chest markings, white margins on black tail. Back shade (grayish or reddish tones)
and amount of yellow below vary regionally. Female duller.
In winter, black markings partly obscured by pale feather
edgings. Briefly held juv. plumage has white spotting above,
lacks adult face pattern. ♪♪ *Tsee-titi*, clear flight call.

Sky Lark *Alauda arvensis* 7¼" Eurasian. Introduced in early 20th century and
now resident on Vancouver I., B.C., and nearby San Juan Is.

Red-whiskered Bulbul

Chat

Catbird

Chats and catbirds are skulkers best known for their singing talent. The chat's distinctive face pattern sets it apart from other birds with yellow breasts. The catbird is gray with a fairly conspicuous black cap. The rusty patch under the tail can be hard to see.

◀**Chat** (Yellow-breasted) *Icteria virens* 7½"
Fairly numerous, but seriously declining in East. In thickets or brush; secretive, solitary. ● Dark, heavy bill; long tail. Yellow throat and breast (can be orange in East from diet of honeysuckle berries). Lores black in male, gray in female. Southwestern birds grayer with longer tail. ♫♫ Jumbled squawks, whistles, rattles given day or night from perch or in fluttering song-flight.

◀**Catbird** (Gray) *Dumetella carolinensis* 8½"
Numerous but shy, solitary in thickets, brush. Behaves like and closely related to thrashers but smaller, with straight bill. ● Slate gray, with black cap and tail, rusty undertail coverts. ♫♫ Thrasher-like jumble of mimicked sounds, odd notes; given day or night. Named for cat-like mewing.

Red-whiskered Bulbul *Pycnonotus jocosus* 7½" Asian. Small population established in 1960s in suburban areas of s. FL.

Warbler-size
Straight bills

CONSULTANT AND ILLUSTRATOR
LARRY MCQUEEN

Warblers and vireos often glean insects from foliage.

There are so many small bug-eating birds that it is hard to believe each has its own foraging preferences. Specialization has evolved to the point that each of five warblers that nest and forage in the spruces of eastern Canada prefers gleaning insects from a different part of the same tree.

Most of the small bug-eaters are warblers. The others are vireos, Old World warblers (different from American warblers), titmice, and the one-of-a-kind wrentit. The first three Keys show vireos, followed by fifteen Keys of warblers. The remaining birds —which are, on average, smaller than the vireos and warblers — appear on the last three Keys of this section.

The titmice, which include the chickadees, eat seeds as well as insects and do not migrate to the tropics as nearly all of the vireos and warblers do. They are welcome and well-known visitors to backyard feeders and often show little fear of humans. A family of chickadees usually forms the core of the roving mixed flocks of small songbirds frequently encountered in winter wood-lands. These flocks include birds such as kinglets, nuthatches, creepers, and other small winter residents.

Old World warblers, the kinglets and gnatcatchers, do not resemble North American warblers and are only distantly related to them. Old World warblers are migrants, but many remain in North America in winter. Gnatcatchers occupy the warmer southern states, while kinglets survive cold northern winters by supplementing their insect diet with a few seeds.

TYPICAL WARBLER

TYPICAL VIREO

Vireos and warblers are best distinguished by bill shape.

Different species of vireos are easily confused with one another, and some are often confused with warblers. A vireo's bill is thicker, more "swollen" than a warbler's and has a hooked tip. Some vireos are also more deliberate feeders than the typical active warbler. Remember to check the bill of any unknown plain or yellowish warbler-like bird; it might be a vireo. Vireos divide fairly cleanly into those with pale eyebrows and plain wings and those with spectacles and wing bars.

To simplify identification, eastern and western warblers have been grouped separately. Those that nest east of the US Rockies are tagged as "E. Warblers" on the Key color bars; those that nest west, as "W. Warblers." Species nesting in both ranges are described fully in both sections. In some species, eastern and western forms show significant distinctions. Within their regions, warblers are grouped by the presence or absence of (1) yellow and (2) wing bars on the spring males. Usually these marks are clear, but in some cases wing bars can be "iffy" and shades of yellow can vary to greenish or orange. In a few cases females or fall birds show yellow when the spring male doesn't. In these cases a small image of the yellow form is placed on the Key that depicts comparable yellow birds, along with a reference to the Key on which the spring male is shown and the species described.

Of the many distant birds that arrive each spring to nest in North America and raise their young on the abundant summer insects, none are more beautiful, varied, or eagerly anticipated than the warblers. By the first of March, with winter still upon most of the continent, species like the black-and-white warbler and the northern parula have already reached northern Florida. More than 50 warbler species join in the migration over the following weeks, blanketing the entire continent. The influx continues with late migrants, such as the Connecticut warbler, still winging to their Canadian nesting sites in early June. Different species travel at different rates, but most birds of any one species will pass through a given area in a week or two.

The greatest numbers migrate up the eastern seaboard, along the Appalachians, or through the Mississippi Valley. In these places, waves of warblers can overwhelm lucky birders. Migrants do most of their flying at night. Days are usually spent feeding and resting, but weather and circumstance dictate the details; migrating birds can show up at any time and at any place.

Although darkness conceals migrating warblers from predators, it also conceals tall structures from the birds. Several million small songbirds a year, it is estimated, collide fatally with radio and television towers and tall buildings. A single structure can claim the lives of more than a thousand birds a year. Ovenbirds, a species of warbler, appear to be one of the most frequently killed.

Most migrating warblers are headed for the cool forests and bogs that stretch across Canada and extend south into the high US Appalachians. Many others nest in southeastern lowlands, especially in river bottoms and wooded swamps. Because most insects prefer wetlands, so do many warblers. But warblers are ubiquitous; even mesquite desert has its associated Lucy's warbler.

Wherever they nest, males usually arrive first and claim a territory by patrolling and singing. It is these males in handsome breeding plumage that usually attract our attention, singing from

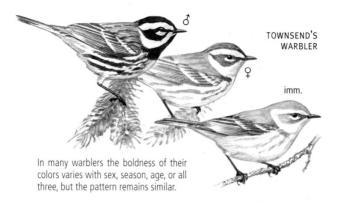

TOWNSEND'S
WARBLER

♂

♀

imm.

In many warblers the boldness of their colors varies with sex, season, age, or all three, but the pattern remains similar.

some conspicuous perch. Some species stay so high in the canopy of mature forests that they are seldom seen, and songs are the only evidence of the male's presence. Females of most species don't sing and are often retiring. Learning the songs of the local nesting species is the best way to identify them easily.

Few warblers actually warble. Their songs tend to be high-pitched notes and trills. Many species have numerous song variations. The song heard coming from a known bird may not be the same as that described in the text. Still, there is a vocal pattern and quality that can be learned and used to identify even those birds with large repertoires. Some species have commonly heard calls – alarm chips or other communications – that are also helpful in identification.

Some females are just as intensely patterned as spring males, but most, along with males in fall plumage and young birds, are less dramatic versions of the spring male. Birds that seem nondescript usually can be identified by faint streaking on the back or breast or by subtle face patterns. Plainness is itself a good mark. Seen clearly, most fall warblers can be identified as readily as those in spring, but too often the glimpses birders are allowed are too brief to make identification certain.

The place where a warbler is seen feeding can be a good clue to its identity. Some are typically high in the canopy, others feed at midlevel, and still others feed on the ground or close to it. Various warblers have adopted feeding strategies similar to those of nuthatches, thrushes, and flycatchers and, in doing so, have come to resemble them in some ways.

After nesting, some species immediately return south while others delay. Fall migration is a more prolonged, less concentrated event than spring migration. Most warblers finally leave the United States – either through Central America or by flying directly across the Caribbean – but nearly all pine warblers remain, as do most yellow-rumped warblers and smaller numbers of several other species.

yellow
extreme

Tennessee warbler
Key 134

Philadelphia Vireo

Red-eyed Vireo

Pale eyebrows and plain wings are the distinguishing marks
of these vireos. Details of the eyebrow and the amount of yellow
on the underparts are the best marks separating them. The
Philadelphia is the only one with a yellow breast, although others
often show yellowish sides. The Philadelphia has a black eyeline
below its eyebrow, while the red-eyed has black borders above
and below. The warbling vireo has only a short gray line behind
its eye, no black in front. The black-whiskered vireo is like the
red-eyed but has a whisker stripe. These vireos are often hidden
in treetops, but all persistently sing or give harsh scold notes.

◀**Philadelphia Vireo** *Vireo philadelphicus* 5¼"
Scarce, esp. in East. In deciduous edges, esp. new growth,
streamside. More active, warbler-like than most vireos; less
restricted to canopy. ● Olive-green above with contrasting
gray crown. Yellow breast; most extensively yellow in fall.
White eyebrow; black eyeline extends through lores. Like
Tennessee warbler (Key 134) but short, hooked bill. ♪ Song
like red-eyed vireo's but weaker, seldom given in migration.

Red-eyed Vireo *Vireo olivaceus* 6"
Abundant but frequently unseen in canopy foliage of

Yellow-green Vireo

Yucatan Vireo

Black-whiskered Vireo

yellow extreme

Warbling Vireo

◀deciduous forests, orchards, shade trees. Forages deliberately, gleaning insects. ● Olive back with contrasting blue-gray crown; white eyebrow bordered above and below with black. White underparts; some show yellowish sides and undertail coverts in fall. Red eye looks dark at a distance; imm. has brown eye. ♪♪ Song a series of short, robin-like phrases given persistently.

Warbling Vireo *Vireo gilvus* 5½"

◀Numerous in crowns of deciduous trees, in woodlands or backyards. Gleans foliage sluggishly. May be 2 species (see dashed line on map). ● Pale gray with only slightly greener tones on back; dull white eyebrow. Slightly brighter in fall with many showing pale yellow sides and undertail coverts, suggesting Philadelphia vireo. ♪♪ Song a drowsy, persistent, rambling warble; sweeter, clearer in eastern birds.

◀**Black-whiskered Vireo** *Vireo altiloquus* 6¼"
Fairly numerous but seriously declining; in mangrove swamps, nearby shade trees, brush. Feeds sluggishly on insects, berries, seeds. Tame. ● Like red-eyed vireo with black whisker stripe (can be indistinct). ♪♪ Song is deliberate, repeated paired phrases similar to red-eyed vireo's.

Yellow-green Vireo *Vireo flavoviridis* 6" Tropical. Records near US-Mexico border. ● Yellower than red-eyed vireo; face marks less distinct, bill longer.

Yucatan Vireo *Vireo magistar* 6" C. American. Records near US-Mexico border.
● Browner than red-eyed vireo; no head-back contrast; eyebrow widest at front.

Yellow-throated Vireo

pine warbler
Key 127

"Cassin's" form
Solitary Vireo

"Blue-headed" form
Solitary Vireo

These vireos, along with some on the following Key, have spectacles and wing bars. The ones on this Key are brighter. The yellow-throated vireo is brightest and resembles the pine warbler (Key 127). Note the vireo's thicker bill and yellow spectacles. The white-eyed vireo also has yellow spectacles, but no yellow on the throat. The solitary vireo has a white throat and spectacles; "Cassin's" is somewhat duller than the "blue-headed" form. The boldest white spectacles are on the black-capped vireo, framing its red eyes.

◀**Yellow-throated Vireo** *Vireo flavifrons* 5½"
Fairly numerous in summer in open stands of deciduous trees, shade trees, orchards. Scarce, declining in northern part of range. Rare in winter. Feeds in canopy; sluggish.
 ● Bright yellow spectacles, throat, breast; gray rump. Similar pine warbler (Key 127) has faint spectacles, streaked sides, olive-yellow rump, slim bill. ♪ *Three-eight,* final phrase in slow series of short, gravelly phrases with long pauses.

Solitary Vireo "Cassin's" form *Vireo solitarius* 5½"
Fairly numerous in mixed woods, esp. pine-oak. Feeds like "blue-headed." ● A bit smaller, browner than "blue-headed";

Thick-billed Vireo

♂

♀

Black-capped Vireo

White-eyed Vireo

juv.

◀ similar to Hutton's (Key 125) but larger, with spectacles.
♪ Hoarser than in "blue-headed," more like yellow-throated's.

Solitary Vireo "Blue-headed" form *Vireo solitarius* 5¾"
Numerous in open coniferous or mixed forest, shade trees.
Feeds sluggishly from canopy to shrubby understory.
Tame. ● Bold white spectacles. Blue-gray head contrasts
with olive back. Throat and underparts white with yellow
◀ sides. ♪ Song a series of short phrases, richer than in red-
eyed vireo; usually given more slowly, with longer pauses.

White-eyed Vireo *Vireo griseus* 5"
Numerous, near the ground in thickets, brambles, brush.
Usually hidden but active, inquisitive. ● Gray above with
yellow spectacles; whitish below with yellow sides. Adult
has white eyes visible at close range; juv., brown. ♪♪ *Spit,*
◀ *and see if I care. Spit.* Loud, scolding song.

Black-capped Vireo *Vireo atricapillus* 4½"
Local, secretive in semi-arid scrub. Seriously declining with
loss of habitat and cowbird parasitism. Active, acrobatic;
flycatches. ● Tiny. Male has white spectacles, black head.
Female duller; juv. browner. ♪ Series of rapid, 2- or 3-note
◀ phrases; call a dry *chid-it.*

Thick-billed Vireo *Vireo crassirostris* 5½" Caribbean. Recorded
in FL Keys. ● Like white-eyed vireo but dark eye, larger bill.

Hutton's Vireo

ruby-crowned kinglet
Key 143

coastal
(fluffed)

southwestern

"Plumbeous" form
Solitary Vireo

Wing bars and spectacles can be faint or absent on some of these vireos. Most are drab gray birds. Only the coastal form of Hutton's and the northern form of Bell's show much yellow on their sides or olive tones on their upperparts. The best mark for Hutton's is its partial eye-ring, clearly broken at the top. "Plumbeous" and gray vireos share range and are easily confused. The gray vireo has fainter spectacles and wing bars, a shorter bill, and the distinctive habit of twitching its long tail. Bell's can be nearly as pale and as faintly marked as the gray vireo, but the two do not share habitat.

◀**Hutton's Vireo** *Vireo huttoni* 5"
Fairly numerous in mixed and deciduous woods, esp. live oaks. Feeds sluggishly at all levels; sometimes flicks wings. Tame, inquisitive. ● Bull-headed, with broken eye-ring, whitish lores, thin wing bars, short tail, blue-gray legs. Coastal birds bright below in fall; all birds dull in worn plumage. Ruby-crowned kinglet (Key 143) smaller with thinner bill, fainter upper wing bar, dark patch below lower wing bar, darker legs,

Empidonax
Key 103

northern form

"least" form

Bell's Vireo

Gray Vireo

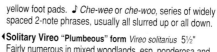

yellow foot pads. ♪ *Che-wee* or *che-woo*, series of widely spaced 2-note phrases, usually all slurred up or all down.

◀**Solitary Vireo** "Plumbeous" form *Vireo solitarius* 5½"
Fairly numerous in mixed woodlands, esp. ponderosa and piñon pines, juniper. Feeds sluggishly at all levels. ● Gray above with prominent white spectacles, 2 bold wing bars. Pale gray below, never more than hint of yellow on sides. ♪♪ Hoarse song as in yellow-throated or "Cassin's" (Key 124).

◀**Gray Vireo** *Vireo vicinior* 5½"
Scarce, declining, in arid scrub; piñon-juniper, oak, chaparral. Forages actively; twitches long tail. ● Gray above, dull white below with faint wing bar and eye-ring. Short, thick bill. ♪♪ Song repeated faster, clearer than in "plumbeous vireo."

Bell's Vireo *Vireo bellii* 4¾"
Fairly numerous but seriously declining in CA and Southwest ◀from loss of riparian habitat, cowbird parasitism. In moist thickets, esp. streamside willows. Active; flicks tail. ● Wing bars and spectacles can be bold or faint. Northern form most colorful; "least" form (in CA), dullest; southwestern birds, intermediate. All are brightest in fresh fall plumage. ♪♪ *Cheedle-cheedle-chu*, series of rapid, nonmusical, scolding notes.

DRAB VIREOS

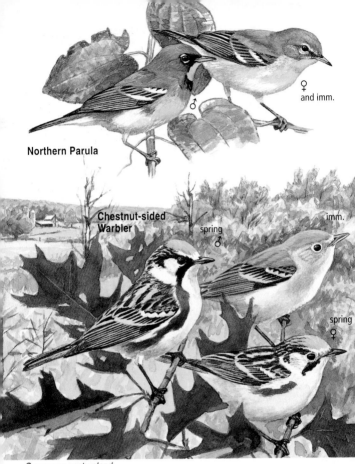

Northern Parula

Chestnut-sided Warbler

spring ♂

imm.

spring ♀

Overgrown pastureland

The northern parula's distinctive pattern includes a blue-gray head with a broken white eye-ring and a bright yellow throat. Males have two breast bands – one black, one orange. The side stripes so prominent on chestnut-sided warblers in spring can be absent on young fall birds, which are a unique lime-green above. Golden-winged warblers have diagnostic yellow wing patches and black face markings (gray in females). On the blue-winged warbler, note the dark eyeline and white wing bars. Golden-wings and blue-wings often hybridize. Offspring with the golden-wing's face pattern are "Lawrence's warblers"; those without, "Brewster's warblers."

◀**Northern Parula** *Parula americana* 4½"
Numerous, expanding to west. Usually near tips of upper branches in mature trees, esp. those near water draped with Spanish moss or *Usnea* lichen (old-man's beard). Agile, often hanging like chickadee. ● Tiny. Blue-gray above with greenish back patch, yellow throat and breast, white belly and two white wing bars, white eye-ring broken by black line. Breast bands lacking or incomplete in female, imm. ♪ *Zeeeeeee-ip*, buzzy, rising trill ending abruptly on single note.

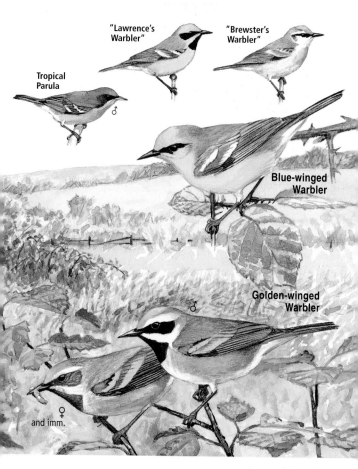

"Lawrence's Warbler"

"Brewster's Warbler"

Tropical Parula ♂

Blue-winged Warbler

Golden-winged Warbler ♂

♀ and imm.

◄Chestnut-sided Warbler *Dendroica pensylvanica* 5"
Fairly numerous but declining in deciduous thickets, early forest regrowth. Sometimes flycatches. ● White underparts with chestnut side stripe in spring, yellow or yellow-green cap, black face markings. Female duller. Fall adults retain some chestnut on sides, resemble spring female. Imm. lime-green above with variable streaking. ♪ *I wish, I wish to see Miss Beecher*, loud, clear song; call a low *chip*.

◄Golden-winged Warbler *Vermivora chrysoptera* 4¾"
Fairly numerous but seriously declining by displacement and hybridization with blue-winged warbler. In shrubby woodland edges. Acrobatic. ● Male has gray back, black throat and mask, yellow forecrown and wing patch. Female and imm. duller, with gray mask and throat. ♪ *Zee-bzz-bzz-bzz*, buzzy song, 1st note higher, 2nd usually in short series.

◄Blue-winged Warbler *Vermivora pinus* 4¾"
Fairly numerous, increasing to north. Habits and habitat like golden-winged warbler's. ● Bright yellow face and under-parts, black eyeline, white wing bars and undertail coverts. Imm. slightly duller. ♪ *Beee-bzzz*, buzzy, 2-note song.

Tropical Parula *Parula pitiayumi* 4½" Tropical. Rare resident of lower Rio Grande Valley. ● No eye-ring. More extensively yellow below than northern parula. Male may have orange wash across breast. Black mask lacking in female.

♀ Blackburnian warbler Key 134

♂

Golden-cheeked Warbler

Black-throated Green Warbler

♀

♂

imm.

The golden-cheeked warbler closely resembles the black-throated green warbler – both have distinctive bright yellow faces – but the golden-cheeked is confined to central Texas. Pine warblers are easily confused with yellow-throated vireos (Key 124) in spring, but note the vireo's prominent yellow spectacles and heavy bill. In fall, pine warblers can be nondescript, but most similar fall warblers, such as the blackpoll (Key 133), have back streaks. The yellow-throated warbler can be told from other warblers with yellow throats by its distinctive black-and-white face markings.

◀ **Golden-cheeked Warbler** *Dendroica chrysoparia* 5½"
Fewer than 4,000 total (est. 1995); in canopy of mature oak and juniper stands, "cedar brakes," in Edward's Plateau of central TX. Has declined seriously with loss of habitat and cowbird parasitism. ● Male has golden face with black crown, throat, upper breast, eyeline, and back. Female and imm. duller; similar to black-throated green but lack well-defined ear patch and yellowish tinge on belly. ♪ *Zee, zee, zeedee-zee*, buzzy song; quality like black-throated green's, but different pattern, variable.

fall blackpoll warbler Key 133

yellow-throated vireo Key 124

Yellow-throated Warbler

Pine Warbler

♀

spring ♂

imm.

◀**Black-throated Green Warbler** *Dendroica virens* 5"
Numerous in canopy of conifers and mixed forest. Separate southern race, "Wayne's warbler," favors cypress swamps.
● Yellow face with greenish ear patch, olive-green crown, back. Black throat and breast of male lacking or limited in female and imm. ♪ *Zee-zee-zee-zee-zee-zoo-zee,* or *zee-zee-zoo-zoo-zee,* buzzy songs.

◀**Pine Warbler** *Dendroica pinus* 5½"
Numerous resident in pines, mixed forest, parks. Early spring migrant. Typically creeps along branches in canopy, gleaning insects. Also forages on lower branches, ground; sometimes flycatches. Eats seeds in winter. Tame. ● Spring male has distinct side streaks, shows brightest yellow underparts. Female, fall birds duller. Imm. females may show no yellow, brownish wash on sides, olive-brown upperparts. ♪ Song a musical trill like chipping sparrow's but slower and shorter.

◀**Yellow-throated Warbler** *Dendroica dominica* 5½"
Fairly numerous, expanding to Northeast. Feeds in canopy of pines, cypress, live oaks, esp. with Spanish moss. Mississippi Valley birds prefer sycamores. Sometimes creeps methodically on lower limbs, trunk. ● Bright yellow throat, upper breast. Gray above, with black-and-white face pattern, black side streaks, white belly. Southeastern birds have yellow lores. ♪ *Tee-ew, tee-ew, tee-ew, tew-wee;* robust song.

Cape May Warbler

spring ♂

♀

imm. ♀

"Myrtle" form Yellow-rumped Warbler

imm.

♀

spring ♂

Canadian boreal forest

These are the eastern warblers with yellow rumps. Spring birds are vivid. Fall birds show enough of the spring patterns to be identified. Note the streaked underparts and faint yellow on the neck of the young Cape May warbler. The "myrtle warbler," the form of the yellow-rumped warbler found in the East, always has a telltale hint of yellow at the shoulder and at least some streaking below. The magnolia warbler always has large white patches in its tail.

◀**Cape May Warbler** *Dendroica tigrina* 5"
Fairly numerous, has increased; once considered rare. Nests in mature spruce forest; usually feeds actively in canopy, often flycatches. Attracted to spruce budworm outbreaks. ● Male (even imm.) has broad white wing patch. Spring male has orange-yellow face and side of neck, chestnut cheek patch, yellow breast with dark streaks. Female and fall birds duller, lack chestnut cheek patch. Imm. female dullest. ♪ *Seet-seet-seet-seet*, thin, very high-pitched.

"Audubon's" form
yellow-rumped warbler
Key 136

♀

imm.

Magnolia
Warbler

spring ♂

◄Yellow-rumped Warbler "Myrtle" form *Dendroica coronata* 5½"
Abundant in summer and migration at edges, clearings of
conifers. Feeds at all heights, flycatches. Most common bird
in fall and winter on much of Atlantic Coast, where bayberry,
wax myrtle, and other berries and seeds provide food for
flocks. Winters farther north than any other warbler. Tame.
● "Myrtle warbler" has yellow rump, crown, side patches;
white throat and eyebrow. Spring male has black breast and
side streaks, black ear patch. Female and fall birds duller,
browner. ♪ Weak, rambling song; *chek,* sharp call.

◄Magnolia Warbler *Dendroica magnolia* 5"
Numerous. Nests in dense, young conifers; either second
growth or at forest edges and clearings. Feeds actively,
wings and tail half-spread; often near center of trees. Fairly
tame. ● Yellow rump, tail black-tipped seen from below.
Spring male has black mask, white eyebrow and wing patch,
yellow underparts with black streaks on breast, sides.
Female duller; fall birds dullest with breast streaks often
replaced by vague grayish breast band. ♪ *Weeta-weeta-
weeta-sixta* (or *one-two-three-six*), loud, clear, rising song.

E. WARBLERS YELLOW / WING BARS

128

Prairie Warbler ♂ ♀

imm.

"western" form spring

Palm Warbler

"yellow" form spring

fall

Michigan jack pine barrens, nesting habitat of Kirtland's warbler

Wing bars are thin or can be lacking on these warblers, but all habitually bob their tails. The prairie warbler often busily flutters its wings as well. These behaviors are especially useful in identifying dull birds in fall. Adult prairie warblers are bright yellow below with distinctive black face marks and side streaks. Streaks extend across the breasts of palm warblers, and spring birds have a rusty cap; some fall birds retain yellow only on their undertail coverts. Few Kirtland's warblers remain to be seen.

◀ **Prairie Warbler** *Dendroica discolor* 4¾"
Fairly numerous, declining; in young forest regrowth or scrub with scattered pines, scrub oaks, cedars; also mangroves in FL. Very active, often flycatches. ● Yellow face and underparts, marked with black; thin yellow wing bars; white undertail coverts. Olive back with chestnut streaks, often concealed even at close range. Female duller; imm. dullest, lacks wing bars. ♪ *Zee-zee-zee-zee*, buzzy notes given in rising series.

cowbird chick

Kirtland's Warbler

♀

♂

◀ **Palm Warbler** *Dendroica palmarum* 5½"
Fairly numerous, usually near ground. Nests in brushy clearings in conifers, esp. bogs, muskeg. Prefers scrub, palmettos in winter; often in small flocks. "Yellow palm warbler" nests in East, winters on Gulf. "Western palm warbler" nests in central Canada, winters in East and FL. ● Chestnut cap in spring, with yellow throat and eyebrow. Breast white or yellow with dark streaking. Fall birds duller, with whitish eyebrow, vague breast streaks, yellow undertail coverts. ♪ Song a buzzy trill; softer, more nervous than in chipping sparrow.

◀ **Kirtland's Warbler** *Dendroica kirtlandii* 5¾"
Always rare; since 1970 has averaged about 200 pairs, increasing in early 1990s. Nests in dense stands of young jack pines. 135,000 acres of habitat managed and access controlled by recovery team. Controlled burning required to regenerate proper habitat. Very tolerant of humans. Cowbird parasitism most serious threat. ● Large. Blue-gray above, yellow below with black side streaks. Broken white eye-ring. Female duller; imm. brownish. ♪ *Chip-chip-che-way-o*, clear, emphatic notes; like northern waterthrush's.

Prothonotary Warbler

Yellow Warbler

♂

♀ and imm.

♂

♀ and imm.

imm. olive extreme

Flooded willow bottomland

Female prothonotary warblers lack the golden glow of the male but have the same blue-gray wings and tail with white tail patches. Some female yellow warblers, especially young ones, are confusingly dull. Their short tails and the striped effect on the wings help distinguish them. The female common yellowthroat lacks the male's mask. Her best mark is a subtle one: the grayish belly contrasting with the yellow on the throat and under the tail.

◀**Prothonotary Warbler** *Protonotaria citrea* 5½"
Numerous in Southeast; less common to north. In wet bottomlands, wooded swamps; often among branches overhanging stagnant or sluggish water. Only eastern warbler to nest in cavities; will use nest boxes. Tame. ● Fairly large, stout, with long bill, prominent eye. Short tail has white patches. Male golden, blending to olive on back and white under tail; blue-gray wings, tail. Female and imm. duller.
♪ *Sweet-sweet-sweet-sweet*, loud, ringing song.

♀ American redstart
Key 134

**Golden-crowned
Warbler**

Common Yellowthroat

imm. ♂

♂

♀

◀**Yellow Warbler** *Dendroica petechia* 5"
Abundant, widespread in shrubs, thickets, esp. near water.
● Yellow overall with short tail, long undertail coverts. Male
bright yellow with chestnut breast streaks. Female and imm.
duller, lack breast streaks. Wing feathers have dark centers
and bright edges, creating striped effect. Dull olive birds
show contrasting pale eye-ring. ♪ *Sweet, sweet, sweet,
I'm so sweet,* loud, energetic song; call a soft, musical *chip.*

Common Yellowthroat *Geothlypis trichas* 5"
◀Abundant in briars, marsh edges, any dense grass or brushy
cover. Active, wren-like, scolding then disappearing. ● Adult
male has white-bordered black mask lacking in female and
only suggested in imm. male. Brightness of yellow underparts varies regionally. Female has olive face (yellow in most
similar species), pale eye-ring. Belly grayish with brown wash
on sides; yellow throat, breast, undertail coverts. ♪ *Wichity-
wichity-wichity,* loud, ringing song; call a throaty *tchek.*

Golden-crowned Warbler *Basileuterus culicivorus* 5" Mexican. Very rare along Rio
Grande Valley in winter.

E. WARBLERS YELLOW / NO BARS

Canada Warbler ♂

♀ and imm.

♀ and imm.

♂ Kentucky Warbler

The bold black markings on these males make them easy to identify. Females and young birds often bear a suggestion of the male's pattern but can be confusing. The faint breast streaks, eye-ring, and yellow in front of the eye of the female Canada warbler are helpful marks, as is the white under the tail. The female hooded warbler shows white in the tail but not on the undertail coverts. The Kentucky warbler's yellow spectacles are always evident, and Wilson's warbler constantly twitches its unmarked dark tail.

◀**Canada Warbler** *Wilsonia canadensis* 5¼"
Fairly numerous in undergrowth of mature forest, usually in cool, moist areas; often at higher elevations or along streams. Feeds actively in understory; often flycatches. ● Male blue-gray above with yellow spectacles (eye-ring can be whitish); yellow below with black necklace. Female and imm. grayer, necklace faint. ♪ Sputtering series of loud, rich notes.

Kentucky Warbler *Oporornis formosus* 5¼"
Fairly numerous, esp. in Mississippi Valley; on ground in low,

Wilson's Warbler

Hooded Warbler

♂

♀ and imm.

◀thick growth of wooded bottomlands, swamp edges, wet upland ravines. Secretive except when male sings from low branch. Walks, often teetering and wagging tail, as it gleans insects from undersides of leaves. ● Yellow spectacles and underparts, black crown and "sideburns," pink legs. Sideburns duller, more limited in female, imm. ♪♪ *Tur-dle, tur-dle, tur-dle,* in series; similar to Carolina wren's; call a strong *chik.*

◀Hooded Warbler *Wilsonia citrina* 5¼"
Numerous in dense understory of moist areas in mature deciduous forest, esp. wooded swamps in South. Active, often flycatches. ● White tail spots. Male has black hood, yellow face. Female duller, often shows traces of hood. ♪ *Weeta-weeta-wee-tée-o,* clear song; call a metallic *tink.*

Wilson's Warbler *Wilsonia pusilla* 4¾"
◀Scarce eastern migrant. Nests in northern thickets, woodland edges, esp. alder and willow tangles, bogs. Feeds actively in low growth; flicks wings and tail; often flycatches. Tame. ● Yellow below, olive above with prominent black eye, yellow forehead. Dark tail often cocked, twitched. Male has black cap, often reduced or lacking in female. Richness of underparts varies with region more than with sex. ♪ *Chi-chi-chi-chi-chet-chet,* sharp, staccato song; call a dry *djep.*

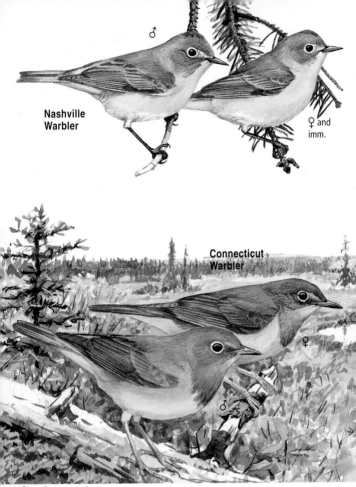

Nashville Warbler

♂

♀ and imm.

Connecticut Warbler

♀

♂

Canadian spruce bog

Other warblers have white eye-rings, but only the Nashville has a gray head contrasting with an olive back and yellow throat. Male mourning and Connecticut warblers have distinctive gray hoods. Female hoods are duller, and yellow shows on the throats of some young mourning warblers. Male mourning warblers have no eye-ring; females and young birds have only thin ones, usually broken. However, the Connecticut warbler has a complete, bold eye-ring. Most orange-crowned warblers in the East are drab with distinct yellow only under their tails. Note the blurred breast streaks.

◀**Nashville Warbler** *Vermivora ruficapilla* 4¾"
Fairly numerous, widespread, esp. in bogs or thickets and tangles of regenerating forest. Feeds actively from ground to treetops; often wags tail. ● Gray head with complete white eye-ring. Olive back, yellow throat and breast, whitish belly. Male's chestnut crown patch seldom seen. Female and imm. duller, heads can be brownish. ♪ *Sweet-sweet-sweet-sweet, chu-chu-chu*, loud, musical song given in 2-part series.

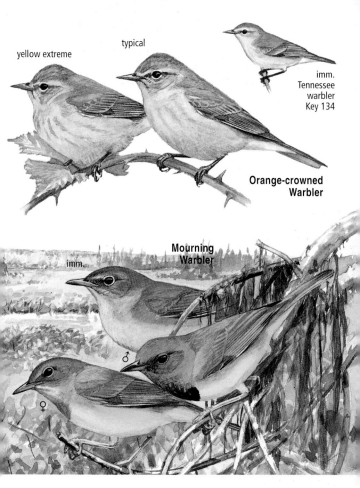

yellow extreme

typical

imm.
Tennessee
warbler
Key 134

**Orange-crowned
Warbler**

**Mourning
Warbler**

imm.

♂

♀

◀**Connecticut Warbler** *Oporornis agilis* 5¾"
Scarce, shy, seldom seen. Spring migration mostly west
of Appalachians; east in fall. Nests in spruce bogs, open
woodlands. Forages in ground litter or on low limbs. Walks
with mincing gait (mourning warbler hops). ● Large with
pink legs. Long undertail coverts. Male has gray hood,
complete white eye-ring. Female duller; imm. dullest.
♪ *Beecher, beecher, beecher, beecher,* loud, shrill song.

◀**Mourning Warbler** *Oporornis philadelphia* 5¼"
Scarce (but more common than Connecticut); near ground
in thickets, forest edges. Shy. ● Male has gray hood, black
on breast, no eye-ring. Hood browner, fainter in female and
imm.; yellow can extend onto throat; many show faint, broken eye-ring. ♪ *Chirry-chirry-chorry-chorry,* loud, liquid song.

◀**Orange-crowned Warbler** *Vermivora celata* 5"
Scarce on Gulf Coast in winter, rare elsewhere in East in
winter and migration; in thickets, esp. near water. Feeds
actively, often flycatches. ● Dull with broken pale eye-ring,
faint dark eyeline. Orange crown usually hidden. Faint
breast streaks, yellow undertail coverts; many show thin
yellowish edge at bend of wing. ♪ Song a thin, weak trill,
dropping in pitch and volume at end. Call a thin *tseet.*

Bay-breasted Warbler

spring ♂

spring ♀

fall

spring ♂

fall

Blackpoll Warbler

spring ♀

Only the blackpoll warbler, which has a solid black cap, and the black-and-white warbler, which has a striped crown, show much similarity. Females resemble males, except for the female cerulean warbler, which is a slightly richer blue-green above than the young bird illustrated. Note the pale eyebrow. In fall, bay-breasted warblers, blackpoll warblers, and young pine warblers (Key 127) present a classic identification problem. All are olive-green above and dirty white to pale yellow below.

◀**Bay-breasted Warbler** *Dendroica castanea* 5½"
Fairly numerous at edges of conifer forest, esp. at outbreaks of spruce budworm. Most migrate west of Appalachians, but fairly numerous to east. Forages at all levels; sometimes fly-catches. ● Spring male has chestnut crown, throat, sides; buff neck patch. Spring female much duller. Fall birds, see opposite page. ♪ *Teetsi-teetsi-teetsi-tee*, high-pitched song.

Blackpoll Warbler *Dendroica striata* 5½"
Numerous. Late migrant; mostly overland in spring, usually in canopy; coastal in fall and at all levels. Summers in conifers; creeps along branches. ● Streaked above and below, more

imm. pine warbler
Key 127

♀ chestnut-sided warbler
Key 126

imm.

♂

Cerulean Warbler

Black-and-white Warbler

♀

spring ♂

black-and-white

cerulean

◄ finely in female. Spring male has black cap, white cheeks. Fall birds, see below. ♪ *Tseet-tseet-tseet,* high-pitched song.

Black-and-white Warbler *Mniotilta varia* 5¼"
Numerous in deciduous and mixed woods. Migrates early when trees bare; gleans insects from tree trunks, large limbs. ● Striped head and body. Male has black cheek patch; female, gray. Spring male has black throat.
♪ *Weesy, weesy, weesy,* high-pitched song.

Cerulean Warbler *Dendroica cerulea* 4¾"
Scarce, declining significantly. Local, in canopy of open deciduous forest near water. ● Male blue above, white below with dark breast band, side streaks. Female and imm. have faint streaks on breast and sides, yellowish tinge on breast and eyebrow; olive- to blue-green above, female with most blue. ♪♪ *Zray, zray, zray, zreeeee,* rapid series ending in trill.

FALL BLACKPOLL, BAY-BREASTED, AND PINE WARBLERS
Blackpoll is streaked above and below, has yellow-green wash on breast, white undertail coverts, usually pale legs. Bay-breasted warbler more faintly streaked, buffier, usually with trace of bay on flanks, undertail coverts; legs usually dark. Pine warbler lacks streaking above, has dark legs and white undertail coverts; most are yellowish on breast.

E. WARBLERS NO YELLOW / WING BARS

133

Blackburnian Warbler

♀ and fall

chestnut-sided warbler fall Key 126

spring ♂

Black-throated Blue Warbler

♂

♀

The brilliant orange throat of the male Blackburnian warbler is much paler in the female and may be barely a blush in young birds. Wing bars on the male Blackburnian merge into a patch. The black-throated blue warbler and American redstart also have wing patches rather than wing bars. The wing patch can be faint on a female black-throated blue, but her pale eyebrow is always present. The Tennessee warbler has plain, unmarked wings and is plain overall, but note the dark eyeline and pale eyebrow. Spring males have a gray cap; females and fall birds have yellowish breasts and can be confused with orange-crowned warblers (Key 132) but have white, not yellowish, undertail coverts.

◀**Blackburnian Warbler** *Dendroica fusca* 5"
Fairly numerous in conifers or mixed forest, esp. in canopy. Declining in Appalachians, possibly from loss of hemlocks to insects. ● Male has orange throat and face, black cheek, white wing and tail patches. Female and imm. paler, yellowish; dullest can suggest imm. cerulean warbler (Key 133). ♪♪ *Sip, sip, sip, titi, tseee,* ascending song ending in thin trill.

orange-crowned warbler Key 132

Philadelphia vireo Key 123

imm.

Tennessee Warbler

spring ♂

American Redstart

◀**Black-throated Blue Warbler** *Dendroica caerulescens* 5¼"
Fairly numerous, but declining. Prefers low deciduous growth, often rhododendrons in Appalachians. • Male dark blue above with small white wing patch, white below with black cheeks, throat, sides. Female pale olive-buff below, dark olive above with dark cheek, sharp white eyebrow, broken eye-ring. Wing patch sometimes small or concealed in female, can be lacking in imm. ♪ *Zwee-zwee-zwee-zwee-zwee?* Buzzy song, last note slurred up.

◀**American Redstart** *Setophaga ruticilla* 5¼"
Abundant in lower level of open deciduous and mixed woodlands. Very active and agile, butterfly-like; often flycatches. • Male black above with salmon patches in wings, sides, tail. Female and imm. olive above with yellow patches, gray head. Male in 1st spring like female but shows at least some salmon on sides. ♪ Song variable, mostly high, thin notes.

Tennessee Warbler *Vermivora peregrina* 4¾"
◀Numerous in openings of coniferous or mixed forest, esp. at spruce budworm outbreaks. Feeds actively; mostly in canopy in spring migration, summer; at all levels in fall. • Short tail, with long, white undertail coverts at all times. Summer male green above with gray crown, black eyeline, white eyebrow. Female and fall birds olive above with yellowish breast, eyebrow. Fall birds show most yellow below and faint wing bar. ♪♪ *Sidit-sidit-sidit-sidit-sit-sit-sit-sit-sit*, loud, staccato song.

E. WARBLERS NO YELLOW / BARS & NO BARS

134

Swainson's Warbler

Worm-eating Warbler

Northern Waterthrush

These five warblers are usually near the ground and can be hard to see, though all are easily heard. All except Swainson's walk rather than hop. Distinctive crowns identify the ovenbird and the worm-eating and Swainson's warblers. Both waterthrushes have dark brown backs, pale eyebrows, and heavy streaking below, which extends onto the throat of the northern waterthrush. The eyebrow is white and broadens behind the eye in the Louisiana waterthrush. It is yellowish and narrow in the northern.

◀**Swainson's Warbler** *Limnothlypis swainsonii* 5½"
Scarce, furtive, declining in canebrakes, dense swamps. Rare in Appalachians in rhododendron thickets. ● Long, pointed bill. Olive-brown above with dull reddish brown crown, pale eyebrow, dark eyeline; slightly buff below. ♫ Song resembles that of Louisiana waterthrush.

Worm-eating Warbler *Helmitheros vermivorus* 5¼"
◀Fairly numerous. Lethargic. Walks stealthily, tail held high, in deciduous underbrush, esp. on sides of wooded ravines. Searches through dead leaves; sometimes creeps over trunks and limbs. Does not eat earthworms. Male often sings from high perch. ● Orange-buff face and breast with

Ovenbird

Louisiana
Waterthrush

black head stripes. ♪♪ Song a thin, insect-like trill, faster
than that of chipping sparrow.

◀**Northern Waterthrush** *Seiurus noveboracensis* 5¾"
Numerous in cool wooded bogs and swamps, where it
sometimes wades. Bobs tail as it walks. ● Brown above,
whitish or buff below with dark streaks on throat, breast,
and sides. Eyebrow usually buff, often tapering behind eye.
♪ *Wit-wit-wit-twee-twee-twee-chew-chew-chew,* loud, ringing song; call a sharp *pik.*

◀**Louisiana Waterthrush** *Seiurus motacilla* 6"
Numerous; usually along flowing hillside streams, sometimes
near still water like northern waterthrush. Active, wades, often
jumps for flying insects. Bobs tail. ● Bill noticeably larger
than in northern. Brown above with white eyebrow, broadest
behind eye; white below with dark streaks on breast, sides;
throat unstreaked. Often shows contrasting buff patch on
flanks. ♪ Song is 3-4 loud, musical notes followed by rapid
jumble of notes; call like northern's but more emphatic.

◀**Ovenbird** *Seiurus aurocapillus* 6"
Numerous, locally abundant, on floor of mature forest with
sparse underbrush. Usually in dry, deciduous woods, but
also in wet areas and, in North, conifers. Wags tail while
walking. ● Olive-brown above with orange crown bordered
in black, white eye-ring; white below with black streaks.
♪♪ *Tcher, tcher, tcher, tcher,* increasing in volume.

spring ♂

Townsend's Warbler

♀

imm.

**"Audubon's" form
Yellow-rumped Warbler**

spring ♂

spring ♀

White wing bars distinguish these and Grace's warbler on the next Key from other yellow warblers in the West. Their distinctive yellow patches separate them from each other. The hermit warbler has a yellow face; Townsend's adds a black ear patch. "Audubon's" and the "myrtle warbler," two forms of the yellow-rumped warbler, have small but easily seen yellow side patches in all plumages, as well as the namesake yellow rump. The yellow on the throat of "Audubon's" is replaced by white in the "myrtle warbler." Young birds are less boldly patterned, but with a good look all are recognizable.

◄**Townsend's Warbler** *Dendroica townsendi* 5"
Numerous in summer in mature conifers, usually high in canopy. Widespread, often in scrub during migration. In winter, fairly numerous in coastal conifers; most winter outside US. ● Yellow face with dark ear patch and crown in all plumages. Male's black bib partially hidden by yellow tips after fall molt. Bib absent in female and imm. ♫♪ Series of high, buzzy notes often finishing on higher pitch.

Hermit Warbler

"Myrtle" form Yellow-rumped Warbler

imm.

spring ♂

spring ♀

◀ **Yellow-rumped Warbler** *Dendroica coronata* 5½"
"Audubon's" and "Myrtle" forms
Abundant in summer in conifers. Widespread in winter;
most common bird in some areas. Active, agile, conspicuous; often flycatches. ● Spring male blue-gray above
with black back streaks, yellow cap; white belly with black
breast band, side streaks. Male "myrtle" has white throat
(yellow in "Audubon's") and black ear patch. "Audubon's"
◀ has more white in wing and spread tail, but less white on
closed undertail. Female and fall birds duller; imm. brownish. Some imm. "Audubon's" can lack yellow on throat but
do not show "myrtle's" distinctly outlined dark ear patch.
♪ Weak, rambling, warbling song. *Chek,* call note.

Hermit Warbler *Dendroica occidentalis* 5½"
Fairly numerous but declining in canopy of mature coniferous
forest, usually at higher elevations than Townsend's where
◀ ranges overlap. ● Yellow forehead, face. Male has black
throat, crown, nape. Throat patch restricted in female, can
be lacking in imm. Distinctive olive back in imm. Hybrids with
Townsend's typically combine unmarked yellow face of hermit
with yellow breast and black side streaks of Townsend's.
♪♪ Song less buzzy than in Townsend's, only 1-2 notes.

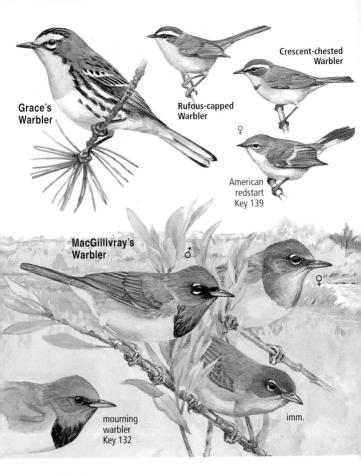

Grace's Warbler

Rufous-capped Warbler

Crescent-chested Warbler

♀

American redstart Key 139

MacGillivray's Warbler

♂

♀

mourning warbler Key 132

imm.

Grace's warbler has white wing bars. Its yellow bib distinguishes it from birds on the preceding Key. The other three species here lack wing bars but have distinctive gray heads and at least partial white eye-rings. The gray on MacGillivray's warbler's head extends to its chest. Nashville and Virginia's warblers are similar, but overlap only in migration. The Nashville is greener above, yellower below. The gray back of Virginia's contrasts with its yellow rump.

◀**Grace's Warbler** *Dendroica graciae* 5"
Fairly numerous but local, usually in canopy of mature pine or pine-oak forest above 6,000 ft. Active, often flycatches. ● White wing bars. Yellow eyebrow, throat, breast; white belly with black side streaks. Gray above with black streaks on back. Female and imm. slightly duller than male. ♪♪ *Chee-chee-che-che-che*, given in rapid series accelerating to trill.

◀**MacGillivray's Warbler** *Oporornis tolmiei* 5¼"
Fairly numerous but shy; in dense thickets of open forest, esp. near water. Hops, does not walk. ● Chunky; pink legs. Male olive above, slate-gray hood, broken white eye-ring; yellow below. Female and imm. have browner hoods, fainter

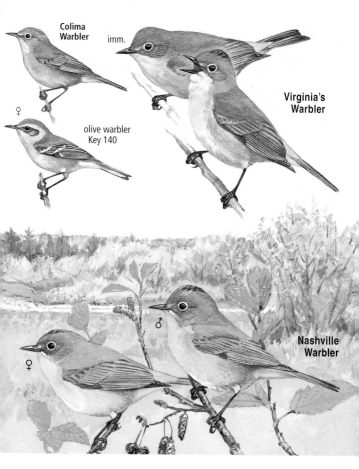

eye-rings. Similar mourning warbler (Key 132) very rare but annual migrant in West; lacks eye-ring. ♪♪ *Cheedle-cheedle-cheedle, turtle-turtle,* loud liquid song; 2nd part lower, variable.

◄ **Nashville Warbler** *Vermivora ruficapilla* 4¾"
Once rare, now fairly numerous; widespread in thickets from wet bogs to dry forest understory. Has increased with deforestation. Active. ● Spring male olive above with gray head, white eye-ring; yellow below with white on belly. Chestnut crown patch seldom seen. Fall birds, females duller. ♪ *See-it,* given loudly in series followed by lower trill, 2-part song.

◄ **Virginia's Warbler** *Vermivora virginiae* 4¾"
Numerous in brush, thickets on high slopes, usually above 6,000 ft. Feeds actively, twitching tail, but shy, often hidden. ● Gray with yellow rump and undertail coverts, white eye-ring. Yellow breast reduced in some females, often lacking in imm. Chestnut crown patch usually concealed. ♪ Song like Nashville's but weak, 2-3 parts, last part usually higher.

Rufous-capped Warbler *Basileuterus rufifrons* 5¼" Mexican. Several records from se. AZ and Big Bend area, TX.

Crescent-chested Warbler *Parula superciliosa* 4¼" Mexican. Several records from se. AZ and Big Bend area, TX.

Colima Warbler *Vermivora crissalis* 5¾" Mexican. Rare in Big Bend area, TX.

Orange-crowned Warbler

yellow extreme

olive extreme

♂

Yellow Warbler

olive imm.

♀ and imm.

The male yellow warbler is bright and has chestnut breast streaks, but some females are much more greenish, and young birds can be confused with orange-crowned warblers. Note the dark eyeline, longer tail, and plain wings of the orange-crowned. The yellow warbler is short-tailed with yellow tail spots, and each wing feather has a dark center, creating a striped effect. Female and young Wilson's warblers and common yellowthroats can also be plain, lacking the black markings of males. However, Wilson's crown is always dark, if not black, and the bird constantly twitches its tail. The female common yellowthroat's pale belly contrasts distinctively with her yellow throat and undertail coverts.

◀**Orange-crowned Warbler** *Vermivora celata* 5"
Numerous in thickets, esp. in old burns, clear-cuts, along streams. Feeds actively near ground. ● Yellow to dull olive below with faint breast streaks; darker above. Crown patch seldom seen. Similar fall Tennessee warbler (Key 134), rare migrant in western states, has white undertail coverts. ♪ Song a thin trill dropping in pitch and volume at end. Call a weak *tzit*.

Fan-tailed Warbler

Common Yellowthroat

♂

♀

imm. ♂

♀

♂

Wilson's Warbler

◀ **Yellow Warbler** *Dendroica petechia* 5"
Abundant, widespread in thickets, esp. waterside. Active, conspicuous. ● Bright yellow to olive-yellow with short tail, yellow tail spots. Male bright with chestnut breast streaks. Female and imm. lack streaks, can be dull. Dull birds show pale eye-ring, not obvious on bright ones. ♪ *Tseet, tseet, tseet, tsitta-tsitta-tseee,* sweet song. Call a musical *chip.*

Wilson's Warbler *Wilsonia pusilla* 4¾"
Numerous, widespread in broad-leaved thickets, esp. along
◀ streams and in alpine meadows. Agile, active near ground, flycatches. ● Bright yellow below, olive-green above with black cap. Some, esp. imm. females, lack black cap. Plain, long, dark tail; often flicked or held cocked. ♪ *Chi-chi-chi-chi-chet-chet,* thin rapid song. Call note a dry *chep.*

Common Yellowthroat *Geothlypis trichas* 5"
Abundant in open, low vegetation, esp. marsh, wet mead-ows. Active, scolds wren-like. ● Male yellow below, dark
◀ olive-brown above with black mask. Female lacks mask; yellow heaviest on throat and undertail coverts; belly paler. Imm. like female but duller. Imm. males show faint mask. ♪ *Wichity-wichity-wichity,* loud, ringing song. Call, *chuk.*

Fan-tailed Warbler *Euthlypis lachrymosa* 5½" Mexican. Recorded in se. AZ.

orange-crowned warbler
Key 138

American
Redstart

♀

♂

These three western male warblers have little in common except that they lack yellow, and that is arguable. The black-throated gray warbler has an inconspicuous spot of yellow before the eye, and the American redstart flashes bright wing and tail patches that are yellow in the female and a rich salmon in the male. Waterthrushes skulk on the ground and suggest thrushes (Key 119) but have breast streaks rather than spots and eyebrows instead of eye-rings. Some Canadian and eastern warblers are black and white like the black-throated gray warbler, but none has a plain gray back.

◄**American Redstart** *Setophaga ruticilla* 5¼"
Scarce in West; in open second-growth deciduous and mixed woodlands. Active, agile; gleans from limbs, trunks, leaves in understory. Often flycatches. ● Male glossy black above with bright salmon patches in wings, tail, on sides. Female and imm. gray with yellow patches. Male acquires full adult plumage by 2nd fall, shows salmon side patches by 1st fall, usually some black on breast by 1st spring. ♪ Song variable; 5-6 notes, last 2 strongly accented.

Black-throated Gray Warbler

♂

imm.

♀

**Northern
Waterthrush**

◀**Northern Waterthrush** *Seiurus noveboracensis* 5¾"
Fairly numerous in summer in North. Shy, secretive in deep
cover of bogs, swamps, wooded shores. Feeds on ground,
often wading at water's edge sandpiper-like. Bobs head and
teeters as it walks. ● Brown above, usually yellowish or
buff below with dark streaks, continuing on throat. Eyebrow
yellowish or buff, usually tapering behind eye. ♪ *Wit-wit-wit,
twee-twee-twee, chew-chew-chew*, loud, ringing song.

Black-throated Gray Warbler *Dendroica nigrescens* 5"
◀Numerous, widespread in open, dry coniferous or mixed
forest and scrub, esp. oak, piñon-juniper, chaparral. Active.
● Male blue-gray above with black-and-white head and
throat, tiny yellow lore spots; white below with black side
streaks. Female can show nearly as much black on face
and throat as male but usually grayer, with some white
on throat. Imm. tinged with brown above; throat white.
♪ *Weezy-weezy-weezy-weezy-chee*, soft, buzzy song
ending on down note; call a thin *chip*.

RARE MIGRANTS The Tennessee (Key 134) and blackpoll (Key 133)
warblers both nest west of Rockies in northern Canada. Nearly all migrate east
of US Rockies, but small numbers occur each spring and fall in western US.

Painted Redstart

juv.

juv.

Red-faced Warbler

There are four warblers with no yellow markings found in the Southwest. The painted redstart and red-faced warbler are conspicuously marked with bright red, and they both flash white patches – in the wings of the painted redstart and on the rump of the red-faced warbler – as they flit about and flycatch. The adult male olive warbler has a burnt-orange breast and head (paler, yellowish in females) with a dark ear patch. Lucy's warbler is the most nondescript; the chestnut rump patch is the best mark, but it can be very pale on young birds. The crown patch is usually concealed.

◄ Painted Redstart *Myioborus pictus* 5¾"
Fairly numerous in wooded canyons, especially at high elevations and along streams. Very active, fanning wings and tail. Often flycatches. ● Bright red belly. Black above with white wing patch, white outer tail feathers, partial white eye-ring. Juv. sooty black, lacks red; molts to adult by fall.
♪ *Weeta-weeta-weeta-weeta-wee*, rapid, warbling song given by both sexes; call a forced *cheer* or *cheele*.

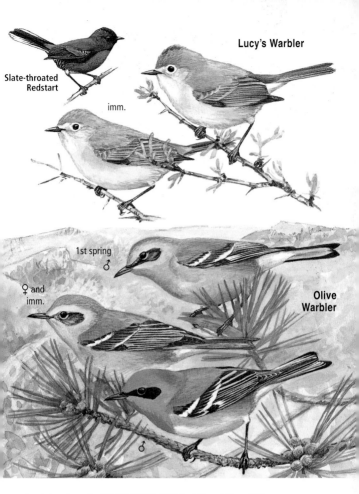

Lucy's Warbler

Slate-throated
Redstart

imm.

1st spring ♂

♀ and imm.

Olive Warbler

◀**Red-faced Warbler** *Cardellina rubrifrons* 5½"
Fairly numerous but local in open forest above 6,000 ft.
Feeds actively; often flycatches. Flicks tail sideways. ● Red
face, black crown and sides of head, white nape and rump.
Juv. brown above; acquires adult plumage by fall. ♪ Song
variable; clear, rapid, similar to yellow warbler's song.

◀**Olive Warbler** *Peucedramus taeniatus* 5¼"
Scarce in summer in canopy of open conifers above 7,000 ft.,
often with western bluebirds. Tame. Feeds deliberately, often
acrobatically. ● Male has burnt-orange head and breast with
black ear patch, white wing bars and tail patches. Female
and imm. duller. Males do not acquire full adult plumage until
2nd fall. ♪♪ *Peter-peter-peter-peter-peter,* loud, clear song.

◀**Lucy's Warbler** *Vermivora luciae* 4¼"
Numerous, local; in desert vegetation, esp. mesquite, willows,
sycamores near streams, washes. Small, shy; often flicks tail.
● Pale gray above, chestnut rump. Whitish below, sometimes
with buff wash. Chestnut crown seldom seen. Imm. duller
with paler rump. ♪ *Weeta-weeta-weeta, che, che, che,* trill
followed by whistled notes; last note often different.

Slate-throated Redstart *Myioborus miniatus* 6" Tropical. Records in se. AZ, sw. NM.

Boreal Chickadee

Carolina Chickadee

Black-capped Chickadee

The look-alike Carolina and black-capped chickadees are usually safely identified by range. Other chickadees can be distinguished by plumage: the boreal by its brown cap, the chestnut-backed by its back color, the mountain chickadee by its white eyebrow. The bridled titmouse has a chickadee-like black bib to go with its titmouse crest. All are active, acrobatic, and frequently fearless.

◀**Boreal Chickadee** *Parus hudsonicus* 5½"
Numerous throughout northern conifer forest, often high in trees extracting seeds from cones. A few come south in winter invasions with black-capped chickadees. ● Like black-capped but dull brown cap and back, rufous-brown sides. ♪ *Chick-a-day-day,* slower, wheezier call than black-capped's.

Carolina Chickadee *Parus carolinensis* 4½"
Numerous, widespread from suburbs to forest edges, coastal plains to Appalachian foothills. Forages nimbly in
◀thickets, lower limbs of trees. ● Black cap and bib, white cheeks and underparts with buff sides, gray back. ♪♪ *Fee-bee, fee-bay,* clear, 4-syllable whistled song. Call a clear *chick-a-dee-dee-dee,* or *dee-dee-dee.*

Black-capped Chickadee *Parus atricapillus* 5¼"
Numerous. Habits and habitat like Carolina chickadee's, but prefers higher elevations where ranges overlap. Many

Mexican Chickadee

Bridled Titmouse

Chestnut-backed Chickadee

Mountain Chickadee

bridled titmouse

◀ hybrids where ranges meet. Irrupts south in large numbers in some winters. ● Like Carolina chickadee but larger. White edges on secondaries and wing coverts of folded wing suggest hockey stick (secondaries can show white in Carolina, not coverts). ♫♪ *Fee-bee,* or *fee-bee-ee,* clear 2- or 3-syllable song. Call like Carolina's but lower, slower.

Mountain Chickadee *Parus gambeli* 5¼"
Numerous in mountain conifers and mixed forest; some at lower elevations in winter. ● Like black-capped chickadee
◀ but with white eyebrow, gray flanks. Form in Rockies has buff tinges on back, sides. ♪ *Dee-dee-dee,* whistled song, 1st note higher; call hoarser than black-capped's.

Chestnut-backed Chickadee *Parus rufescens* 4¾"
Numerous in coastal rain forest, dense streamside woods, shaded groves; also suburbs. Often forages high in tall trees. ● Blackish brown cap, rich chestnut back and sides (sides
◀ can be gray with little or no chestnut in some CA birds). ♪ *Tseek-a-zee-zee,* higher, buzzier call than black-capped's.

Bridled Titmouse *Parus wollweberi* 5¼"
Numerous in oaks. In mountains, foothills in summer; lower elevations in winter. ● Prominent crest, black-and-white face markings, black bib. ♪ Song variable, 1-2 syllables usually repeated in series; chickadee-like call, often scolds.

Mexican Chickadee *Parus sclateri* 5" Mexican. Only chickadee in mountains of extreme se. AZ, sw. NM. ♪ Hoarse call.

Plain Titmouse

Beardless-Tyrannulet

"Black-crested Titmouse"

Tufted Titmouse

Titmice sport crests like some jays. The plain and tufted titmice have separate ranges, and in southern Texas there is a distinctive "black-crested" form of the tufted titmouse. Wrentits are drab, long-tailed birds that are secretive and scolding like wrens rather than bold and acrobatic like chickadees and tits. Wrentits are best identified by their ringing calls. The yellow head is an easy mark for the adult verdin. In contrast, the little bushtit is best told by its lack of markings: no crest, no eye-ring, no wing bars. Only near Mexico can a few individuals with black cheeks ("ears") be found.

◀**Plain Titmouse** *Parus inornatus* 5¾"
Numerous, conspicuous in open woods, nearby suburbs; esp. oak and piñon-juniper woodlands. Forages acrobatically like chickadee but alone or in pairs, not in flocks.
● Unmarked gray (coastal birds gray-brown, may be separate species), paler below, with short gray crest. ♪ Song variable, similar to tufted titmouse's; calls in chickadee pattern.

◀**Tufted Titmouse** *Parus bicolor* 6½"
Numerous, expanding range north. Widespread in shade trees, deciduous woods, esp. moist woods. In mixed flocks in winter. ● Gray, with prominent crest, black forehead, buff flanks. "Black-crested" adult has black crest, gray or

"black-eared" form

coastal ♂

Bushtit

interior ♂

♀

juv.

Verdin

Wrentit

buff forehead. Hybrids at zone of contact. ♪ *Peter-peter,* whistled song, variable 1- or 2-syllable note given in series; calls like chickadee, often scratchier, scolding.

◀**Wrentit** *Chamaea fasciata* 6½"
Numerous in dense brush, chaparral. Neither a wren nor a tit but suggests both. Active, noisy, but secretive, usually sings from hidden perch. ● Brown (form in s. CA grayer than shown) with indistinct breast streaking, white eye. Long tail often cocked, pumped in flight. ♪♪ *Yip-yip-yip,* staccato series accelerating to a descending trill, given all year.

◀**Verdin** *Auriparus flaviceps* 4½"
Numerous in dense thorn scrub of low desert, alone or in family groups. ● Gray-brown with yellow face. Shoulder patch not conspicuous when wing folded. Juv. resembles bushtit but tail shorter, base of sharp bill yellowish. ♪ *Tseeé-tsee-tsee,* loud, whistled, 3- or 4-note song; chipping calls.

◀**Bushtit** *Psaltriparus minimus* 4½"
Numerous in noisy flocks when not nesting; forages actively in brush, shrubs from backyards to foothills. ● Gray-brown, with long tail. Female has pale eye. Coastal birds have brownish caps. Some southern interior males have black ear patch. ♪ *Pit,* thin call, often doubled.

Beardless-Tyrannulet (Northern) *Camptostoma imberbe* 4½" Fairly numerous in se. AZ, rare in summer in lower Rio Grande Valley. Secretive. ● Indistinct eyebrow, slight crest, buff wing bars. ♪♪ *Pee-yeep,* shrill call, repeated.

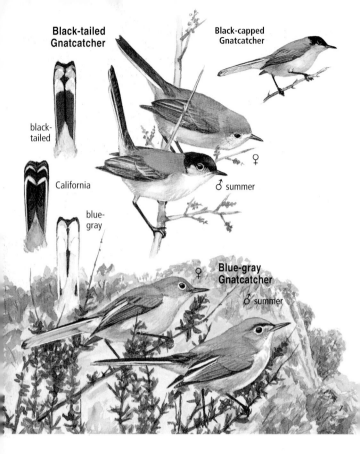

Black-tailed Gnatcatcher

Black-capped Gnatcatcher

black-tailed

California

blue-gray

♀

♂ summer

Blue-gray Gnatcatcher

♀

♂ summer

Gnatcatchers are tiny, elongated birds; all are fidgety and wag their long tails expressively. Their head markings vary with sex and season, but undertail markings are constant for each species and usually easy to see. The bright crown stripes of the golden-crowned kinglet are always present, but the red crown patch on the male ruby-crowned is usually hidden, and the bird resembles Hutton's vireo (Key 125). Look for the tiny bill and the dark "kinglet patch" below the lower, and often only, wing bar.

◀**Black-tailed Gnatcatcher** *Polioptila melanura* 4½"
Numerous in thorn brush, dry washes of low desert. Habits like blue-gray gnatcatcher's. ● Browner wings, shorter bill than in blue-gray; much less white in tail. Male has glossy black cap in summer; resembles female in winter but grayer, can show thin remnant of cap. ♪ Variable buzzy notes given in series: harsh *jeee-jeee,* thin *tsip-tsip.*

◀**Blue-gray Gnatcatcher** *Polioptila caerulea* 4½"
Numerous, widespread in open woods and thickets, usually alone or in pairs. Actively gleans insects from underbrush to treetops; also flycatches and hovers at foliage to glean. Inquisitive. ● Tail black above with white outer edges, mostly white below. Male has blue-gray upperparts with

white eye-ring, whitish underparts; narrow black border on forecrown in summer. Female and imm. grayer. ♪ *Pseee*, thin, twangy call note; song a mix of buzzes, thin warbles.

◄Golden-crowned Kinglet *Regulus satrapa* 4"
Abundant. Habitat and habits like ruby-crowned kinglet's.
● Like ruby-crowned, but orange (male) or yellow (female) crown patch bordered by black and white stripes. ♪ *Tsee-tsee-tsee*, very high-pitched call.

◄Ruby-crowned Kinglet *Regulus calendula* 4¼"
Abundant in conifers in summer; widespread in migration, winter. Gleans insects, larvae from twigs, branch tips. Feeds actively, flicking wings, hovering; alone or in small, often mixed flocks. ● Plump body, stubby tail, tiny bill, broken eye-ring. Olive-green above with dark patch below lower wing bar. Legs black, feet yellow or yellowish. Red crown of male erected only when excited. ♪ *Did-it*, scolding call.

California Gnatcatcher *Polioptila californica* 4½"
◄About 2,500 in CA coastal scrubland. Has declined due to habitat destruction, cowbird predation. ● Like black-tailed gnatcatcher but darker, browner, with little white on underside of tail. ♪ *Mew*, scratchy, whining; harsh scold notes.

Black-capped Gnatcatcher *Polioptila nigriceps* 4¼" Mexican. Rare in summer in se. AZ; has nested. ● Tail as in blue-gray gnatcatcher, but male has black cap in summer. Female much like female blue-gray; eye-ring narrower, bill longer.

Bananaquit *Coereba flaveola* 4½" Tropical. Several records in se. FL.

Groove-billed Ani

Elegant Trogon ♂ ♀

Smooth-billed Ani

ILLUSTRATOR **JOHN O'NEILL**

<u>Large</u> <u>conical</u> <u>bills</u> These are tropical birds – anis, parrots, and trogons. Anis are sometimes mistakenly dismissed with a passing glance as grackles (Key 112), but their huge conical bills are distinctive. The anis have separate ranges, although both birds wander.

The one parrot that had been adapted to North America, the Carolina parakeet, is now extinct. But Americans have been busily creating cities and tropical gardens that now support small breeding populations of parrots descended from escapes. Much of the natural flora along the Atlantic coast of southern Florida has been replaced by exotic fruits and showy blooms drawn from tropical regions throughout the world. A similar transformation has occurred in the arid lands of southern California. The parrots shown are those that have established breeding colonies or visit from Mexico. Many other escapes may be seen. Small parrots are illustrated here with the large ones, rather than with smaller birds.

◀**Groove-billed Ani** *Crotophaga sulcirostris* 12"
Fairly numerous. In pairs or small flocks in brush, fields, marshes. Often with livestock; feeds on insects stirred up. Also takes fruit, seeds. Flies weakly on short wings; hops clumsily on ground, long tail often oddly cocked. ● Grooves in upper mandible hard to see, can be absent. Black with purplish gloss on wings and tail; greenish gloss on body. Juv. browner. ♪ Variety of slurred whistles, other notes.

Eared Trogon

Budgerigar

Rose-ringed Parakeet

Monk Parakeet

Green Parakeet

Thick-billed Parrot

Canary-winged Parakeet

Red-crowned Parrot

Yellow-headed Parrot

◀**Smooth-billed Ani** *Crotophaga ani* 13"
Fairly numerous, but declining with loss of habitat. Habitat and habits like groove-billed ani's. ● Like groove-billed except upper mandible is smooth with high, curved ridge on culmen; bronze sheen on head and nape. ♪ *Que-ee-eeek?* Rising, querulous call; others like groove-billed's.

Elegant Trogon *Trogon elegans* 12" Tropical. Rare but annual breeder in mountains of se. AZ. Sits still, tail down, posture erect.

Eared Trogon *Euptilotis neoxenus* 14" Tropical. Recorded in Chiricahua Mountains of se. Az. ● Female like male but gray breast and head.

Budgerigar *Melopsittacus undulatus* 7" Popular cage bird from Australia. Escapes widely seen. Breeding populations in s. FL cities. Plumage highly variable; most common form illustrated.

Rose-ringed Parakeet *Psittacula krameri* 16" Native to Asia, Africa. Populations in Miami, Los Angeles. ● Very long tail. Female lacks rose collar.

Monk Parakeet *Myiopsitta monachus* 12" S. American. Small population in s. FL.

Green Parakeet *Aratinga holochlora* 13" Mexican. Rare, but annual visitor to s. TX. Escapes elsewhere. ● Unmarked green overall, pointed tail.

Thick-billed Parrot *Rhynchopsitta pachyrhyncha* 15" Mexican. Visitor to AZ until 1935. Now rare, endangered in Mexico. Reintroduction program begun in US in 1986 failed because captive-raised birds could not succeed in wild.

Canary-winged Parakeet *Brotogeris versicolurus* 9" S. American. In s. FL, s. CA.

Red-crowned Parrot *Amazona viridigenalis* 13" Mexican visitors recorded in extreme s. TX. Small populations established in se. FL, Los Angeles.

Yellow-headed Parrot *Amazona oratrix* 14" Mexican. Small populations in se. FL, Los Angeles. ● Imm. has less yellow on head.

Cardinal-size
Conical bills

CONSULTANT **LOUIS BEVIER**
ILLUSTRATOR **JOHN DAWSON**

Flexor tendons in a bird's leg cause the toes to clamp to a perch even while the bird sleeps.

Perching birds grasp with their toes. Tendons cause the toes to clamp as the leg flexes. The cardinals, towhees, and grosbeaks in this section have three toes forward and one back, like other songbirds. However, their bills are distinctively large and conical, allowing them to feed on a wider range of seeds than the smaller-billed sparrows and finches, as well as many softer foods, such as buds, fruits, and insects, when found.

Seeds are available throughout the winter, even in the conifer forests of the frozen Far North. Bird feeders also assist some of these birds through stressful winters, and species like the cardinal have expanded their winter range northward in response to the availability of food at feeders.

Cardinals search from the ground up for seeds, berries, or bugs. They can be bold but are often wary of people. Towhees are ground-dwellers that are particularly wary around humans. They hop and scratch the ground with both feet simultaneously, trying to uncover seeds and insects in the leaf litter and other ground debris. Their scratching in the underbrush is often heard before the birds are seen. They also take berries and seeds from plants.

Grosbeaks are usually seen in trees, sometimes in shrubs or thickets. They typically move deliberately, and the pine grosbeak, in particular, can be quite tame. Evening grosbeaks feed chiefly on the seeds and buds of maple and box elder, while blue grosbeaks forage primarily on insects. All exhibit a great degree of feeding versatility. They are usually seen in flocks, and their distinctive colors and patterns make them fairly easy to identify even in flight.

Cardinals and towhees are very territorial and aggressive among their own kind. Their own reflection can trigger a fight that they find difficult to resolve.

Pyrrhuloxia

♀ ♂

Cardinal

♂ ♀

Pyrrhuloxias, sometimes called "gray cardinals," are a southwestern relative of the familiar cardinal. Female cardinals are
browner than female pyrrhuloxias, but the best mark is the bill.
The pyrrhuloxia has a curved, parrot-like bill – yellow in adults.

◀**Pyrrhuloxia** *Cardinalis sinuatus* 9"
Fairly numerous in thorn scrub, thickets; also hedgerows,
farmlands, esp. in winter. Habits like cardinal's. ● Male
gray with prominent scarlet markings incl. long scarlet-
tipped crest. Red more restricted on female. Stout, curved
yellow bill can darken in winter. Juv. like female but duller,
with pale wing bars, dark bill. ♪ Like cardinal's.

◀**Cardinal** (Northern) *Cardinalis cardinalis* 9"
Abundant, expanding in New England. Widespread in thickets from woodland edges to backyards. Feeds on ground
or in shrubs on seeds, fruit, insects. Aggressive. ● Male
scarlet with black on face, pink bill, prominent crest. Female
olive-brown with red tinges. Juv. like female but dark bill.
♪ *Whe-cheer*, or *wheet-wheet-wheet*, repeated whistle.

Spotted Towhee

♂

♀ brown-headed
cowbird
Key 114

♀

♂

Eastern Towhee

juv.

Towhees are wary, brush-loving birds with long, rounded tails. All scratch at ground litter noisily to uncover seeds and insects. Both the eastern and spotted towhees (once lumped as the rufous-sided towhee) have dark hoods and rufous sides, and the spotted has prominent white wing bars and spots on its back. The California, canyon, and Abert's towhees are plain but easily distinguished birds. The California towhee, the most nondescript, has a separate range. The canyon towhee shows two good marks: a dark breast spot and a rusty cap. Abert's has warmer colors than the canyon and California towhees and a distinctive black face patch.

◀**Spotted Towhee** *Pipilo maculatus* 8½"
Numerous, widespread in woodland undergrowth and brush, incl. chaparral, streamside thickets, gardens.
● Male has black hood, wings, and back (streaked in some races), with white wing bars and white-tipped scapulars; rufous sides; black tail with white corners; red iris. Female gray-brown, not as brown as female eastern towhee. Juv. streaked brown with brown iris; wings and scapulars as in adult. ♪ *Teeeee*, trilled song; call a low *creee*.

Abert's Towhee

Canyon Towhee

California Towhee

Eastern Towhee *Pipilo erythrophthalmus* 8½"
Still numerous but more rapidly declining than any other bird in East. Habitat similar to that of spotted towhee. ● Like spotted towhee but little white on upperparts. Female has brown hood, back. Race in FL has white iris. ♪ *Drink-your-tea-ee-ee-ee*, last note trilled; call a plaintive *chwee*.

California Towhee *Pipilo crissalis* 8½"
Numerous, widespread in brushy cover, esp. parks, suburbs, where sometimes hides under parked cars as if in brush. ● Dull gray-brown, darkest on tail. Face and throat paler, cinnamon-buff. Rusty undertail coverts. ♪ *Pink*, metallic note given singly or in accelerating series.

Canyon Towhee *Pipilo fuscus* 8½"
Fairly numerous in scrubby, arid hillsides. ● Buffy throat and upper breast outlined in fine dark streaks. Pale belly, central breast spot, rusty undertail coverts. Rusty cap contrasts with grayish back. ♪ *Chilli, chilli, chilli*, musical song.

Abert's Towhee *Pipilo aberti* 9½"
Fairly numerous in desert valley brush: mesquite, salt cedar, streamside willows. Also in backyards, farmlands. ● Brown, paler below. Black on forehead, chin, and in front of eyes. ♪ *Peek*, metallic call; or given in series as song.

TOWHEES

juv.

Crimson-collared Grosbeak ♂ ♀

♂ **Yellow Grosbeak**

Green-tailed Towhee

Evening Grosbeak ♂ ♀

The green-tailed towhee's rusty cap, white chin, and dusky mustache are all good marks. Grosbeaks, including the two on the next Key, have huge bills. Most plumages are distinctive and attractive, but female rose-breasted and black-headed grosbeaks resemble large, streaked sparrows. The female black-headed is buffier overall and has only faint side streaks. Male rose-breasted and black-headed grosbeaks attain adult plumage in their second year; young males have plumage varying from female-like to nearly adult male.

◀**Green-tailed Towhee** *Pipilo chlorurus* 7¼"
Fairly numerous in open lands with dense brushy cover. Nests mostly in mountains. In lowlands in winter, often with sparrows. Wary but curious; runs to cover. ● Green in wings and tail visible only in good light. Gray face and breast with white throat and dark mustache. Rusty cap, yellow wing linings. Juv. streaked, lacks crown patch. ♪ *Meuw*, cat-like call.

Evening Grosbeak *Coccothraustes vespertinus* 8"
Fairly numerous in summer in conifers, mixed forests.

Rose-breasted Grosbeak

rose-breasted

Black-headed Grosbeak

◀Irregular in winter in wandering flocks, searching for seeds and buds, esp. of conifers, maples. Takes sunflower seeds at feeders. Tame, noisy. ● Male brown and yellow with yellow forehead and eyebrow, large white patch in black wing. Female grayer, 2 white wing patches. ♪ *Cleep!* Loud call.

Black-headed Grosbeak *Pheucticus melanocephalus* 8"
Numerous in woodlands, parks, and suburbs. Feeds mostly
◀in trees; moves deliberately. ● Adult male has deep orange breast, sides, rump, collar; black head and back; white patch in wings. Female and juv. have buff, unstreaked breasts.
♪ Long, melodious, thrush-like song; call a sharp *peek*.

Rose-breasted Grosbeak *Pheucticus ludovicianus* 8"
◀Numerous. Habitat and habits like black-headed's. ● Adult male black and white with red breast and wing linings, partially obscured in fall by buff feather tips. Female brown above with whitish eyebrow and median stripe, breast streaks, yellow wing linings. Male in 1st fall has buff breast, suggests female black-headed except for fine breast streaks and some red in breast and wing linings. ♪ Song like black-headed's.

Yellow Grosbeak *Pheucticus chrysopeplus* 9" Mexican. Nearly annual in se. AZ.

Crimson-collared Grosbeak *Rhodothraupis celaeno* 8½" Mexican. Records in TX.

Pine Grosbeak

Blue Grosbeak   1st spring ♂

A flock of pine grosbeaks usually includes some distinctive rosy males. Male blue grosbeaks are larger than the similar indigo bunting (Key 149) and have brown wing bars. Females have blue hints in the wings and rump, but young fall birds can be all-brown.

◄Pine Grosbeak *Pinicola enucleator* 9"
Fairly numerous in coniferous forest edges. At high elevations in US in summer. Irruptive flocks in winter mostly imms. Tame. ● Male red with white wing bars, larger than in white-winged crossbill (Key 151). Female gray with olive head, rump. Imm. male has reddish head. ♪ *Tee-tee-tew*, whistled flight call.

Blue Grosbeak *Guiraca caerulea* 7"
Fairly numerous in thickets, hedgerows, esp. near ◄water or farmlands. Expanding range in Northeast. Secretive, but male sings from conspicuous perch. ● Male deep blue (looks black in poor light) with brown wing bars. Female and juv. brown with rusty wing bars. Male acquires adult plumage by 2nd winter. ♪ *Chink!* Explosive call note; song a series of warbled phrases.

Sparrow-size
Conical bills

CONSULTANT **LOUIS BEVIER**
ILLUSTRATOR **DALE DYER**

Birds that eat seeds can find food throughout the winter.

Almost all the small, conical-billed seed-crunchers are sparrows or finches, including birds called buntings, redpolls, and longspurs. The exceptions are the bobolink, a member of the blackbird family, which has become a seed specialist, and several Old World species now established in North America.

Sparrows and finches are the same size as warblers and other small bug-eaters with straight bills. But even when bill shapes cannot be distinguished, the seed-crunchers can often be separated from the bug-eaters. Many sparrows and finches have distinctive brown streaks on their backs or breasts. Few straight-billed birds show this pattern. Habitat and behavior also provide clues. Where there are seeds but no bugs, such as in fields in winter, only seed-eating birds will be found. Finches and sparrows are often on the ground or near it in bushes and seedy weeds. Finches are also seen in trees, hanging on birch catkins or pinecones looking for seeds, but most birds flitting about a treetop are hunting insects.

During the summer, sparrows and finches typically supplement their diet with insects found near the ground. Most young birds require the concentrated protein. However, goldfinches eat seeds almost exclusively, with the satisfying result that cowbird chicks do not survive long in a goldfinch nest. All native finches and sparrows defend nesting territories. Most form flocks in winter, and some forage in small groups even when nesting.

Although closely related, finches can be separated from sparrows. The best mark is the finches' undulating flight. Finches also typically have heavier bills. Crossbills (which are finches) have the most distinctive bills – crossed at the tips and used for extracting seeds from pine- and spruce cones.

Some finches and sparrows, such as longspurs, nest in grasslands or other open areas, where there are no high perches from which males can sing in spring. These males often advertise by "skylarking" – giving their songs as they flutter in place in midair.

The most colorful birds are illustrated on the first Keys in this section, followed by those with less colorful but notable patterns. At the end of the section are the confusing, small, brown-streaked sparrows that seem to have few, if any, field marks.

Painted Bunting

juv.

♂

♀

fall ♂

1st spring ♂

spring ♂

Indigo Bunting

♀

The brilliant adult male buntings would seem easy to identify, but in poor light both indigo and varied bunting males look black. Most of the females are shy and share a drab brown plumage that lacks the heavily streaked back typically seen on sparrows. Only the female painted bunting, with its bright green upperparts, is distinctive. Fortunately, the birds seen are usually singing males, often on sunny perches that reveal their colors. The male indigo bunting resembles the larger blue grosbeak (Key 148), but the grosbeak has a much heavier bill and brown wing bars. The lazuli bunting might at first be confused with a western bluebird (Key 120).

◄**Painted Bunting** *Passerina ciris* 5½"
Fairly numerous in dense shrubs, thickets, woodland edges, gardens, esp. streamside. In flocks during migration. Shy, often unseen, except when male sings. ● Male brilliant red, blue, green. Female bright green above, yellowish below. Juv. drab with hints of green above or yellow below. Male in 1st spring like female but brighter; may show hints of adult male color. ♪ Song a clear, rich warble, similar to that of warbling vireo.

Blue Bunting ♂ ♀

Varied Bunting ♂ ♀

western bluebird
Key 120

Lazuli Bunting ♀ ♂

◀**Indigo Bunting** *Passerina cyanea* 5½"
Numerous in summer in forest regrowth, woodland edges. A few stragglers winter in s. FL. ● Spring male iridescent blue, purplish on head. Female brown above, paler below with faint breast streaking, whitish throat; blue tinges in wings, tail, sometimes on shoulder, rump. Fall male has fresh plumage with brown tips concealing most blue. Most 1st-spring males are patchy and have brown wing bars. Juv. like female. ♪ Song a short series of paired, jumbled notes.

◀**Lazuli Bunting** *Passerina amoena* 5½"
Fairly numerous in weedy fields, grassy clearings. ● Male blue with rufous breast and flanks, white belly, bold wing bars. Female has bolder wing bars than female indigo bunting; buffy breast band contrasts with white belly. Juv. has breast streaks. ♪ Song faster than indigo's; some notes unpaired.

Varied Bunting *Passerina versicolor* 5½"
◀Scarce, local in mesquite scrub, esp. near water. ● Stubbier bill than in indigo bunting, curved upper mandible. Male black with red, blue, purple gloss; feathers brown-tipped in winter. Female like female indigo. ♪ Song like painted bunting's.

Blue Bunting *Cyanocompsa parellina* 5½" Mexican. Several records in s. TX, one in LA. ● Thick, strongly curved bill. Male's forehead paler than indigo bunting's.

COLORED BUNTINGS

149

American Goldfinch

winter ♂

summer ♂

summer ♀

♀ Lawrence's winter

American

UNDERTAILS

Lawrence's

Lawrence's Goldfinch

winter ♂

summer ♂

summer ♀

Male goldfinches in summer are strikingly distinctive. (Note the two forms of the lesser goldfinch.) Winter flocks and females call for a close look. The American is white under the rump, and males have a yellow shoulder patch. The lesser is yellow under the rump and has a white wing patch. A sure mark for Lawrence's is the extensive yellow in the wings. The yellow on a pine siskin is more subdued; it is the streaking that is distinctive. Calls and tail patterns are diagnostic and especially useful in identifying flying flocks.

◀ **American Goldfinch** *Carduelis tristis* 5"
Numerous, widespread in thickets, weedy fields, woodland edges. Fond of thistle seeds. Usually forages in flocks even when nesting. Flocks fly in distinctive roller-coaster style.
● Summer male bright yellow with black cap, wings, tail; white rump, undertail coverts. Female duller, olive above, lacks black cap. Winter and juv. like summer female but browner above. White spots on outer tail feathers extend to tip of tail. ♪ *Po-tato-chip*, flight call. Song a long series of phrases given randomly.

Eurasian Siskin

Pine Siskin

pine siskin

♀ lesser

black-backed ♂

♀

green-backed ♂

Lesser Goldfinch

◀**Lawrence's Goldfinch** *Carduelis lawrencei* 4¾"
Scarce, unpredictable on dry weedy slopes, chaparral.
● Gray with yellow breast, wings, rump. Male brighter with
black face, greenish back. Duller in winter with browner
back. Juv. shows little yellow, faint streaks. White tail spots
are at midtail. ♪ *Tink-ul*, bell-like flight call.

Lesser Goldfinch *Carduelis psaltria* 4½"
◀Fairly numerous in thickets, woodland edges, esp. dry
brushy fields. Flight style similar to American goldfinch's.
● Male bright yellow below with black cap, black or green
back (some intergrades). Female paler below with greenish
back, lacks black cap. White tail spots at base of tail. Juv.
resembles female. ♪ *Tee-yeé*, or *teé-yer*, flight call.

Pine Siskin *Carduelis pinus* 5"
◀Numerous, in conifers, mixed woods (feeding on birch, fir,
alder seeds) as well as in thickets, weedy fields. In large
wandering flocks in winter. Flocks fly in distinctive undulating
pattern, bunching and separating. ● Sharply pointed, slender bill for a finch. A few have faint greenish backs, suggest
female **Eurasian Siskin** *(C. spinus)* but have more yellow in
wings, less on breast, fainter streaking below. ♪ *Weeer*,
descending flight call; also *shreee*, ascending buzzy trill.

YELLOW FINCHES

Red Crossbill

♂

juv.

♀

♀ winter

Gray-crowned Rosy Finch

♂ winter interior

♂ winter coastal

The twitters and chips of a flock of crossbills flying overhead are usually the first clues to these wandering birds' presence. Only at close range are the crossed bill tips visible. Crossbills are tame, and the white-winged often feeds especially deliberately and fearlessly. Most rosy finches summer above the timberline near snowbanks, moving to lower elevations in harsh winters. Males show pink on the wings and body. Females are duller, some with barely a hint of color. Note the contrast of the pale underwings in flight. The rosy finches can be difficult to separate by plumage.

◄**Red Crossbill** *Loxia curvirostra* 6¼"
Fairly numerous in conifers, esp. pines. Flocks wander widely and separately, specialize in different cones; may be several species. Irrupts south when cone crop fails, feeding on seeds, fruits, buds. ● Bill tips crossed. Male usually brick red but can be orange or yellow. Female grayish olive, brightest on underparts, rump; may show some red; throat usually gray. Imm. streaked. ♪ *Jip,* or *jip, jip-jip,* harsh flight call.

imm. ♂

♂

White-winged Crossbill

♀

Brown-capped Rosy Finch

♀

summer

♂

♂

summer

Black Rosy Finch

◄**Gray-crowned Rosy Finch** *Leucosticte tephrocotis* 6¼"
Fairly numerous in alpine areas. Winters in large flocks,
sometimes mixed. ● Black forehead, gray crown, brown
body and cheeks. Pink on shoulder, rump, belly, flanks. Bill
black in summer, yellow in winter. Female may have only
trace of gray, little or no pink. Birds in Aleutians, Coast
Range, Cascades have larger gray patch incl. cheek. Imm.
gray-brown overall. ♪ *Tchew,* nasal call.

Black Rosy Finch *Leucosticte atrata* 6¼"
Scarce, local. Habits as in gray-crowned. ● Blacker than
gray-crowned. Female blackish overall, little gray on crown.

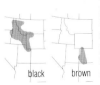

black   brown

Brown-capped Rosy Finch *Leucosticte australis* 6¼"
Scarce, local. Habits as in gray-crowned. ● Like gray-
crowned but head brown, red extends higher onto breast.

White-winged Crossbill *Loxia leucoptera* 6½"
◄Fairly numerous in West, abundant in East. In conifers, esp.
spruce. Habits like red crossbill's. ● Crossed bill tips, broad
white wing bars (upper bar can be hidden). Male bright pink;
female olive-gray with yellowish tinge, diffuse streaking. Imm.
male yellow with red or pink patches. Juv. streaked. ♪ *Chit-
chit,* often in series; harsher, flatter than in red crossbill.

Male finches are one identification problem, females another, and the redpolls yet a third. The amount of red on male finches varies widely, and in house finches the red can have an orange cast. Best mark for the male house finch is the brown streaking on the belly. Female house finches can be told by their plain faces. Note the sharp contrast on the face of the female purple finch. The facial contrast is less in the female Cassin's but still more than in the house finch. Redpolls have neat red caps and black chins. The hoary redpoll is paler but hard to distinguish from the common redpoll.

◄**Cassin's Finch** *Carpodacus cassinii* 6¼"
Fairly numerous in open conifers at high elevations in summer. In flocks at lower elevations in winter. ● Bright red crown of male, often held slightly erect, contrasts with brown nape and paler red throat. Belly white, rump red. Female has sharper streaks on whiter breast than in purple finch; streaks continue onto undertail coverts; faint eyebrow and cheek patch. ♪♪ *Tee-dee-up*, or *see-up*, flight calls.

Purple Finch *Carpodacus purpureus* 6"
Fairly numerous in open woodlands, suburban conifers;

Hoary Redpoll

Brambling
♂

♀

Common Redpoll

♂

♀

House Finch

♂

◄declining in East. ● Male extensively wine red, incl. back; belly whitish. Female has well-defined eyebrow and cheek patch, heavily streaked underparts but clear undertail coverts. ♪♪ *Pick*, sharp, metallic flight call.

House Finch *Carpodacus mexicanus* 6"
Abundant backyard bird, also in scrub in West. Introduced in East in 1960s; increasing westward, ranges may have united.
● Slimmer than Cassin's or purple finches with shorter wings,
◄smaller notch in tail. Male has red (rarely orange to yellow) forehead and eye stripe, bib, rump; brown streaks on sides, belly. Female has plainer face and back than Cassin's or purple finches. ♪ *Cheep*, flight call, often given in series.

Common Redpoll *Carduelis flammea* 5¼"
◄Irregular winter visitor to US, often in large flocks. Abundant in summer on tundra. ● Red cap, black chin; dark streaks above, on sides. Male has pink breast. Can be pale, suggest hoary redpoll. ♪ *Chit-chit-chit*, raspy call.

Hoary Redpoll *Carduelis hornemanni* 5¼"
Habits like common redpoll's; much rarer in US. ● Like
◄common redpoll but typically frostier, with shorter bill. Lacks streaks on rump, undertail coverts. ♪ Like common's.

Brambling *Fringilla montifringilla* 6¼" Eurasian. Migrant in w. Aleutians. Handful of other widespread N. American records.

summer ♂
Dickcissel
♀
imm.

summer ♂
Bobolink
♀

The black and yellow markings of the summer male dickcissel suggest a meadowlark (Key 115). The black male bobolinks and lark buntings are also distinctive in summer, but females and winter birds of all three species are duller and finch-like. Lark buntings show distinctive broad, whitish wing patches year-round. Snow buntings on their Arctic nesting grounds are a striking black and white. In winter, flocks appear surprisingly dark on the ground. When flushed they reveal their white underparts and wing patches.

◀**Dickcissel** *Spiza americana* 6¼"
Numerous but seriously declining; irregular in grain- or weed fields, prairies. Large flocks in migration. Disappeared from most of East in 19th century. ● Male has yellow breast, black bib (obscure in fall), rufous shoulder. Female duller, lacks bib; suggests female house sparrow (Key 163) but has large dull bill, usually shows rufous shoulder and some yellow on face. Imm. streaked. ♪ *Brrrrt*, buzzer-like flight call. Song is 2-3 *dick* notes followed by hoarse trill.

Snow Bunting

summer ♂

winter

winter ♂   summer ♂   **Lark Bunting**

♀

◀**Bobolink** *Dolichonyx oryzivorus* 7"
Fairly numerous, declining; in grainfields, tall grasslands. Flocks in fall migration favor weedy grainfields, esp. corn, rice. ● Summer male black with white rump and scapulars, buff nape. Pattern obscured in spring by buff feather edges. Female, fall birds buff with crown stripes; streaks on back, sides. ♪ *Pink!* Sharp flight call. *Bob-o-link,* bubbling song.

◀**Lark Bunting** *Calamospiza melanocorys* 7"
Numerous in prairies, esp. dry plains, sagebrush, even barren land. Flocks in migration, winter. Takes many insects, esp. grasshoppers. ● Summer male black with white wing patches. Female and imm. gray-brown above with whitish wing patches, white below with dark streaks. Winter male like female but retains black chin; acquires summer plumage gradually. ♪ *Hoo-ee,* soft call note. Song is long, varied.

◀**Snow Bunting** *Plectrophenax nivalis* 6¾"
Numerous but irregular winter visitor, usually in large flocks on snowy fields, beaches, dunes, barren lands. Walks. ● Extensive white on body and in wings; males whitest. Rusty above and on breast in winter, with dark back streaks. Rusty feather tips wear away over winter. ♪ *Tew,* whistled call note; also, soft rattle.

FINCH-LIKE

153

Lapland Longspur

winter ♂

winter ♀

Lapland
summer ♂

summer ♂

winter
♂

winter
♀

Chestnut-
collared
Longspur

Male longspurs are strikingly patterned in summer. The chestnut-collared and McCown's longspurs nest on the Great Plains, but the Lapland and Smith's nest in the Arctic, largely unseen. Females and winter birds have a nondescript, sparrow-like pattern, which makes them hard to see even though winter flocks gather on open grasslands – even barren ground – and creep about searching for seed. Flocks are often flushed before being seen. Their flight is high and undulating, but the birds soon land, becoming invisible again. Tail patterns are distinctive and the surest winter plumage mark.

◀ **Lapland Longspur** *Calcarius lapponicus* 6¼"
Numerous in winter on short-grass plains, barren ground, beaches. Often flocks with horned larks (Key 121) or snow buntings (Key 153). ● White in tail limited to outer feathers; less than in other longspurs and not always apparent. Rufous wing panel in all plumages. Female and winter birds have dark-outlined cheek patch, white belly. Summer birds have reddish nape, black face and breast. ♪ *Tew*, descending note similar to flight call of snow bunting; also, dry rattle.

winter ♂

Smith's Longspur

Smith's summer ♂

summer ♂

McCown's Longspur

♀

◀**Chestnut-collared Longspur** *Calcarius ornatus* 5½"
Fairly numerous on prairies in summer, open fields in winter.
Declining with loss of habitat to cropland. In flocks in winter.
● Small with small bill. Black wedge on white tail. Summer
male black below with chestnut nape, intricately patterned
head. Winter male shows some black on breast, chestnut
on nape; some have white shoulders. Female and imm.
plain buff below and lack any chestnut on nape. ♪ *Chiddle*,
musical flight call, different from dry rattle of other longspurs.

◀**McCown's Longspur** *Calcarius mccownii* 6"
Scarce, local, on barren ground, short-grass plains. Feeds
heavily on grasshoppers in summer. Often flocks with
horned larks (Key 121) in winter. ● Tail white with inverted
black T. Summer male pale gray with black crown, breast,
mustache; rufous shoulder; large black bill. Female and
winter males buff to whitish below with pinkish bill; most
show some rufous on shoulder, some black on breast.
♪ Flight call a coarse rattle.

◀**Smith's Longspur** *Calcarius pictus* 6"
Fairly numerous but local in winter in dry short-grass prairie.
● White outer tail feathers. Winter birds buff below with fine
breast streaking. White shoulder patch often obscured by
body feathers. Summer male buff below with black-and-
white face pattern. ♪ Flight call a dry rattle.

All forms of the dark-eyed junco have white-edged tails, which they flick in flight and when alarmed. Most have pink bills, dark hoods, and white bellies. Some intergrades between the forms shown occur. The black-chinned sparrow lacks the junco's white tail margins and has the characteristic streaked back of a sparrow.

Dark-eyed Junco *Junco hyemalis* 6¼"
Numerous to abundant. Feeds on ground, hopping about searching for exposed seeds and insects at forest edges and clearings. Winters in small flocks, often mixed, in open woodlands. Fairly tame; when disturbed flies to lower tree branches, flashing white tail feathers. ● All forms have pale, usually pink, bills except for southernmost "gray-headed" form, which has dark upper mandible.

"Slate-colored" is abundant eastern form, rare in West. Male slate gray with white underparts. Female and winter birds can be brownish above.

"White-winged" form larger than others with more white in tail; most have 2 broad white wing bars; fairly numerous in

Yellow-eyed Junco

spring ♂

Black-chinned Sparrow

♀ and fall

"Oregon"

♀

♂

"Oregon" pink-sided

"gray-headed"

"Oregon"

ponderosa pine of Black Hills, SD. Other forms occasionally show white wing bars.

"Gray-headed" form fairly numerous in southern Rockies, has pale gray head and sides with black lores, rufous back.

"Oregon" form numerous throughout West. Male has black hood, rusty brown back, pinkish to buff sides. Female duller with grayer hood.

"Pink-sided" variation of "Oregon" form in northern Rockies has broader pink sides, pale gray hood, and black lores. Juvs. of all forms brownish, heavily streaked. ♪ *Tik,* or twittering alarm notes. Song a musical trill like chipping sparrow's.

Black-chinned Sparrow *Spizella atrogularis* 5¾"
Scarce, local, usually seen singly on high, arid, brushy slopes. Sometimes in winter flocks of mixed sparrows. Secretive. ● Gray with streaked brown back, pink bill. ◀Summer male has black chin, lores. ♪ *Sweet, sweet, sweet,* musical song accelerating to a trill.

Yellow-eyed Junco *Junco phaeonotus* 6¼" Mexican. Numerous at high elevation in conifers and pine-oak forests of extreme se. AZ, sw. NM. Tame. ● Yellow eyes.

summary ♂
winter
imm.

Harris' Sparrow

juv.
White-crowned Sparrow
imm.
"Gambell's" form

These large sparrows with distinctive crowns are all fairly tame ground-feeders that form small flocks, often mixed, in winter. The contrast of Harris' sparrow's large pink bill against its black bib and crown is a good mark. The white-crowned and white-throated have striped heads, including forms with brownish head patterns. The white-throated has a well-defined white throat patch, a dark bill, and a shorter neck than the white-crowned; its yellow lores can be faint. The crown patch of the golden-crowned sparrow is faint on some winter birds, but nearly all show a hint of yellow.

◄**Harris' Sparrow** *Zonotrichia querula* 7½"
Fairly numerous but local in winter around brush, hedge-rows, woodland edges, esp. streamside. ● Large size. Pink bill contrasts with black crown, throat. In winter, black crown obscured by grayish feather tips; black bib may show white flecks or white neck patch. Imm. has white throat, buff head, less breast spotting than adult. ♪ *Weenk*, alarm note.

juv.

White-throated Sparrow

tan-striped form

Golden-crowned Sparrow

imm.

juv.

◀**White-crowned Sparrow** *Zonotrichia leucophrys* 7"
Numerous, widespread in diverse brushy habitats; in winter
esp. residential areas, roadsides, parks. Abundant in West.
● Black-and-white striped crown; gray cheek, nape, breast.
Bill varies regionally from pink to yellow, with dusky tip;
lores can be black or white. Imm. has tan crown with red-
dish brown stripes. Juv. similar to imm. but streaked below.
♪ *Tseep,* high, thin call. Song musical, whistled, ends in trill.

Golden-crowned Sparrow *Zonotrichia atricapilla* 7"
◀Fairly numerous in summer in shrubs near timberline, esp.
near bogs, wet ravines; coastal in AK. Winters in dense
brush. ● Golden crown with black borders; duller in winter,
finely streaked in imm. Dusky upper mandible, pale lower.
Juv. like imm. but streaked below. ♪ *Oh-dear-me,* descending whistled notes; *tchup,* call note.

White-throated Sparrow *Zonotrichia albicollis* 6¾"
Abundant in summer at brushy edges in coniferous or mixed
◀forest. Winter flocks in dense woods, backyard brush. More
secretive than white-crowned sparrow. ● White throat, black
and white or brown and tan crown stripes, yellow lores, dark
bill. Juv. has muted adult head pattern, streaked breast.
♪ *Old Sam Peabody Peabody Peabody,* thin, whistled song.

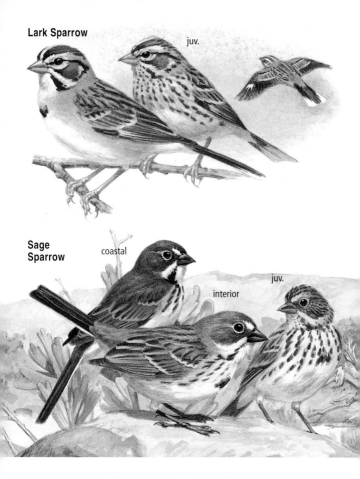

Lark Sparrow

juv.

Sage Sparrow

coastal

interior

juv.

The lark sparrow has an unmistakable head pattern and a clear breast with a dark central spot. The white flash in the corners of the tail is a good mark as the birds flush from rural roadsides. Vesper sparrows (Key 161), sage sparrows, and black-throated sparrows also have white in their tails, but only a narrow, often inconspicuous, outer margin. On the sage sparrow the dark head with white markings and the dark breast spot are the best marks. The black-throated sparrow's black bib is unmistakable.

◄**Lark Sparrow** *Chondestes grammacus* 6½"
Numerous in West in grassy areas with scattered trees, shrubs. Scarce in East, where it once nested widely. Often perches on posts or wires. Usually feeds in flocks even when nesting; large flocks in winter. ● White margins and corners on tail, chestnut head markings, black chest spot. Juv. has streaked chest without spot, faint head pattern of adult. ♪ Long, varied song, musical for sparrow.

Sage Sparrow *Amphispiza belli* 6¼"
Fairly numerous but secretive in scattered brush of dry flatlands; on scrubby chaparral slopes in CA. Race on San

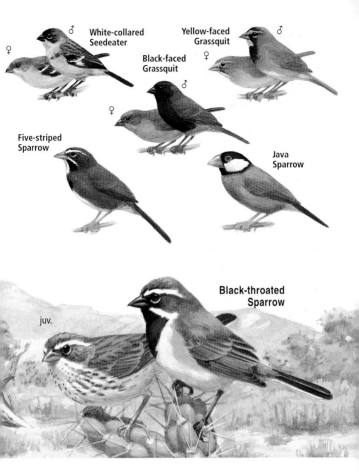

White-collared Seedeater ♂
White-collared Seedeater ♀
Yellow-faced Grassquit ♂
Black-faced Grassquit ♂
Yellow-faced Grassquit ♀
Black-faced Grassquit ♀
Five-striped Sparrow
Java Sparrow

Black-throated Sparrow

juv.

◀Clemente I., CA, is threatened. Often flicks tail; runs to cover when approached. Small flocks in winter. ● Gray head with white eye-ring, eyebrow. Black whisker marks and central breast spot, streaked sides. Long black tail with white margins. Coastal form darker above. Juv. streaked. ♪ High, thin call note, often repeated rapidly as twitter.

Black-throated Sparrow *Amphispiza bilineata* 5½"
◀Numerous. The common sparrow of hot, dry desert. Flicks tail like sage sparrow. Flies rather than running to cover. Small flocks in winter. ● Black bib, bold face pattern. Long blackish tail with more white on outer feathers than in sage sparrow. Juv. streaked above and below; dull face pattern. ♪ Song is 2 quick, high, clear, rising notes followed by trill.

White-collared Seedeater *Sporophila torqueola* 4½" Mexican. Rare in lower Rio Grande Valley.

Yellow-faced Grassquit *Tiaris olivacea* 4½" Tropical. Recorded in s. FL, s. TX.

Black-faced Grassquit *Tiaris bicolor* 4½" W. Indian. Handful of s. FL records.

Five-striped Sparrow *Amphispiza quinquestriata* 6" Mexican. Rare in extreme se. AZ in dense desert scrub on high, dry, rocky slopes.

Java Sparrow *Padda oryzivora* 6" Javan. Introduced and established around Miami, FL. ● Imm. brownish with dark, but very large, bill.

The sparrows that follow are sometimes called "LBJs," or "Little Brown Jobs," because of their similar and obscure dark markings. Many of them are also secretive, running through cover rather than flushing or flushing briefly in weak flight, only to drop quickly back to cover. The furtive sparrows are best seen and identified in spring, when males reveal themselves to sing.

There is no need to despair about identifying a drab sparrow once you have it in your vision. Drabness itself is a very good field mark, since it eliminates from consideration all the prominently marked species. And, of course, no bird is totally featureless. A sparrow's breast can be streaked or clear, the crown can be a solid-colored cap or variously striped and streaked, and the bill can vary in size and color. Many sparrows that have clear breasts as adults show streaks in juvenal plumage. However, in most such species the breast streaks are lost soon after the young bird leaves the nest, and the streaked juvenal plumage is seldom seen.

Because it is so difficult to get binoculars focused on many of these sparrows, it is especially useful to learn the shapes, habitats, and behaviors of the various genera. Then if you can catch sight of a plumage mark or two, you can often cinch an identification.

Spizella
Key 158

Birds of the genus *Spizella* are small with plain breasts and fairly long, notched tails. They are typically found in shrubby, second-growth areas or woodland edges and openings rather than in marshes or grasslands. They are not shy, but instead feed openly, on or near the ground, in small flocks except when nesting. They often retreat to trees when alarmed.

Not all plain sparrow-like birds are sparrows. Young birds, females, and winter plumages of several other species can be quite sparrow-like and nondescript.

♀ RED-WINGED BLACKBIRD

♀ BOBOLINK

JUV. BROWN-HEADED COWBIRD

♀ DICKCISSEL

Aimophila
Key 159

Like the *Spizella*, the *Aimophila* sparrows have plain, unstreaked breasts. They differ by being larger, with long, rounded (not notched) tails, and by foraging warily, alone or in pairs – never in flocks. Habitats are specific and fairly limited for each species. None is normally seen in marshes or wet areas.

Melospiza
Key 160

The *Melospiza* have rounded tails (a little shorter than in the *Aimophila*), which they pump distinctively in flight. Only one, the swamp sparrow, has a plain breast; the others are streaked. All prefer dense or damp vegetation. They tend to be secretive and are seldom in flocks. Illustrated with the *Melospiza* is the fox sparrow, a distinctively large sparrow with heavy breast streaking and a blunt-tipped tail.

Ammodramus
Keys 161-62

The *Ammodramus* sparrows are small and tend to have flat foreheads and short tails. Tail feathers are distinctively pointed on most. All are streaked below except for the grasshopper sparrow, and all are secretive; none flock. Some species are typically birds of grasslands (Key 161), and others prefer marshes or wet areas (Key 162). The savannah and vesper sparrows are illustrated with the grassland *Ammodramus*. They are streaked below, like most *Ammodramus,* but their foreheads are not flattened and their tails are notched rather than spiky. The vesper sparrow has distinctive white outer tail feathers. Small flocks of savannah or vesper sparrows are common in winter.

One small brown sparrow is abundant, tame, and easy to identify – the house sparrow (Key 163).

AMERICAN PIPIT

♀ INDIGO BUNTING

♀ LAPLAND LONGSPUR

♀ HOUSE FINCH

PINE SISKIN

PLAIN SPARROWS

Tree Sparrow

juv.

Field Sparrow

juv.

Three of these sparrows have easily seen rusty red caps and fairly obvious marks: a chest spot in the tree sparrow, a bright pink bill in the field sparrow, and a white eyebrow over a black eyeline in the chipping sparrow. In winter young chippies lack the bright cap; but the black eyeline continuing in front of the eye and the gray rump distinguish them from the clay-colored and Brewer's sparrows, which have brown rumps. Separating the clay-colored from Brewer's sparrow is a job for good binoculars.

◀**Tree Sparrow** (American) *Spizella arborea* 6¼"
Numerous, but large declines in East. In small flocks in winter at wooded edges, weedy fields, feeders. Nests on tundra near treeline. ● Rusty cap, partially obscured in winter by gray feather tips. Central breast spot, white wing bars. Upper mandible dark; lower, yellow. Juv. has streaked brown crown, streaked breast. ♪ *Tee-dle-eet,* musical call.

Field Sparrow *Spizella pusilla* 5¾"
Numerous but declining; in overgrown fields, brush, briars.
◀Shier than other *Spizella;* usually avoids backyards. Small flocks in winter. ● Pink bill contrasts with gray face. White eye-ring gives blank expression. Rusty crown and streak behind eye, pink legs. White wing bars, unstreaked gray

juv.

1st winter

summer

Clay-colored Sparrow

Brewer's Sparrow

Chipping Sparrow

1st winter

juv.

summer

underparts. Juv. duller with streaks on breast. ♪ Song is several plaintive, musical whistles accelerating to a trill.

◀**Chipping Sparrow** *Spizella passerina* 5½"
Abundant on lawns or lawn-like cover at forest edges, mountain meadows. Small flocks during winter and migration, usually mixed. ● Rufous crown in summer, with white eyebrow, black eyeline extending to bill, black bill, gray rump. Face and crown duller in winter, esp. 1st winter; bill dull pink. Juv. holds breast streaks until late fall. ♪ Song a series of dry *chips*, usually given rapidly.

◀**Brewer's Sparrow** *Spizella breweri* 5½"
Fairly numerous in sagebrush flats; alpine meadows in Canadian Rockies. Winter flocks, often mixed, in desert scrub. ● Gray-brown, nondescript; dull pink bill. Fainter head pattern than in clay-colored sparrow, esp. in summer; crown brown with fine black streaks, no defined median stripe. Faint white eye-ring, brown rump. Juv. finely streaked below. ♪ Song a series of varied buzzy and musical trills.

Clay-colored Sparrow *Spizella pallida* 5½"
Fairly numerous in summer on dry, brushy plains. Scarce in US in winter, often in mixed flocks. ● Distinct, contrasting head stripes, eyebrow. Also note dark cheek patch, gray nape and side of neck. Buffier below in winter, esp. 1st winter; crown can be faintly streaked. Dull pink bill, brown rump. Juv. streaked below. ♪ Song a series of insect-like buzzes.

Bachman's Sparrow

Botteri's

Cassin's

juv.

juv.

Cassin's Sparrow

Cassin's sparrow skylarking

Bachman's and Cassin's sparrows are similar and nondescript except for their large bills and long, rounded tails. Cassin's shows a bit of white in the corners of its tail. Separate songs, ranges, and habitats make these two easy to separate in spite of similar plumages. Both are furtive and best located by their songs in spring. Bachman's continues singing until fall. The rufous-crowned sparrow differs from other rusty-capped sparrows in its large bill, tail shape, and the black and white whisker marks.

historical range

◀**Bachman's Sparrow** *Aimophila aestivalis* 6"
Scarce, seriously declining, range contracting to south from historical maximum reached in early 1900s. Once numerous in grassy undergrowth of mature pine forests. With felling of mature forest, now found in similar grassy areas with little brush: overgrown fields, utility clear-cuts, burns. Seldom flushes. ● Reddish brown streaked crown and back, reddish eyeline. Grayish to strongly buff underparts. Juv. streaked below, thin eye-ring. ♪♪ 1-2 long whistled notes followed by trill or warble on different pitch. Whistled notes and trill vary with repetition.

Botteri's Sparrow

Rufous-winged Sparrow

Olive Sparrow

juv.

Rufous-crowned Sparrow

◄Cassin's Sparrow *Aimophila cassinii* 6"
Fairly numerous in dry, open areas with thin vegetation, scattered cactus or brush. ● Gray-brown with darker streaking on crown and back, blurry flank streaks. White tail corners (best seen when skylarking), barred center tail feathers. Juv. similar, streaked below. ♩♩ *Ti-ti-tseeeeee, tay, tay,* long, liquid trill with distinct beginning and ending notes.

◄Rufous-crowned Sparrow *Aimophila ruficeps* 5¾"
Fairly numerous, local, on rocky outcrops of slopes with scattered brush, grass. Shy, scurries to cover, seldom flushes; but curious, responds to squeaking noises. Tame in some areas, visiting feeders. ● Rufous crown with pale median line, pale gray eyebrow, black and white whisker marks. Overall reddishness varies regionally. Juv. buffier with streaked breast, crown. ♩♩ *Dear,* sharp call often doubled or tripled.

Botteri's Sparrow *Aimophila botterii* 6" Mexican. Scarce in se. AZ, Gulf coast of s. TX. ● Like Cassin's but lacks flank streaks, white corners to tail, distinct barring on central tail feathers. Does not skylark. ♩♩ *Chip* notes, accelerating into a trill.

Rufous-winged Sparrow *Aimophila carpalis* 5¾" Mexican. Scarce, local in south-central AZ. ● Grayish head with rusty crown stripes, eyeline, shoulder; 2 black whiskers. ♩♩ *Seep,* high, loud call note.

Olive Sparrow *Arremonops rufivirgatus* 6¼" Tropical. Numerous in thickets in southernmost TX. ● Dull olive above with rusty brown crown stripes, eyeline.

Song Sparrow

juv.

winter

juv.

Swamp Sparrow

summer

Song sparrows, fox sparrows, and savannah sparrows (Key 161) all have breasts with heavy streaking that typically merges into a central spot. The fox sparrow's greater size is usually obvious; its long, blunt tail is another good mark. The song sparrow's tail is rounded and pumped in flight, and the bird has a prominent dark whisker stripe. Lincoln's sparrow may show a small breast spot, and so may the swamp sparrow. Like song sparrows, both pump their tails in flight. The swamp sparrow has a rusty back and wings in all plumages and a bright rusty cap in summer. Young swamp sparrows have a buff wash and fine streaking on their breasts and are easily mistaken for Lincoln's sparrows.

◀**Song Sparrow** *Melospiza melodia* 6¼"
Abundant, widespread in diverse brushy habitats from desert scrub to marsh to backyards. Pumps tail distinctively in flight. ● Variable; some forms darker, paler, or redder than shown. All have dark whisker, heavy breast streaking. Juv. buff below with finer streaking, may not show central spot. ♪ *Tchip*, low, nasal call note.

regional variations

Fox Sparrow

Lincoln's Sparrow

◀**Swamp Sparrow** *Melospiza georgiana* 5¾"
Numerous in summer in freshwater marshes. Also in diverse
brushy habitats with other sparrows in migration, winter. Shy.
● Rusty above with bright cap in summer, brownish crown,
pale median stripe in winter. Gray wash on breast sets off
white throat, brown flanks. Breast can be finely streaked,
show dusky spot. Juv. has unstreaked throat; darker crown,
redder back and wings than Lincoln's sparrow. ♪ *Chip*, call,
like eastern phoebe's. Song a trilled *weet-weet-weet*.

◀**Lincoln's Sparrow** *Melospiza lincolnii* 5¾"
Numerous in West, scarce in East. In forest wetlands in
summer; bogs, pond margins, wet meadows. Often in drier,
brushy areas during migration, winter. Skulks. ● Buff breast
and malar area. Finer breast streaks than in similar adult
sparrows, extending onto throat. Gray and reddish head
stripes. Juv. similar. ♪ *Tik!* or *tuk!* Given in series as alarm.

Fox Sparrow *Passerella iliaca* 7"
◀Numerous, but wary in dense undergrowth; often first heard
scratching in brush. ● Large with much variation in plumage;
all forms heavily streaked below. Eastern form (foreground)
is brightest red with streaking on crown and back. Darkest
western form has few reddish tones, mostly in tail. ♪ Song
a series of whistles, slurs, buzzes; more complex, melodious,
variable than in other sparrows. Call notes vary regionally.

PLAIN SPARROWS ROUNDED TAILS

Vesper Sparrow

large-billed form

Savannah Sparrow

dark

typical

"Ipswich sparrow"

Grasshopper sparrow at nest

These sparrows are usually found in grasslands. All except the grasshopper sparrow have streaked breasts. The vesper sparrow's rusty shoulder patch is a good mark but not always obvious; better are the white eye-ring and white outer tail feathers, conspicuous in flight. Savannah sparrows show regional variation, but all forms have a short, notched tail; most show yellow before the eye; and many have a central breast spot. In some areas, savannah sparrows occupy wet grass. Baird's sparrow has an ochre crown and nape. Like the grasshopper sparrow, it is usually hidden except when the male sings. Besides a clean buff breast, the grasshopper sparrow has a clean face, giving it an odd, beady-eyed look for a sparrow.

◀**Vesper Sparrow** *Pooecetes gramineus* 6¼"
Fairly numerous but seriously declining in East; in short-grass or nearly barren habitats, esp. pastures, meadows, roadsides, where posts and wires provide males with singing perches. Prefers dry regions. ● White outer feathers on fairly short, slightly notched tail. Streaked underparts, white eye-ring, rufous shoulder patch. ♪♪ *Here-here, where-where, all-together-down-the-hill*, 2 sweet, slurred notes followed by similar higher pair, ending in a tumbling trill; given persistently.

Grasshopper Sparrow

juv.

Baird's Sparrow

◀**Savannah Sparrow** *Passerculus sandwichensis* 5½"
Abundant, widespread, wherever dense, dry, grassy cover
adjoins wetlands or water: tundra, grassy dunes, marsh
edges, streamside. Secretive. ● Can be very similar to
song sparrow (Key 160) but tail short, notched; not long,
rounded. Yellow lores may be absent. Rare large-billed
form in s. CA has faint back streaking. "Ipswich" form large,
very pale; winters on coastal dunes in Northeast. ♩♪ *Sip,
sip, sip, seeeee, saaay,* 2-3 chip notes followed by 2 buzzy
trills. *Seep,* distinctive flight call.

◀**Baird's Sparrow** *Ammodramus bairdii* 5½"
Scarce, declining; in dry, tall-grass prairie in summer.
Numerous before plowing reduced habitat. Few winter in US.
● Narrow median crown stripe widens at nape, forming dull
ochre triangle with fine black streaking on side crown, nape.
Two black whisker stripes. Necklace-like band of breast
streaks can be faint or absent. Juv. similar. ♩♪ *Zip, zip, zip,
zrrr-r-r-r,* several high notes followed by lower trill.

◀**Grasshopper Sparrow** *Ammodramus savannarum* 5"
Fairly numerous in diverse dry grass habitats: prairies, hay-
fields, grassy scrub. Serious declines in East; habitat loss
threatens FL race. ● Bright buff breast and face without
obvious streaks or whisker marks. Dark crown with whitish
median stripe, white eye-ring, yellowish lores (yellow does
not extend behind eye). Juv. has streaked breast. ♩♪ Song
is grasshopper-like buzz, often with beginning *pit* note.

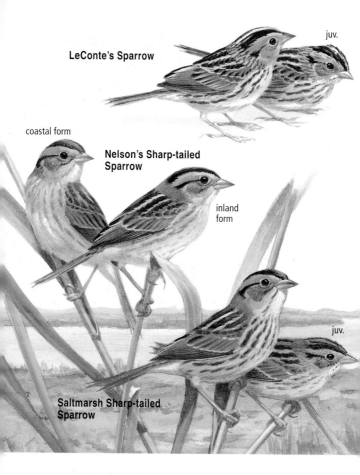

LeConte's Sparrow

juv.

coastal form

Nelson's Sharp-tailed Sparrow

inland form

juv.

Saltmarsh Sharp-tailed Sparrow

These sparrows with short, pointed tail feathers nest in marshes or wet fields. All are streaked below and timid, running mouse-like through thick cover and seldom flushing. When seen, they are usually singing, and the songs are diagnostic. LeConte's and the two sharp-tailed sparrows each have a buff-orange breast and face with a contrasting gray cheek patch. Only LeConte's has a white central crown stripe. The sharp-tails have separate summer ranges. Seaside sparrows are larger and darker, with yellow lores. The olive-green head and crown stripe of Henslow's sparrow are obvious against its rusty wings and back.

◄ **LeConte's Sparrow** *Ammodramus leconteii* 5"
Fairly numerous in summer in matted grasses around prairie marshes, boreal bogs; also drier fields in winter. ● White central crown stripe with ochre at forehead; gray nape with chestnut streaks. Buff-orange breast and eyebrow, streaked sides. Juv. paler, breast streaked. ♫♫ *Bzzzz*, insect-like song.

Nelson's Sharp-tailed Sparrow *Ammodramus nelsoni* 5¼"
Fairly numerous, but declining with loss of marsh. Local and

Henslow's Sparrow

Gulf form

Atlantic form

"Cape Sable" form

Seaside Sparrow

juv.

secretive in tall grass of salt and freshwater marshes. Recently split from saltmarsh sparrow. ● Inland form brightly contrasting; shows distinct back streaks but usually only faint streaks on sides. Coastal form duller, back streaks obscure, faint streaks below usually incl. breast. Juv. like juv. saltmarsh. ♩♩ *Sheeee,* fairly loud, hissing buzz.

Saltmarsh Sharp-tailed Sparrow *Ammodramus caudacutus* 5¼"
Fairly numerous in salt marsh. ● Like inland form of Nelson's but darker streaking across breast, less contrast on back. Juv. browner. ♩♩ Soft series of notes, trills, buzzes.

Seaside Sparrow *Ammodramus maritimus* 6"
Numerous but local in salt marshes, especially along mud channels. ● Long bill, yellow lores, white throat bordered by dark whisker stripe. Atlantic form dark olive-gray above with dusky streaking below. Gulf form buffier. Juv. duller, lacks yellow lores. "Cape Sable sparrow" *(A. m. mirabilis)* is isolated, greenish FL race; endangered. ♩♩ *Tup-tup, zee´-reeeee,* buzzy song, opening notes soft.

Henslow's Sparrow *Ammodramus henslowii* 5"
Rare, local, declining; in wet weedy fields; also drier grassy areas, esp. in winter. ● Olive-green head; rufous back, wings, tail. Juv. similar to adult but with only faint side streaks below. ♩♩ *Tsi-lik´,* weak song, often given at night or in rain.

Eurasian Tree Sparrow

fall ♂

House Sparrow

♀

spring ♂

The house sparrow is the common sparrow of cities, suburbs, and farms. The male's black bib and chestnut head markings are largely obscured by pale feather tips in fresh (fall) plumage. By spring the pale tips wear away, revealing the crisply detailed colors on the head, throat, and breast.

◄**House Sparrow** *Passer domesticus* 6¼"
So abundant around human population centers that it is often considered a pest. Old World species; introduced widely in N. America, first in NY in 1851. Early western introductions in San Francisco, CA (1871), and Salt Lake City, UT (1873). Range and numbers quickly expanded, but always in habitat modified by man, incl. isolated towns and farms with isolated flocks. Slightly declining in East since 1985. Active, aggressive. Small regional variations have already evolved. ● Male has gray crown with chestnut border and nape, whitish cheek, gray underparts with black throat and breast, white wing bar; bill is black in summer, yellow in winter. Female and juv. plain-breasted with rusty upperparts, pale eyebrow, pale bill. ♪ *Chee-ip,* insistent call.

Eurasian Tree Sparrow *Passer montanus* 6" Eurasian. Introduced, now numerous, stable around St. Louis, MO, and nearby IL. Often in mixed flocks with house sparrows. ● Sexes alike, similar to male house sparrow but brown crown and rump, black ear patch, small black throat patch, buffier underparts. ♪ Similar to house sparrow's.

Arctic birds

CONSULTANT **THEDE TOBISH**
ILLUSTRATOR **ALAN MESSER**

For the purposes of this guide, Arctic birds are those not normally seen in the lower 48 states or the more populated areas of Canada along its US border. Many of these birds migrate from winter homes in Asia or Europe to nest on the Arctic tundra of North America. The long hours of sunshine during the Arctic summer transform a barren, icy winter landscape into a brief abundance of blooms, insects, birds, and other wildlife.

Few birds remain when the days grow short and the snows return. Perhaps the most surprising winter Arctic resident is the common raven. Even at Point Barrow, the northern tip of Alaska, ravens endure the frigid winters, feeding on carrion left by predators like polar bears and refuse discarded by humans. At openings in the ice pack or along the edges, gulls or alcids (birds of the auk family) may be found in midwinter.

The Aleutian Islands stretch from the southwestern Alaskan mainland over a thousand miles, almost into Asia. These and other remote, rocky islands in the Bering Sea provide nesting sites for numerous seabirds. The Near Islands of the western Aleutians also provide salvation for Asian migrants that overshoot nesting areas to the south, and for others in passage to nesting areas farther north in Asia. Dedicated birders travel to the westernmost Aleutian island, Attu, in particular, to record these vagrants. A great variety of Asian visitors to North America have been recorded, and new ones are seen regularly. Arctic species also recorded in the lower 48 states are labeled "US rec."

Siberia

Pt. Barrow

St. Lawrence I.

Alaska

Attu I.   St. Matthew I.

Nunivak I.

Pribilof Is.

ARCTIC BIRDS

Aleutian Is.

Most of the Bering Sea islands identified are too small to see when drawn to scale and are shown greatly enlarged.

The horned puffin has the enormous bill that is characteristic of all puffins. Distinctive curved crests sprout from the foreheads of both whiskered and crested auklets, but only the rarer whiskered auklet has three white facial plumes. The other two auklets, the parakeet and the least, lack crests. Note the white underparts of the parakeet and the small size and tiny bill of the least. Kittlitz's murrelet is very similar to the marbled murrelet (Key 12); its best marks are its shorter bill and, in winter, whiter face.

◀**Horned Puffin** *Fratercula corniculata* 15"
Numerous. Nests under boulders, in rock crevices or burrows. Near shore in summer, at sea in winter ● White face and underparts. Shares range with tufted puffin (Key 11), which has dark underparts.

Whiskered Auklet *Aethia pygmaea* 7¾"
◀Rarest auklet. Nests in crevices, under boulders. Feeds in tide rips near shore. ● Dark gray; darkest on head, palest on belly. Slim dark crest on forehead, 3 white plumes on face, stubby bill. Plumes shorter in winter. Juv. lacks plumes, has whitish belly and 2 faint white streaks on face.

winter marbled murrelet
Key 12

winter

summer

winter

Kittlitz's

summer

Kittlitz's Murrelet

Parakeet Auklet

winter

winter

least

summer

Least Auklet

summer

winter

summer

◄**Crested Auklet** *Aethia cristatella* 10"
Numerous, sometimes in large flocks. Nests in colonies among boulders, often with other auklets. ● Dark gray, above and below. Chunky with stout red-orange bill and side plate. Dark crest in summer, white plume behind eye. In winter, brown bill, shorter plume. Juv. lacks plumes.

◄**Parakeet Auklet** *Cyclorrhynchus psittacula* 10" (US rec.)
Fairly numerous, alone or in small groups. Nests among boulders or in puffin burrows. ● Large head and heavy, conical orange-red bill; white plume behind eye, white belly. Foreneck gray in summer, white in winter. Juv. like winter.

Least Auklet *Aethia pusilla* 6¼" (US rec.)
◄Abundant, nesting in huge colonies on bare slopes or among boulders. ● Tiny with stubby bill, difficult to see in flight. Clean white throat in summer, with variable mottling below; small white plumes on forehead and behind eye. In winter, black above, white below with white scapulars.

◄**Kittlitz's Murrelet** *Brachyramphus brevirostris* 9½" (US rec.)
Scarce, local, often near glaciers. Nests on rocky alpine tundra and steep sea cliffs. ● Like marbled murrelet (Key 12) but bill shorter, outer tail feathers white; paler brown above in summer, whiter below. In winter, black cap does not extend to eye or nape; has dark neck band.

Ross' Gull

winter

pelagic
cormorant
Key 30

Red-faced
Cormorant

Spectacled Eider ♂

♀

The best marks for Ross' gull are its wedge-shaped tail and small
black bill. Adult ivory gulls are white with yellow-tipped bills.
Red-faced cormorants have thicker, paler bills than the pelagic
cormorants (Key 30) they resemble. Emperor geese are distinctive; their white heads and hind necks are often stained rusty.
Male eiders are nearly all field mark. The brown females have the
same shapes as their distinctive mates but much subtler patterns.

◀**Ross' Gull** *Rhodostethia rosea* 14"
Fairly numerous migrant in flocks on pack ice in fall. Nests
in Greenland, has nested in Canadian Arctic. ● Wedge-
shaped tail, red legs, small black bill. Thin black necklace
and pink wash reduced or absent in winter. Imm. has W
pattern on mantle, black on tip of tail. Adult by 2nd yr.

◀**Red-faced Cormorant** *Phalacrocorax urile* 31" (US rec.)
Alaskan species. Numerous but local in colonies on steep
sea cliffs, rocky islands; frequently with other seabirds.
● Heavy, yellowish bill. Orange-red face patch extends onto
forehead, duller in winter. Large white flank patches except
in late summer, fall. Imm. brown with dull red face patch.

imm.

Ivory Gull

summer

Emperor Goose

♀ ♂ **Steller's Eider**

◀**Spectacled Eider** *Somateria fischeri* 21"
Rare, rapidly declining. On shallow coastal waters, nearby tundra ponds in summer. Often in small flocks. Winters offshore, range poorly known. ● Base of bill feathered to nostril. Male has green head, orange bill, white "goggles" with black rims, black-and-white body pattern. Female barred and brown with dark bill, outline of goggles.

◀**Steller's Eider** *Polysticta stelleri* 17" (US rec.)
Scarce in summer on tundra ponds. Winters in bays, near coasts, often in large flocks. Wings whistle in flight. ● Purple speculum bordered with white, small crest on back of head. Male white above with black markings; buff breast and underparts. Female dark brown, mallard-like but squarer head.

◀**Emperor Goose** *Chen canagica* 26" (US rec.)
Fairly numerous in small flocks on coasts, nearby tundra ponds, marshes. ● White head, hind neck; black throat. Scaly blue-gray body, yellow-orange legs. Juv. dark-headed, gradually becoming white. ♪ *Cla-ha, cla-ha,* musical honks.

◀**Ivory Gull** *Pagophila eburnea* 17" (US rec.)
Scarce, local on pack ice, often in small flocks. Nesting range uncertain. Bold. ● White with black legs; black bill, yellow tip. Imm. has dark tips on tail, primaries; dark spotting above, heaviest on face. Adult by 2nd yr. ♪ *Keeer,* tern-like call.

Dotterel

juv.

Far Eastern Curlew

Bristle-thighed Curlew

The dotterel is a plover – a very distinctive one, with a bold white eyebrow, white breast stripe, and dull rusty breast and flanks in summer. The ringed plover is very similar to the semipalmated plover (Key 58) but usually has a broader breast band. The safest way to tell them apart is by voice. Long, curved bills define the curlews and godwits. The bristle-thighed curlew resembles a whimbrel (Key 52); the rusty orange rump and tail are its best marks. The bar-tailed godwit resembles a marbled godwit (Key 51) but is smaller and browner with relatively short legs.

◀**Dotterel** (Eurasian) *Charadrius morinellus* 8¼" (US rec.)
Rare, irregular in summer in mountain tundra of w. AK.
Tame. ● Broad white eyebrows meet at nape. White breast
band, dull rusty breast and flanks in summer; female
brighter. Winter birds duller. Juv. pale buff below, breast
band inconspicuous. ♪ *Pip-pip* or *pip-pip-pip*, soft flight call.

Bristle-thighed Curlew *Numenius tahitiensis* 17"
Rare. Nests only on tundra in w. AK. First nest not found

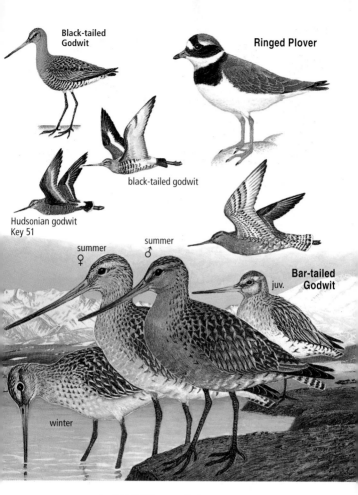

Black-tailed Godwit

Ringed Plover

black-tailed godwit

Hudsonian godwit
Key 51

summer ♀

summer ♂

Bar-tailed Godwit

juv.

winter

◀until 1948. Winters on Pacific islands, migrates offshore.
● Like whimbrel (Key 52) but with orange-rufous rump and
tail. Bill pale pink at base. ♪ *Chiu-it,* whistled call.

Bar-tailed Godwit *Limosa lapponica* 16" (US rec.)
Scarce; on marshy tundra in loose colonies; also visits mudflats, beaches. ● Long, upturned, dark-tipped bill. Short
◀legs; in flight, only feet extend beyond tail. Barred rump and
tail. Summer male reddish brown below; female paler, larger,
with longer bill. Winter adults buffy gray above fading to white
on belly. Juv. like winter but buffier. European form, recorded
on Atlantic Coast, has less barring on whitish rump.

Ringed Plover (Common) *Charadrius hiaticula* 7½" (US rec.)
◀Eurasian. Numerous in Canadian Arctic. Rare spring migrant
on w. AK islands; has bred on St. Lawrence I. Habits like
semipalmated plover's (Key 58). ● Slightly larger than
semipalmated; breast band usually broader; white mark
above eye larger. ♪♪ *Too-li,* mellow call, rising inflection.

Black-tailed Godwit *Limosa limosa* 16" (US rec.) Eurasian. Rare but regular in
w. Aleutians. ● Similar to Hudsonian (Key 51); wing linings white, bill straighter.

Far Eastern Curlew *Numenius madagascariensis* 25" Several records in Aleutians,
Pribilofs. ● Similar to long-billed curlew (Key 52); browner, wing linings white.

Siberian Tit

Wheatear

summer ♂

wheatear

♀

spring ♂

winter

summer ♀

Willow Ptarmigan

The Siberian tit suggests a large boreal chickadee (Key 141) but is grayer above and has pale buff, not rufous, sides. The bluethroat is shy; the distinctive rufous patches in the tail are often more evident than the blue throat. The wheatear also has a diagnostic rear patch – a white one on the rump and tail. McKay's bunting is a whiter version of the snow bunting (Key 153) and must be carefully distinguished from it. Rock and willow ptarmigan are also much alike. Both are white in winter with black tails that distinguish them from the white-tailed ptarmigan (Key 88).

◀**Siberian Tit** *Parus cinctus* 5½"
Rare; in summer in willow, spruce, birch near treeline; in river valleys during winter. Range poorly known. Seldom in flocks.
● Distinct gray-brown cap, white cheek patch, pale buff sides, fairly long tail. ♫ *Dee-deer*, slurred call, given in series.

Wheatear (Northern) *Oenanthe oenanthe* 5¾" (US rec.)
◀Fairly numerous, active in rocky alpine tundra, barren fields.
● White in rump and tail. Summer male has black mask and wings, variably buff breast. Female, fall male duller. Juv. bright buff below, often with scaled look. ♪ *Chak-chak*, loud call.

snow bunting Key 153

Bluethroat

♂ ♀

McKay's Bunting

summer ♂

summer ♀ McKay's bunting

summer ♂ winter ♂

summer ♀ winter ♂ winter ♀

summer ♂ **Rock Ptarmigan**

◀**Willow Ptarmigan** *Lagopus lagopus* 15"
Numerous in flocks on shrubby tundra, esp. thickets of willow, alder. ● Bill larger than in rock ptarmigan. White with black tail in winter. Dark, barred feathers appear on head and neck in spring, gradually extend over body except wings. Summer male usually rustier, darker than male rock ptarmigan.

◀**Rock Ptarmigan** *Lagopus mutus* 14" (US rec.)
Numerous on flocks in open tundra, esp. upland areas.
● Smaller bill than willow ptarmigan. Winter males have black lores. Females similar to female willow ptarmigan.

McKay's Bunting *Plectrophenax hyperboreus* 6¾"
Fairly numerous in summer on Bering Sea is. Scarce, local
◀in flocks in winter on barren coasts. ● Summer male white with dark bill; less black in wings and tail than in snow bunting (Key 153), little or no black on back. Females, winter birds also whiter than snow bunting; juv. like juv. snow.

Bluethroat *Luscinia svecica* 5½"
◀Scarce. Skulks in scrub willow thickets, esp. near streams.
● Rufous patch in tail conspicuous in flight. White eyebrow. Male has brightly patterned throat and breast with rufous center spot. Female streaked below with white throat, black border. Juv. like female but brighter buff below, border on throat often broken. ♪ Loud, varied, melodious song.

ARCTIC LANDBIRDS

Wood Warbler

Dusky Warbler

Black-backed Wagtail

juv.

summer ♂

Arctic Warbler

spring ♂

imm.

juv.

White Wagtail

The arctic warbler is similar to the Tennessee warbler (Key 134) but darker above with a stouter bill, long whitish eyebrow, and dingy, unstreaked underparts. Wagtails and pipits are slender, shy birds that walk methodically rather than hop. Both the white and yellow wagtails bob their heads and wag their tails while walking. Yellow wagtails in fall can be whitish below but always lack the white forehead and wing bars of the white wagtail. It is the rusty face and breast that best separates the red-throated from other pipits in summer. In fall the color is reduced or lacking, but the bird retains its distinctive black streaking above and its pink legs.

◀ **Arctic Warbler** *Phylloscopus borealis* 5"
Numerous in riparian willow thickets. Nests on ground, feeds mainly in canopy. ● Olive-green above, pale legs. Long, whitish eyebrow and underparts can be tinged with yellow in spring. Fall adults and juvs. yellower below and on eyebrow, brighter green above. Narrow wing bar often wears off by midsummer. ♪ Song a long, flat trill on single pitch.

◀ **White Wagtail** *Motacilla alba* 7¼"
Scarce, in open areas near water, buildings, debris. ● Gray back, long black tail with white edges. Spring male has most black on crown, nape, bib; female has less. Juv. gray with dusky breast band becoming black in imm.; white wing bars (lacking in imm. yellow wagtail). ♪ *Chiz-zick´*, flight call.

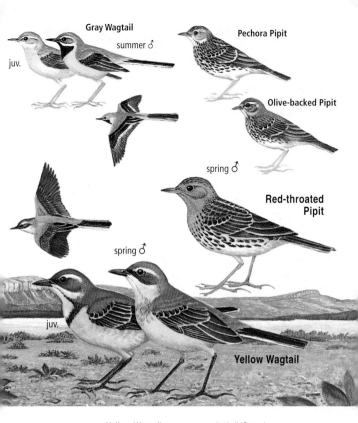

Yellow Wagtail *Motacilla flava* 6½" (US rec.)
Numerous in coastal tundra thickets. ● Male yellow below with white throat, hint of dusky breast band; olive-brown above with white eyebrow, black tail, white outer tail feathers. Female and fall birds duller, usually yellowish or buff below. Juv. has dark breast band. ♪ *Tzeeet*, drawn-out flight call.

Red-throated Pipit *Anthus cervinus* 5½" (US rec.)
Rare in summer on open coastal tundra. Regular migrant in w. Aleutians. ● Spring birds have rusty pink face and breast lacking in some fall birds, juvs. Pink legs and black back streaks differ from dark legs, faint brown streaks of American pipit (Key 121). ♪ *See-eep*, emphatic flight call.

Dusky Warbler *Phylloscopus fuscatus* 5" (US rec.) Several AK records. ● Like arctic warbler but dusky brown above, buff-white eyebrow, lacks wing bars.

Wood Warbler *Phylloscopus sibilatrix* 5" One record in w. Aleutians. ● Like arctic warbler but bright yellow on throat, breast, eyebrow; olive-green above.

Black-backed Wagtail *Motacilla lugens* 7¼" (US rec.) Nearly annual on Bering Sea is. ● Like white wagtail but has black back (dark gray in female) and larger white wing patch. Juv. same as juv. white wagtail.

Gray Wagtail *Motacilla cinerea* 7¾" Rare on Bering Sea is. in spring. ● Like yellow wagtail but more slender, longer tail, yellow rump. Male has black throat.

Pechora Pipit *Anthus gustavi* 6¼" Several records on Bering Sea is. ● Back streaked with rich colors and 2 white streaks. Buff on face, outer tail feathers.

Olive-backed Pipit *Anthus hodgsoni* 6½" Rare in w. Aleutians. ● Olive-green above, faint back streaks. Buff lores, face; white on eyebrow and below ear patch.

Red-legged Kittiwake *Rissa brevirostris* 15" (US rec.) Rare nester in Pribilofs, Aleutians. Pelagic, seldom seen in winter. ● Like black-legged kittiwake (Key 4) but red legs, shorter bill, darker wings contrasting with white trailing edge. 1st-winter red-legged kittiwake lacks black collar of 1st-winter black-legged.

Aleutian Tern *Sterna aleutica* 15" Local nester on AK coasts and Bering Sea is. ● White forehead, black cap, black bill. Juv. has buff-brown cap and upperparts; base of lower mandible dusky red.

Oriental Pratincole *Glareola maldivarum* 10" Recorded on Attu and in Gambell. ● Swallow-like shorebird. Throat outlined in black, rufous underwing, forked tail.

Slaty-backed Gull *Larus schistisagus* 25" (US rec.) Rare in Aleutians and w. AK; also other AK coastal records. ● Like western gull (Key 18), but bill more slender, wide white trailing edge to wing.

Black-tailed Gull *Larus crassirostris* 19" Records for w. Aleutians, St. Lawrence I., AK. ● Black band on white tail; dark wing tips; yellow bill with black ring, red tip.

Whooper Swan *Cygnus cygnus* 60" (US rec.) Rare in winter in w. and c. Aleutians; other AK records. ● Like trumpeter swan (Key 25), but base of bill yellow.

Pink-footed Goose *Anser brachyrhynchus* 26" European. One Newfoundland record. ● Like bean goose but smaller with darker head and neck, pink legs.

Bean Goose *Anser fabalis* 31" Rare in spring on Bering Sea is; several other AK records. ● Gray-brown; bill blackish with yellow or pink band.

Eurasian Coot *Fulica atra* 16" Few records from Pribilofs, e. Canada. ● Like American coot (Key 41), but frontal shield all-white, undertail coverts dark.

Chinese Egret *Egretta eulophotes* 27" Recorded in w. Aleutians. ● Like snowy egret (Key 44) but larger with thicker yellow bill and short, bushy crest.

Yellow Bittern *Ixobrychus sinensis* 14" Recorded in w. Aleutians. ● Like least bittern (Key 48), but male has yellow-brown back, female lacks black cap.

Spot-billed Duck *Anas poecilorhyncha* 22" Several AK records. ● Like female mallard (Key 32), but bill dark with yellow tip.

Common Pochard *Aythya ferina* 18" Regular spring, summer visitor to Pribilofs, w. and c. Aleutians. ● Like canvasback (Key 36), but head more rounded; dark bill has broad pale band.

Smew *Mergellus albellus* 16" (US rec.) Eurasian. Rare in fall and winter in w. Aleutians. ● Male largely white with conspicuous black eye patch, short crest. Female darker with rusty cap, white cheeks and throat.

Garganey *Anas querquedula* 15" (US rec.) Eurasian. Regular migrant in w. and c. Aleutians; other AK records. ● Male has brown head, broad white eyebrow. Female lacks blue-gray on forewing; face has contrasting stripes.

Baikal Teal *Anas formosa* 17" (US rec.) Rare spring migrant to several Bering Sea is.; also records in w. AK. ● Head of male is distinctive. Note white spot at base of bill of female.

Falcated Teal *Anas falcata* 19" Rare in spring and fall in w. and c. Aleutians; also recorded in Pribilofs. ● Male has large, pendant, iridescent crest; white throat. Female like female wigeon or gadwall (Key 33) but dark bill; suggestion of crest.

Common Sandpiper *Actitis hypoleucos* 8" Rare migrant in Aleutians and Bering Sea is. Teeters. ● Like winter spotted sandpiper (Key 59) but longer tail.

Terek Sandpiper *Xenus cinereus* 9" (US rec.) Rare migrant in Aleutians, Bering Sea is.; also mainland AK records. ● Long, upturned bill; short orange legs.

Black-winged Stilt *Himantopus himantopus* 15" Recorded in w. Aleutians. ● Like black-necked stilt (Key 51), but male has less black on neck; female, none.

Wood Sandpiper *Tringa glareola* 8" (US rec.) Fairly numerous on w. Aleutians, less so on Bering Sea is., AK mainland. ● Like solitary sandpiper (Key 59), but rump white, wing linings paler, upperparts heavily spotted with buff; distinct call.

Green Sandpiper *Tringa ochropus* 9" Recorded in w. Aleutians. ● Like solitary sandpiper (Key 59), but rump and base of tail white.

Marsh Sandpiper *Tringa stagnatilis* 9" Recorded in w. Aleutians. ● Size of lesser yellowlegs (Key 53) but green legs, long and needle-like bill, white wedge on back.

Spotted Redshank *Tringa erythropus* 12" (US rec.) Rare migrant in w. Aleutians. ● Legs and lower mandible red in all plumages. Winter birds dull gray-brown.

Greenshank (Common) *Tringa nebularia* 13" Rare spring migrant in w. Aleutians. ● Like greater yellowlegs (Key 53) but green legs, white wedge on back.

Little Ringed Plover *Charadrius dubius* 7" Recorded in w. Aleutians. ● Lacks white wing stripe of semipalmated (Key 58). Note differences in bill and head.

Mongolian Plover *Charadrius mongolus* 7½" (US rec.) Rare migrant in w. Aleutians. Has bred on mainland of w. AK. ● Male (shown) brighter than female. Rufous breast band lacking in winter.

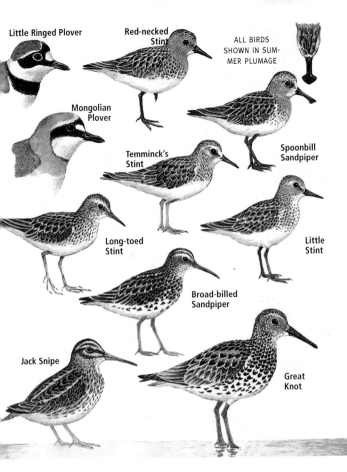

Little Ringed Plover

Red-necked Stint

ALL BIRDS SHOWN IN SUMMER PLUMAGE

Mongolian Plover

Temminck's Stint

Spoonbill Sandpiper

Long-toed Stint

Little Stint

Broad-billed Sandpiper

Jack Snipe

Great Knot

Red-necked Stint *Calidris ruficollis* 6¼" (US rec.) Scarce migrant in Bering Sea area, rare breeder in coastal AK. ● Variably rusty face, upper breast; may be pale.

Spoonbill Sandpiper *Eurynorhynchus pygmeus* 6" Recorded in nw. AK and B.C. ● Like red-necked stint but spatulate bill.

Temminck's Stint *Calidris temminckii* 6" Rare migrant on Bering Sea is. ● Uniform gray-brown above. Only peep with white outer tail feathers.

Long-toed Stint *Calidris subminuta* 6" Scarce migrant in w. Aleutians, rarer on other islands. ● Like least sandpiper (Key 61) but rustier above; legs longer, greenish.

Little Stint *Calidris minuta* 6" (US rec.) Recorded in migration in Bering Sea area. ● Like pale red-necked stint; rustier than least sandpiper (Key 61), legs black.

Broad-billed Sandpiper *Limicola falcinellus* 7" Juvs. recorded in w. Aleutians in fall. ● Distinct bill shape. Forked eyebrow in all plumages.

Jack Snipe *Lymnocryptes minimus* 7" (US rec.) Recorded in AK, Labrador. ● Like a tiny snipe (Key 55) with short bill, no rufous in tail, no bars on flanks.

Great Knot *Calidris tenuirostris* 11" Recorded in spring on Bering Sea is. ● Bright rusty scapulars, breast and sides heavily spotted with black, rump white.

Gray-tailed Tattler *Heteroscelus brevipes* 10" (Not shown) Rare migrant in Bering Sea is. and Aleutians; also AK mainland records. Best told from wandering tattler (Key 56) by unmottled belly, distinct call. ♪♪ Mellow, 2-note whistle.

European Golden-Plover *Pluvialis apricaria* 12" (Not shown) Eurasian. Recorded in Nfld. ● Like American golden-plover (Key 57) but paler underwing, white axillars.

ARCTIC SHOREBIRD RARITIES

170

Steller's Sea-Eagle *Haliaeetus pelagicus* 37" Records in w. AK, Bering Sea is.
● Huge orange-yellow bill, white shoulders. Adult tail long, white, wedge-shaped.

White-tailed Eagle *Haliaeetus albicilla* 33" (US rec.) Rare in w. Aleutians, where it has bred. Several old records in w. AK. ● Short, white, wedge-shaped tail.

Eurasian Hobby *Falco subbuteo* 12" Recorded in w. Aleutians. ● Like small peregrine falcon (Key 77) with chestnut thighs and undertail coverts.

Eurasian Kestrel *Falco tinnunculus* 13" (US rec.) Recorded in w. Aleutians. ● Like American kestrel (Key 78) but larger with spotted upperparts, single facial stripe.

Common House-Martin *Delichon urbica* 5¼" Several records in Bering Sea area.
● Like tree swallow (Key 81) but white rump.

Common Swift *Apus apus* 6½" Recorded in Pribilofs. ● Forked tail, white throat.

Fork-tailed Swift *Apus pacificus* 7½" Recorded in w. Aleutians and Pribilofs.
● Forked tail, white throat, white rump.

White-throated Needletail *Hirundapus caudacutus* 8" Recorded in w. Aleutians.
● Square tail, white throat and forehead, white undertail coverts and tertials.

Jungle Nightjar *Caprimulgus indicus* 12" One record in w. Aleutians. ● Like a nighthawk (Key 67) but shorter white wing bar, unbarred breast.

Oriental Turtle-Dove *Streptopelia orientalis* 13" Recorded on Bering Sea is.
● Striped neck patch, rufous on mantle.

Hoopoe *Upupa epops* 11" Recorded once in w. AK. Crest usually flattened.

Oriental Scops-Owl *Otus sunia* 7½" (Not shown) Recorded in w. Aleutians, where it is only *Otus* owl. ● Smaller than screech-owls (Key 65), less streaked below.

Red-breasted Flycatcher *Ficedula parva* 4½" Recorded in w. Aleutians, St. Lawrence I. ● White patches in tail. Male has orange throat lacking in female.

Mugimaki Flycatcher *Ficedula mugimaki* 5" One record in w. Aleutians. ● Male orange-red and black with white markings. Female brownish, lacks white marks.

Narcissus Flycatcher *Ficedula narcissina* 5" Two records in w. Aleutians. ● Male black and yellow with white wing patch. Female drab brown with white throat.

Gray-spotted Flycatcher *Muscicapa griseisticta* 5½" Rare migrant in w. Aleutians in spring. ● Gray-brown above with white eye-ring, lores. Streaked below.

Siberian Flycatcher *Muscicapa sibirica* 5" Recorded in w. Aleutians. ● Like gray-spotted flycatcher but smaller, broad dusky band on breast, lacks white lores.

Asian Brown Flycatcher *Muscicapa latirostris* 5" Recorded in w. Aleutians. ● Like Siberian flycatcher but much paler underparts, pale base to bill.

Brown Shrike *Lanius cristatus* 8" (US rec.) Recorded in Bering Sea is. and AK mainland. ● Small shrike; brown above with black mask.

Great Spotted Woodpecker *Dendrocopos major* 9" One record in w. Aleutians. ● Black back with large white scapular patches, red lower belly.

Eurasian Wryneck *Jynx torquata* 6½" One record in nw. AK. ● Mottled brownish gray above with dark stripe from forehead down back; barred below.

Common Cuckoo *Cuculus canorus* 13" (US rec.) Several records in Bering Sea area. ● Falcon-like. Gray; barred black below. Female has rare rufous phase.

Oriental Cuckoo *Cuculus saturatus* 13" (Not shown) Records in w. Aleutians. ● Like common cuckoo but ochre undertail coverts; barred rump on rufous female.

Siberian Rubythroat *Luscinia calliope* 6" Rare in w. Aleutians; several other AK records. ● Brown; white eyebrow, whisker. Throat often white, not red, in female.

Red-flanked Bluetail *Tarsiger cyanurus* 5½" Recorded in w. Aleutians. ● Male blue above with rusty flanks. Blue mostly replaced by gray-brown in female.

Lanceolated Warbler *Locustella lanceolata* 4½" Recorded in w. Aleutians. Skulks. ● Smaller than Middendorff's grasshopper-warbler; fine streaks above and below.

Siberian Blue Robin *Luscinia cyane* 5½" One record in w. Aleutians. ● Male blue above, white below. Female brown above, dingy whitish below, with blue in tail.

Siberian Accentor *Prunella montanella* 5½" (US rec.) Fall records in AK and Bering Sea is. ● Black crown and ear patch; ochre eyebrow and breast.

Stonechat *Saxicola torquata* 5" Recorded on St. Lawrence I., mainland AK. ● Male black and white with rusty breast. Female duller.

Redwing *Turdus iliacus* 8" Newfoundland records. ● Rusty flanks, wing linings.

Middendorff's Grasshopper-Warbler *Locustella ochotensis* 6" Several records in Bering Sea area. Skulks. ● Stocky with wedge-shaped, pale-tipped tail.

Dusky Thrush *Turdus naumanni* 9½" (US rec.) Records in Bering Sea area and Pt. Barrow, AK. ● Rusty wings, 2 scaly dark breast bands. Female duller.

Eyebrowed Thrush *Turdus obscurus* 8½" Rare in w. Aleutians, recorded on other Bering Sea is. ● White eyebrow, rusty orange breast and flanks. Male has gray throat; female, white.

Yellow-breasted Bunting *Emberiza aureola* 5½" Recorded on w. Aleutians. ● Yellow below. Male has black face and throat, brown collar and upperparts. Female streaked above and below; shows yellow wash on breast.

Yellow-breasted Bunting ♂ ♀

Reed Bunting ♂ ♀

Rustic Bunting ♂ ♀

Gray Bunting ♂ ♀

Little Bunting ♂

Pine Bunting ♂ ♀

Oriental Greenfinch ♂

Bullfinch ♂

Hawfinch

Reed Bunting *Emberiza schoeniclus* 6" Recorded in w. Aleutians. ● Stubby, thick bill. Rusty bend of wing, white outer tail feathers. Male has black head and bib, white whisker. Female has head stripes.

Pallas' Bunting *Emberiza pallasi* 5½" (Not shown) Recorded in nw. AK. ● Like reed bunting but smaller bill, blue-gray bend of wing, pale rump.

Rustic Bunting *Emberiza rustica* 5¾" (US rec.) Scarce in migration in w. Aleutians; other AK records. ● White outer tail feathers. Male has black-and-white head pattern; rusty breast, upperparts, rump. Female similar but duller.

Gray Bunting *Emberiza variabilis* 6" Recorded twice in w. Aleutians. ● Male gray, female brown above with chestnut rump. No white in tail.

Little Bunting *Emberiza pusilla* 4¾" (US rec.) Recorded in w. AK. ● Like savannah sparrow (Key 161) but chestnut crown and cheeks. Female duller.

Pine Bunting *Emberiza leucocephala* 7" Recorded in w. Aleutians. ● Male has white crown patch, ear patch, chestnut throat (all obscure in winter). Female duller.

Oriental Greenfinch *Carduelis sinica* 6" Recorded in w. Aleutians. ● Male dull greenish with yellow patches in wings and tail. Female browner.

Bullfinch (Eurasian) *Pyrrhula pyrrhula* 6½" Several records in Bering Sea area and AK mainland. ● Male has black cap, rosy cheeks and breast, white rump, gray body. Female browner, lacks rose color.

Hawfinch *Coccothraustes coccothraustes* 7" Several records in Bering Sea area. Very shy. ● Stocky with massive bill. Bold white wing patches. Female duller.

Common Rosefinch *Carpodacus erythrinus* 5¾" (Not shown) Recorded in w. AK. ● Like purple finch (Key 152) but lacks strong head stripes.

Index

Key 24
full image 10" x 17"

Reduced to only 38 square inches on the Key, Barry Van Dusen's terns are breathtaking when reproduced at their original 170 square inch size.

The artists' original paintings are much larger than those printed in the Keys. Details of three paintings are shown here at original size.

Key 135 full image 9½" x 16"
All of Larry McQueen's warblers and Dale Dyer's sparrows are painted at life size making them especially life-like.

Key 33 full image 9½" x 16"
The exquisite detail of Jonathan Alderfer's gadwalls can be appreciated best at the original painted size.

LANDBIRDS

The families of landbirds have adapted to exploit every source of food across the continent. Some even feed off other birds. Many are easily recognized by their distinct feeding adaptations. Owls, woodpeckers, and turkeys, for instance, are not likely to be confused with the many perching landbirds we know as songbirds.

Nocturnal Owls and nightjars are night hunters and are often seen at dusk or by moonlight.

Aerialists Hawks hunt from the wing. Swifts and swallows are also aerialists, and hummingbirds are the most acrobatic flyers of all.

Ground-walkers Many species occasionally perch on the ground, but only a few, such as grouse and quail, live there. They walk rather than hop. Many have plump bodies and are commonly hunted as game birds.

Tree-climbers Woodpeckers use their remarkable bills to hammer or probe under bark for food. They and similar birds are usually seen clinging to the sides of trees.

63	**NOCTURNAL**	Owls (large)
65		Owls (small)
67		Nightjars
69	**AERIALISTS**	Eagles, Falcons, Hawks, Vultures
79		Swallows, Swifts
82		Hummingbirds
85	**GROUND-WALKERS**	Pheasant, Roadrunner, Turkey
86		Grouse, Partridge, Quail, White-tailed Ptarmigan
90		Doves, Pigeons
92	**TREE-CLIMBERS**	Woodpeckers
97		Creeper, Nuthatches